National Development
1776-1966

A selective and annotated
guide to the most important
articles in English

by

H. Kent Geiger

Department of Sociology
University of Wisconsin

The Scarecrow Press, Inc.
Metuchen, N.J.   1969

Preface

This book consists of 350 annotated references to the most important literature of national development published in English through 1966.

I have been assisted in the task of identifying, evaluating, analyzing and annotating the published literature in this field by a large number of persons. My greatest obligation is to my students, who have contributed their skills and time as part of their class work or as project assistants, and out of their own interest and belief in the importance of careful bibliographic research. Among the last-named group I am particularly grateful to Bohdan Czarnocki for helpful suggestions about procedures and format, to John W. Gartrell for assistance in making selections, to Jerome S. Kraus for administrative help, to Oguz B. Nayman for annotations, and to Michael S. Taylor for counsel and assistance in the processing and analysis of the materials. Others to whom I am grateful for their aid in the preparation of this report, include especially Mrs. Mildred A. Busse, Secretary of the University of Wisconsin Russian Area Studies Program, and Mrs. Patricia A. Moll of the Department of Sociology secretarial staff, who contributed typing services and also carried a large share of the responsibility for the collection and tabulation of the data, from the very beginning stages of the project. Special thanks have already been extended personally to the many social science professors and department chairmen who supplied me with their course reading lists, but I should like to note here my appreciation for their generous cooperation.

The project began as an instructional activity, but in the end it could only be done within a reasonable period of time with financial assistance. I am happy to acknowledge the generous support, both financial and social, extended by the members of the Executive Committee of the Sociology of Economic Change Program offered by the Departments of Sociology and Rural Sociology and by the Office of International Studies and Programs, University of Wisconsin, Madison campus.

Table of Contents

List of Tables

v

A. Introduction

This bibliography is composed of the most important publications in the English language dealing with national development. Cultural, economic, political and social aspects of development are all represented, and each item of the total of 350 has been annotated and evaluated. Of the 350, 213 are books, defined as publications of 50 pages or more, and 137 are articles published in scholarly journals or chapters in edited anthologies.

The books and articles were published within the span of years from 1776 to 1966. In the former year Adam Smith's classic, An inquiry into the nature and causes of the wealth of nations, appeared and 1966 was the closing date for this bibliographic research project. The median year of publication is 1960, and the modal year 1963. See Table I for more detail.

The items are presented in chronological order, by year of publication of first edition or version, though information about later editions or versions is included in the reference. Books and articles first published in the same year are ordered alphabetically by author's or editor's last name. The index contains entries by author or editor, first word in title, and categories based upon analysis of the annotations.

After each annotation the evaluation is recorded. The evaluation refers to scores or frequencies assigned to each publication as a result of four different procedures. Gei refers to the selection and evaluation procedure followed by me and my students, and the numbers 1, 2 and 3 refer to our judgments about the quality of the item in question, 3 being the score accorded the few truly outstanding book-length publications about national development. The other digits registered are 7 and 8. The first refers to publications I classified as belonging to a peripheral field rather than to the new field of development, and the second to anthologies, which my students and I did not evaluate. Items for which a dash appears over the Gei were not inspected by us.

Table I

Growth of the Literature of National Development

	N	Percent
1766-1899	11	3
1900-1949	28	8
1950-1959	124	35
1960-1966	187	54
		100
1960	27	8
1961	31	9
1962	25	7
1963	37	11
1964	28	8
1965	18	5
1966	21	6
		54

The second evaluation procedure produced the results appearing over the term cit, and the numbers refer to the frequency with which the corresponding publication was cited -- referred to -- in footnotes and bibliographic references occurring in a 20% sample of all English language publications treating national development and published in 1966. It is my presumption that frequency of citation of a publication is a good measure of its quality as a contribution to knowledge, therefore, items cited frequently are considered higher in quality.

A third evaluation procedure consists of a frequency score combining the judgments of a large number of professors who are currently giving instruction on national development in the best graduate departments of anthropology, economics, political science and sociology of American universities. The score recorded over the term lis refers to the number of times the publication was required or recommended in 69 courses offered by 37 different departments in 18 universities.

The fourth procedure is more complex. The score recorded over the term rep refers to the result of a computation according to a formula which takes into account three different features of a publication. Was the article or (portion of a) book reprinted from some prior source of publication in an anthology dealing with national development? If so, how many years elapsed between the date of original publication and the date of republication? And, finally, how many years elapsed between the date of reprinting in an anthology and the year 1966? Republication in an anthology is deemed a sign of merit, and the magnitude of the merit is considered to rise in proportion to the length of time elapsing between date of original publication and date of reprinting, and to fall, for our purposes, in proportion to the number of years between publication of the anthology and 1966. As in the three preceding scores, the higher the number the higher the quality as evaluated by this method.

The over-all scores described above are on the left side of the page. On the right side are four additional scores, or dashes. These refer to the frequencies with which the given publications were recommended to students by professors in their course reading lists, but broken down according to particular academic disciplines. Thus, a score of 2 over the term ant means that the publication was listed in two different reading lists for anthropology courses, a score of 1 over eco means that the same item

9

was listed once among the economics reading lists, and so on. As a result of this mode of evaluation the reader can by inspection determine which publications among the 350 included are most discipline-specific, and which, on the other hand, are most inter-disciplinary.

B. How 250 Items were Selected by Each of Four Methods

Since a large part of the value of this publication rests upon its claim to be a valid and reliable guide to the literature of development, it is important to describe the selection procedures in some detail. The first method (hereafter method #1) is the traditional one -- an individual professor, aided by his students, reads, compares, discusses, evaluates and makes his choices. The predecessor to this publication was distributed in mimeo form in March, 1967. Its 200-odd items were all monographs, and they represented my efforts to delineate the field of development by identifying the most important books within the field. At that time I attempted also to establish boundaries, by proposing publications which I felt belonged to neighboring or "peripheral" fields but not properly in the area of development. Among such fields were general theories of social change, community studies, comparative economic systems, historical and general treatments of revolution, and so on.

In continuing my bibliographic analysis, I wished to continue also my own study of the literature, in which activity evaluation is a very necessary part, and to organize further my own thinking about what form the field of national development ought eventually to take. It was possible to do this and also to enlist the aid of a large number of graduate students in a variety of departments in connection with my responsibilities as the instructor in a cross-disciplinary course on the subject offered at the University of Wisconsin. As part of the requirements for this course, entitled "Societal development," students were asked to inspect and evaluate a substantial number of publications, and to contribute annotations for those they considered to be of the highest quality. These selections and annotations were then further inspected, evaluated, retained or discarded, and if retained, edited by me to the point where they were suitable for publication.

Thus the bulk of the work done to construct a bibliography through method #1 was accomplished in the normal

10

routine of course instruction and the students' learning experience. My students and I together chose 250 publications as outstanding after well over 2000 items had been inspected with some care, and probably close to 5000 items contained in an initial "master file" of all identifiable publications in the field had been reviewed more cursorily. To compose the 250 items, I arbitrarily elected to choose 150 books and 100 articles. These 250 items, with the exception of 17 chosen for special distinction, were given a score of 2. The 17 "very best" were scored as 3. These numbers are recorded in column one of Table II, and in Table III the reader will find reasonably accurate estimates of the publications inspected but not included in the method #1 set of 250. Scores of 1, 7 and 8 refer to rejection on the grounds of average or low quality, being in a peripheral field or a text book, and being an anthology, the latter two groups being excluded a priori by method #1.

Evaluation by one or more external authorities was used to measure the adequacy of the judgments made in compiling this work. Consequently, it was an indispensable part of our procedure to finish the selection of the best 250 by method #1 before the results of the other procedures became known, and this is what was done.

The second selection and evaluation method is the method of citation frequency. My aim here, as also in methods #3 and #4, was to select by a different procedure as close to 250 items as possible, so that the set chosen by each method could be compared with those chosen by the other methods. This was accomplished in this case by including references to published materials which appear most frequently in the form of footnotes and bibliographic citations in the most recent publications on the subject of development.

The most recent publications were defined as those appearing in 1966, so the first step was to identify all such items and to treat them as a population to be sampled. By consulting standard bibliographic sources, such as the International Index (more recently appearing as Social Sciences and Humanities Index), the Bulletin of the Public Affairs Information Service and the Cumulative Book Index, as well as drawing from the project's master file, it was possible to obtain an initial group of 993 English language items dealing with national development and published in 1966. Upon closer inspection 480 of this total were discarded as inappropriate for one or another reason,[1] which left as a basic population 513 published items.

11

Table II

Distributions of Scores or Frequencies for
Approximately 250 Outstanding Publications Selected
by Each of Four Methods

Geiger and Students		Citation Frequency for 1966 Sample		Recommended by Professors		Reprinted in Anthologies	
(1)		(2)		(3)		(4)	
Score	N	Freq.	N	Freq.	N	Score	N
2	233	2	212	3	124	7-9	81
3	17	3	28	4	60	10-12	45
		4	5	5	34	13-15	19
Total	250	5	4	6	17	16-18	7
		6	5	7	3	19-21	20
		7	-	8	6	22-24	2
		8	2	9	3	25-49	15
		9	-	10	3	50-74	7
				11	-	75-99	8
				12	2	100-	36
		Total	256	13	1		
						Total	240
				18	1		
				24	1		
				Total	255		

12

Table III

Distributions of Scores or Frequencies for
Publications Inspected or Identified but not Selected
as Outstanding by Each of Four Methods

Geiger and Students		Citation Frequency for 1966 Sample		Recommended by Professors		Reprinted in Anthologies	
(1)		(2)		(3)		(4)	
Score	N	Freq.	N	Freq.	N	Score	N
1	1500*	1	3772	1	3032	4-6	188
7	300			2	466	1-3	216
8	200					(-2)- 0	137
				Total	3498	(-5)-(-3)	91
						(-8)-(-6)	26
						-(9)	4
						Total	662

*Estimates

13

Of these 513 items 86 are books and 427 are articles. 384 items deal with development in a general or cross-national way, and 129 treat single countries or regions, but in terms appearing to be relevant to the creation or testing of general concepts and propositions. There was, of course, an unavoidable element of arbitrary judgment involved here; another researcher might well have chosen an initial population larger or smaller by 100, and of somewhat different composition.

Once the population was identified, the question of sampling arose. Trial runs suggested that a 20 per cent sample would generate a total pool of citations close to 5000, so a 20 per cent sample was taken. It consists of 104 publications, 18 books and 86 articles.

All references to published items appearing in these publications, with the exception of three which could not be located, were copied on 3 x 5 cards, and then the frequencies with which particular items appeared were tallied. In this way a total of 4366 references were taken, and when items appearing more than once were tallied, the method produced 4028 references to different publications. The choice of sample size proved to be fortunate, because items with frequencies of appearance of two or more times amounted to 256, a remarkably close approximation to the target number of 250. The specific breakdowns by number for each frequency appear in Table II.

Although the initial 256 publications seemed fortunately close to 250, it soon became apparent that the final outcome would be less happy, for it was necessary to discard 39 of these, 38 because they were references to publications appearing in foreign languages and one because the reference was to an entire scholarly journal, with no specific articles or issues designated. These eliminations left a total of 217 outstanding publications finally eligible as selected by method # 2.

The third method of selection and evaluation promised in advance to be the best, and the results now at hand have born out the expectation. Method # 3, like method # 2, is based on a frequency count, but in this case the count is made for publications appearing as references in the unpublished reading lists of professors offering courses on development in the leading graduate departments of outstanding American universities.

The first step, as in the preceding method, was to

14

list a population of courses. Such a population was constructed by identifying the graduate departments offering the most effective graduate training program in the four social sciences concerned,[2] and then, from inspection of catalogs, listing all courses open to graduate students and dealing with national development.

That procedure led to a population of 159 different courses, 118 of them dealing with development in a general way, and 41 concentrating upon the development experience of particular regions. Courses concentrating only on one, or two, countries (Brazil, China and Japan, etc.) were excluded.

From this population a sample of 91 different courses was selected, 72 of them being general treatments, and 19 focussing on particular regions in which national development is a problem of great concern. The distribution of both population and sample by discipline and topical emphasis is shown in Table IV. The name of the professor currently responsible for each of these courses was then taken from the university catalog, and a letter was sent explaining the project and soliciting the professor's cooperation. He was asked to supply the reading list most recently distributed to students enrolled in the course. The first letter was sent on August 18, 1967; a second, follow-up request for those not responding to the first letter was sent on October 30, 1967. Included in the second letter was a check list of reasons to be noted by those unable or unwilling to supply reading lists.

The results of the operation were quite satisfactory. The over-all rate of return on the original sample was 68 per cent, with negligible differences among the disciplines, as shown in Table V. The rate of response, to include those professors who answered our request but did not furnish reading lists, was much higher--86 per cent. A detailed breakdown of the reasons offered for not contributing lists, and of non-response, is presented by discipline and topical emphasis in Table VI. It should be noted especially that a total of ten of the reading lists analyzed were not part of the originally chosen sample, but were volunteered by the professor contacted, or by a colleague. These voluntarily contributed reading lists referred in the main to newly offered courses or to courses taught as substitutes for those originally in the sample, and since the course contents seemed appropriate, all were included for analysis. The professors in political science departments had the lowest rates of return and response, but also the highest rate of voluntarily contributed lists, which may reflect the rapidity

15

Table IV

Sample Design for Solicitation of Professors'
Reading Lists on National Development, August, 1967

Topical Orientation of Course	Number of Courses in Population and Sample									
	Anthrop.		Econ.		Pol. Sci.		Sociol.		All	
	pop.	sam.	pop.	sam.	pop.	sam.	pop.	sam.	pop.	sam.
General treatments	18	18	55	18	28	19	17	17	118	72
On specific areas: Africa	3	2	3	2	7	2	-	-	13	6
Latin America	2	2	5	2	2	2	2	2	11	8
Other*	-	-	10	2	6	2	1	1	17	5
Totals	23	22	73	24	43	25	20	20	159	91

* Middle East, Southeast Asia, etc.

Table V

Rate of Return and Final Sample Size

Used for Analysis of Professors' Reading Lists

Rate of return	anthrop.	econ.	pol. sci.	sociol.	all
Original sample size	22	24	25	20	91
Sample lists returned for analysis	16	17	15	14	62
Percent of original sample	73	71	60	70	68
Other lists volunteered	1	2	5	2	10
Total of lists received	17	19	20	16	72
Excluded as inappropriate	1	2	-	-	3
Total of lists analyzed	16	17	20	16	69

Table VI

Response Pattern to Soliciation of Professors'

Reading Lists by Discipline and Topical Emphasis of Course

	Anthrop.		Econ.		Pol. Sci.		Sociol.		
	gen'l.	area	gen'l.	area	gen'l.	area	gen'l.	area	All
Lists (sample) returned	14	2	13	4	10	5	11	3	62
Other responses: course not offered	2	-	-	1	1	-	1	-	5
no list used	1	-	2	-	-	-	2	-	5
list not available	-	1	-	-	3	-	1	-	5
prof. not located	-	-	1	-	-	-	-	-	1
No response	1	1	2	1	5	1	2	-	13
Total	18	4	18	6	19	6	17	3	91
Lists analyzed: from sample	13	2	11	4	10	5	11	3	59
volunteered	1		2		5			2	10
Total	14	2	13	4	15	5	11	5	69

with which persons in that discipline introduce changes in their academic curricula. In any case, a final total of 69 lists was analyzed, with each reference taken on a 3 x 5 card. In many cases, instructional reading lists contained references to selected portions of books, in addition to entire books and to articles. When this was so, the reference was tallied to refer to the entire book. The result was 5053 cards, which, after repetitions were tallied, produced a total of 3753 different references. Specific numbers for each frequency class are shown in Table II and III. The proper cutting point needed to select the best 250 items again proved easy to pick, for the publications recommended three times or more by the professors turned out to number 255.

The fourth method of selection and evaluation aggregates the knowledge and decisions of individual scholars who have edited anthologies of previously published articles and portions of books. Republication of material in an anthology is taken as a measure of high quality. There was no shortage of anthologies at hand, which we may well interpret as an indication of the tremendous interest created by the phenomenon of so many less advanced nations entering, or seeking entry, into the modern era. One hundred and eighty-four anthologies dealing partly or entirely with development were located without too much difficulty. Those that were least highly specialized, in both an area and topical sense, numbering 125, were taken for analysis. The reference for each item in the anthologies was listed on a separate sheet of paper and scored as R (for reprinted) or OP (standing for "original publication," meaning that the chapter in the anthology appeared there for the first time). All items scored R were then taken for further analysis. There were 977 of these, involving 914 different publications, of which 52 had been reprinted more than one time. For twelve references the information given, particularly the date of first publication, was incomplete, requiring their discard.

At this point a problem presented itself: how was I to use this method to select the 250 best, as had been done with the use of the first three methods? The solution chosen was to introduce an additional characteristic of the republished item, a property I have termed its "age credential." Age credential takes into account two facts about the quality or status of a reprinted publication both of them connected with its age. Due to the rapid advance of knowledge it is well known that a scientific publication tends on the average quickly to lose its worth. In general, old publications are less important, or of lower quality, than new ones.

19

On the other hand, some select few publications prove to be exceptions to the rule, maintaining a position of high regard for years, in rare cases, even for centuries. When this occurs the publication is generally accepted as a "classic." A classic, then, is here defined as a publication which has, contrary to the general pattern, withstood the test of time with extraordinary success.

In the case of reprinted materials, each item has, in fact, two relevant ages, one its age measured by the years elapsing between year of original publication and year of republication in an anthology, and the second its age measured by the time elapsing between date of republication and the present, which in this study is taken as the year 1966. In accordance with the arguments presented above, the first age lends prestige to the item as it increases, but the second detracts, as it increases. Taking these pluses and minuses to be of equal weight, the age credential for each republished item is given by the formula: (date of publication of anthology - date of original publication of item) - (1966 - date of publication of anthology). In consequence, an old item newly reprinted earns a high score, while a younger item reprinted a considerable time ago earns a low score. For example, an article published originally in 1955 and reprinted in an anthology in 1965 would have its score computed as follows:

$$(1965 - 1955) - (1966 - 1965) = 10 - 1 = 9$$

In accordance with this formula, each of the 902 reprinted items was given a score. The scores for items reprinted once ranged from a high of 182 (for Smith, . . . the wealth of nations) to a low of - 11 (for an article published first in 1953, then reprinted the following year in an anthology).

There is, of course, a more essential characteristic to be considered, namely the frequency of reprinting. Forty-three items were reprinted twice, 7 three times, and two items were reprinted in four different anthologies. I decided arbitrarily to assign high value without question to all materials reprinted more than once, and to give them a correspondingly high score. This was computed by multiplying their age credential score (taken as an arithmetic mean, when the dates of republication differ) by a multiple reprint weight score. The weight score was constructed to reflect the probability with which any item chosen randomly from the original pool of 902 items would be reprinted any number of times from one to four. [3]

20

The distributions, formula and adjusted weight scores are shown in Table VII.

This procedure generated some very high scores. The highest was 2762, the score assigned to W. W. Rostow, "The take-off into self-sustained growth," first published in 1956, and subsequently republished in four different anthologies. For the group of 52 publications reprinted twice or more the median score is 110 and the mode is 20, the latter being a reflection of the fact that age credential scores of less than one were all scored as one for this group.

The proper cutting point in the case of method # 4 proved to be at the point of score seven; references with scores of seven and higher totalled to 240. As with the other methods the distributions are presented in Tables II and III.

C. How the Final Selection of 350 Was Made

Throughout the design and data collection stages of the project it had been my assumption that a final set of publications numbering between 300 and 500 could be selected mainly on the basis of agreement among the four different methods used. The hope was not fulfilled; only two publications were selected by all four methods, 24 were chosen by three methods, and 102 were selected by any combination of two methods. The exact combinations which comprise the total of 128 simultaneously selected items are shown in Table VIII. The most frequent combination is method # 1 and method # 3, Geiger and students together with nominations taken from the course reading lists.

It is of some interest at this point to inquire about the relative efficacy of each of the four methods. There is no completely suitable way to do this, for an independent standard for evaluation is lacking. We can, however, assume that the total of 128 represents the best judgment currently available as to which are the truly basic publications of national development, and compare the observed magnitude of the contribution of each of the four methods to this total in relation to the magnitude of an "expected" contribution of each, i.e., if that of each were equal to that of every other. As shown in Table IX, the number of nominations by each method, from # 1 to # 4, included in the total of 128 is 79, 72, 99 and 34. Dividing each of these numbers by the mean of all four and multiplying by 100 provides a measure of the relative efficacy of each method. For methods # 1 to # 4 respectively the

21

corresponding scores are 111, 101, 139 and 48. Other ways of estimating the value of each method in relation to the other three are shown in Table IX.

It is clear that method #3, frequency of citation on the professors' reading lists, ranks highest, and that selection by method #4, reprinting and age analysis, ranks lowest. It should be kept in mind, of course, that the capacity of each method to contribute to the presumed best or ideal set of publications is limited by restrictions, both inherent ones and those arbitrarily imposed by my a priori procedures. For example, anthologies are generally composed mainly or even exclusively of previously published articles rather than reprinted portions of books, so that this method is of limited use in indicating which books are important. Method #2, that of frequency citation, is handicapped by the fact that all foreign language references had to be deleted, and method #1 by the decision to exclude all anthologies and textbooks from among the best 250. Thus, the rate of final acceptance of articles nominated by each of the four methods of selection would probably show better the relative strength of each method.

The fact that only 128 references were nominated in common by two or more of the four methods made it necessary to introduce additional criteria of selection to compose the final set. The first of these was the decision to include in the final set all publications (N = 150) referred to in three or more of the course reading lists. The main consideration was my desire to reveal in the final set the best subsets of publications for each of the four major disciplines involved.

A second criterion was to include the "best" as chosen by each of the other three methods of selection but which were so chosen only by these individual methods. These are described in rows C - E of table X, and totalled to 34+ 14 + 5 = 53.

At this point the final set numbered 331. To bring the total to 350, and to include certain publications the compiler felt deserved representation, two additional sub-sets, numbering 8 and 11 respectively were added. The first of these is identified with the symbol (2) in the first column of the evaluation scores; the second group, coming from the citation frequency (method #2) group of references, is identified with the same symbol, but in the second column of the evaluation scores.

22

Once the final set of 350 references had been selected it was necessary to go back to the original master files for each of the four methods of selection to ascertain the scores received by each of the 350 publications which had not been among the 250 original nominations made according to each of the four methods. These were recorded in the proper column at the end of the annotations, and also have been tallied and summarized in Tables XI - XIV. These tables, then, serve as a summary description of the scores actually recorded in the first four columns at the end of the 350 annotations to follow.

D. Identifying the Classics in the Development Literature

Perhaps "classics is too enthusiastic a term to apply to the select few publications among the 350 described in these pages. Perhaps in a new field like national development the time has been too short to permit the establishment of such a category. "Elite" publications, "best of the best," members of a documentary "upper-upper class," or simply "most important" all convey the same idea, that of a group of items ranking at the top of a stratified hierarchy.

We can now describe two groups of publications, numbering 26 and 52, and each selected in a different way, as the most important. The first group consists of publications chosen by three or more out of the four different selection methods as among the best 250 of each. These 26 together with their scores, are found in Table XV. If one were to seek for a still smaller and more highly selected group of the best, he might do well to add the scores obtained by the second and third methods, columns two and three in the table. For example, the number of publications with a combined frequency score of ten and higher is eight; any person seeking quick access to the core concepts and ideas of development would do well to start with and work hard at mastering these eight publications.

A second group of "best among the outstanding" can be identified by listing some standard number of all those chosen as best among the original 250 nominations selected by each method. The standard number chosen in this case is 17, the reason being that the compiler-editor of this work, who was also the main architect and evaluator of method #1, selected that many as his personal favorites. These are the items checked in the first column of Table XVI. In column two of the same table appear, also identified by check-marks, those publications cited four times or more by method #2, that of frequency citation. The closest approximation to the target number of 17 was 16. In column three are checked the authors and titles of publications recommended eight times or more in the course reading lists supplied by American university professors. Finally, in column four are to be found checked those items as selected by method #4 with scores of 182 and higher. Here, as with method #2, an N of 16 proved to be the closest approximation to 17. Again, of course, if a still smaller and more select group is of use, items with two or more checks opposite them, eleven in number come extra-highly recommended more than once.

For many persons using this publication the question of most pressing concern will be: which are the most significant publications in my own field? Our final table supplies an answer for each of the four social sciences. To construct this array of publications only the recommendations contained in the course reading lists were utilized. Those publications most frequently cited in the course lists for each discipline, and which totalled most proximately to ten, a procedure which entailed the use of three different frequency ranges, are identified in Table XVII. Scores in parentheses refer to frequencies with which publications not in the "best ten" under the particular discipline in question, but which were selected as among the best ten of some other discipline, are recommended by that (the former) discipline.

A notable feature of this set of 39 references is the remarkable extent to which the "best" literature of development can be distinguished as "discipline-specific" or "interdisciplinary." At one extreme stand books such as Spicer's Human problems in technological change, apparently esteemed only by anthropologists, and Chenery and Clark's Interindustry economics, valued highly by economists but ignored by the other three disciplines. At another extreme is Hagen's On the theory of social change: how economic growth begins, a publication identified by American university professors as among the top ten in all four disciplines.

24

Table VII

Frequency Distribution and Formula for Assigning

Multiple Reprint Weight Scores to

Items Reprinted More than Once*

Frequency with which item is republished	Number of different publications	Per Cent	Adjusted Weight Score	N of references taken
1	850	94.2	1	850
2	43	4.8	20	86
3	7	.8	121	21
4	2	.2	425	8
5	-	-		
Total	902	100.0		
DK	12			12
				977

Weight formula for frequencies > 1: $\dfrac{\text{N for frequency of 1}}{\text{N for observed frequency} > 1}$

$\dfrac{f}{1}$					
2	850/850	=	1	=	1
3	" / 43	=	19.8	=	20
4	" / 7	=	121.4	=	121
	" / 2	=	425	=	425

* For further information on the meaning of the formula, see text.

Table VIII

Combinations by which Publications Nominated by

Two or More of Four Different Methods were

Included in the Final 350

| | Geiger | | | | |
| | Citation Frequency | | Citation Frequency | | |
	Lists	Lists	Lists	Lists	Totals
Reprinted	2	1	1	8	12
Reprinted	19	9	39	x	67

| | Geiger | | | | |
| | Citation Frequency | | Citation Frequency | | |
	Lists	Lists	Lists	Lists	
Reprinted	3	11	8	x	22
Reprinted	27	x	x	x	27
Totals	51	21	48	8	128

26

Table IX

Measures of the Efficacy of Each of the

Four Methods Used to Select 128 Publications*

	Percent of 128 Chosen by Each Method		Percent of Original $250^{\pm}$ Included in 128	
	N	Percent	N	Percent
Geiger and students	79	62	79	(79/250=) 32
Frequency citation	72	56	72	(72/256=) 28
Professors' lists	99	77	99	(99/255=) 39
Reprinted	34	27	34	(34/240=) 14

* Calculated from the information provided in Tables VIII and II.

Table **X**

Composition by Mode of Selection of

Final 350 Outstanding Publications in the

Field of National Development

Mode of Selection	N
(A) Selected simultaneously by two or more of four methods	128
(B) Recommended on three or more professors' reading lists, and not selected by mode (A)	150
(C) Reprinted in anthologies two or more times and/or received a score of 80 or higher, and not selected by mode (A)	34
(D) Cited three or more times in footnotes or references of 20 percent sample of 1966 publications, and not selected by mode (A)	14
(E) Assigned a score of three by Geiger, and not selected by mode (A)	5
(F) Assigned in final stage by Geiger, and not otherwise selected	8
(G) Cited two times in footnotes or references of 1966 sample, starting with oldest publication not yet included, and adding to make a total of 350	11
Total	350

Table XI

Frequencies of Scores Assigned by

Geiger and Students to Publications Included in

Final 350

Score		N	Per Cent
-	not inspected	151	43
1	inspected but not chosen for 250	48	14
2	chosen for inclusion in 250	67	19
(2)	chosen in final stage	8	2
3	chosen as best books	17	5
7	identified as test or in peripheral field	28	8
8	anthologies	31	9
		350	100

Table XII

Distribution of Citation Frequencies of

Publications Included in the Final 350

Frequency	N	Per Cent
-	181	52
1	72	21
2	44	13
(2) added to make 350	11	3
3	26	7
4	5	1
5	4	1
6	5	1
7	-	
8	2	1
9	-	
	350	100

Table XIII

Distribution of Frequencies with which Publications Included in the Final 350 were Recommended on Professors' Reading Lists

Frequency	N	Per Cent
-	57	16
1	31	9
2	13	4
3	119	34
4	59	17
5	34	10
6	17	4
7	3	1
8	6	2
9	3	1
10	3	1
11	-	
12	2	1
13	1	-
18	1	-
24	1	-
	350	100

Table XIV

Distribution of Scores Assigned on the

Basis of Republication and "Age Credential"

for Books and Articles in the Final 350

Score	Number of Times Reprinted					N	Per Cent
	0	1	2	3	4		
1000-			1	2	2	5	2
500-999			2			2	-
400-499			1	1		2	-
300-399			2	1		3	1
200-299			2			2	-
175-199		1	5			6	2
150-174		1	2			3	1
125-149		2	1			3	1
100-124		2	7	1		10	3
75-99			8			8	2
50-74			2			2	-
25-49			1			1	-
0-24		20	11			31	9
-25- -1		3				3	1
-	269					269	77
Totals	269	29	43	7	2	350	100

32

Table XV

Most Important Publications in the Literature

of National Development: Summary Table of Items

Chosen Simultaneously for Inclusion in "Best 250"

by Three or Four* out of Four Methods (N= 26)

Author, short title and date	Score or Frequency			
	Gei	cit	lis	rep
Bellah, Tokugawa religion, 1957	3	3	4	-
Bendix, Nation-building and citizenship, 1964	2	2	5	-
Bendix, Work and authority in industry, 1956	2	2	3	-
Deutsch, "Social mobilization and political . . . ," 1961	2	2	8	5
Emerson, From empire to nation, 1960	2	3	4	2
Epstein, Economic development and social change in . . . , 1962	2	2	3	-
Erasmus, Man takes control, 1961	3	2	7	-
Fanon, The wretched of the earth, 1961	3	2	6	-
Furtado, Development and under-development, 1961	2	2	3	-
Geertz, Peddlars and princes, 1963	2	2	5	-
Hagen, On the theory of social change, 1962	3	5	24	-
Harbison and Myers, Education, manpower and . . . , 1964	2	4	4	-
Hirschman, Journeys toward progress, 1963	2	3	13	-
Hirschman, The strategy of economic development, 1958	2	5	12	-
Lerner, The passing of traditional society, 1958	3	8	18	-
Lewis, "Economic development with un-limited . . . ," 1954	1	3	4	641
Lewis, The theory of economic growth, 1955	7	8	3	100
Lipset, "Some social requisites of democracy," 1959	2	2	4	-

33

Author, short title and date	Score or Frequency			
	Gei	cit	lis	rep
McClelland, The achieving society, 1961	3	2	5	-
Myrdal, Rich lands and poor, 1957	2	6	8	-
Nurkse, Patterns of trade and development, 1961	2	1	3	20
*Nurkse, Problems of capital formation in . . . ,1953	2	2	6	9
Nurkse, 'Some international aspects of . . . ," 1952	2	2	1	140
*Rostow, The stages of economic growth, 1960	3	6	9	20
Rostow, 'The take-off into sustained . . . ," 1956	1	2	3	2672
Schultz, Transforming traditional agriculture, 1964	2	3	6	-

* Chosen by four out of four methods.

Table **XVI**

Most Important Publications in the Literature of

National Development: Summary Table of Items

Indicated Outstanding by Each of Four Methods (N= 51)

Author, short title and date	Gei	cit	lis	rep
Almond and Coleman, The politics of the developing areas, 1960		x		
Almond and Verba, The civic culture, 1963			x	
Apter, The politics of modernization, 1965	x		x	
Banfields, The moral basis of a backward society, 1958		x		
Bellah, Tokugawa religion, 1957		x		
Black, The dynamics of modernization, 1966		x	x	
Boeke, "Dualistic economics," 1930				x
Bronfenbrenner, "The appeal of confiscation in . . . ," 1955				x
Clark, The conditions of economic progress, 1940		x		
Currie, Accelerating development, 1966	x			
Denison, The sources of economic growth in . . . , 1962		x		
Deutsch, "Social mobilization and political . . . ," 1961			x	
Doob, Becoming more civilized, 1960	x			
Eckstein, "Individualism and the role of the state in . . . ," 1958				x
Erasmus, Man takes control, 1961	x			
Erlich, The Soviet industrialization debate . . . , 1961	x			
Fanon, The wretched of the earth, 1961	x			
Foster, Traditional cultures, and the impact . . . , 1962			x	
Geertz, Old societies and new states, 1963			x	

35

Author, short title and date	Gei	cit	lis	rep
Gluckman, Custom and conflict in Africa, 1955				x
Goode, "Reconstruction of foreign tax systems," 1952				x
Hagen, On the theory of social change . . ., 1962	x	x	x	
Harbison and Myers, Education, manpower and . . ., 1964		x		
Heller, "Taxation in underdeveloped countries," 1954				x
Hirschman, Journeys toward progress, 1963			x	
Hirschman, The strategy of economic development, 1958		x	x	
Hoselitz, Sociological aspects of economic growth, 1960		x		
Johnson, Revolutionary change, 1966	x			
Johnson, Political change in Latin America, 1958			x	
Kuznets, Modern economic growth, 1966	x	x		
Lagos Matus, International stratification . . ., 1963	x			
Lenin, The development of capitalism in Russia, 1899		x		
Lerner, The passing of traditional society, 1958	x	x	x	
Lewis, The theory of economic growth, 1955			x	x
McClelland, The achieving society, 1961	x			
Marx, Capital, 1867		x		x
Matossian, "Ideologies of delayed industrialization . . .," 1958				x
Moore, Social origins of dictatorship and democracy, 1966	x			
Moore, Social change, 1963			x	
Myint, The economics of the developing, 1964			x	
Myrdal, An international economy, 1956		x		
Myrdal, Rich lands and poor, 1957		x	x	
Pye, Politics, personality and nation-building, 1962			x	
Rosenstein-Rodan, "Notes on the theory of the 'big push,' . . .," 1957				x
Rosenstein-Rodan, "Problems of industrialization of . . .," 1943				x
Rostow, The stages of economic growth, 1960	x	x	x	x

Author, short title and date	Gei	cit	lis	rep
Singer, "The distribution of gains between . . . ," 1950				x
Smith, An inquiry into. . . the wealth of nations, 1776		x		x
Spicer, Human problems in technological . . ., 1952			x	
United Nations, Land reform, 1951				x
Viner, International trade and economic . . ., 1952				x
Totals	17	16	17	16

Table XVII

Most Important Publications in the Literature of National
Development by Discipline: Summary Table of (Approximately)
Ten Items Recommended Most Frequently for Students of
Anthropology, Economics, Political Science and Sociology by
Professors in Major Graduate Departments (N= 39)

| Author, short title and date | Discipline | | | |
	ant	eco	pol	soc
Almond, "A functional approach to comparative . . .," 1960	(1)	-	5	-
Almond and Verba, The civic culture, 1963	-	-	7	(1)
Apter, Ghana in transition, 1955	-	(1)	5	-
Apter, The politics of modernization, 1965	(1)	-	6	5
Aron and Hoselitz, Social Development, 1965	-	-	-	4
Black, The dynamics of modernization, 1966	(1)	-	(4)	4
Chenery, "Comparative advantage and development policy," 1961	-	4	-	-
Chenery and Clark, Interindustry economics, 1959	-	5	-	-
Coale and Hoover, Population growth and economic . . ., 1958	-	4	-	-
Deutsch, "Social mobilization and political . . .," 1961	-	-	5	(3)
Eisenstadt, The political systems of empires, 1962	-	-	5	-
Erasmus, Man takes control, 1961	6	-	-	(1)
Foster, Traditional culture and the impact . . ., 1962	7	-	(2)	(1)
Goodenough, Cooperation in change, 1963	7	-	-	-

38

Author, short title and date	Discipline			
	ant	eco	pol	soc
Hagen, On the theory of social change . . ., 1962	5	7	7	5
Harbison and Myers, Education, man- power and economic . . ., 1964	-	4	-	-
Harbison and Myers, Manpower and education, 1965	-	4	-	-
Hirschman, Journeys toward progress, 1963	(4)	4	(2)	(3)
Hirschman, The strategy of economic development, 1958	-	7	(1)	4
Hoselitz, Sociological aspects of economic growth, 1960	-	-	(2)	4
Hoselitz and Moore, Industrialization and society, 1963	-	-	1	4
Johnston and Mellor, "The role of agri- culture in . . .," 1961	-	4	-	-
Lerner, The passing of traditional society, 1958	6	-	8	4
Lewis, Development planning, 1966	-	4	(1)	-
Meier, International trade and develop- ment, 1963	-	4	-	-
Meier and Baldwin, Economic Development: theory . . ., 1957	-	4	(1)	-
Morgan, "The long-run terms of trade between . . .," 1959	-	4	-	-
Myint, The economics of the developing countries, 1964	(1)	5	(1)	(1)
Nurkse, Problems of capital formation in . . ., 1953	-	4	(1)	(1)
Paul, Health, culture and community, 1955	5	-	-	-
Prebisch, "Commercial policy in the underdeveloped . . .," 1959	-	4	-	(1)
Pye, Politics, personality and nation- building, 1962	(2)	-	8	-
Redfield, The folk culture of Yucatan, 1941	5	-	-	-
Redfield, The primitive world and its transformations, 1953	5	-	(1)	-
Rosenstein-Rodan, "International aid for . . .," 1961	-	4	-	-
Schultz, Transforming traditional agri- culture, 1964	-	4	-	(2)

Author, short title and date	Discipline			
	ant	eco	pol	soc
Scott, Mexican government in transition, 1964	-	-	5	(1)
Spicer, Human problems in technological change, 1952	8	-	-	-
Weiner, Modernization, 1966	(2)	-	(1)	4

Discipline	Frequency range	N
anthropology	5-8	9
economics	4-7	18
political science	5-8	10
sociology	4-5	9

Notes

1. Forty-seven were documents issued in mimeo form with limited distribution, 85 were on subjects related but not central to development (the population explosion, urbanization in the American South, etc.), 70 dealt with foreign aid and assistance programs, and so on.

2. Included are the departments rated "extremely attractive," or "attractive" in the report on graduate education in American universities prepared by the American Council on Education. See pp. 33, 35, 41 and 43 in Allan M. Cartter, An assessment of quality in graduate education: a comparative study of graduate departments in 29 academic disciplines, Washington, D. C.: American Council on Education, 1966. There were 56 departments so rated, 16 in political science, 15 in economics, 14 in sociology and 11 in anthropology. To increase the size of the population I added 7 additional departments to the anthropology group. These were rated as "acceptable plus" in the report, and their addition brought the number of eligible departments up to 63.

3. The probability of being reprinted a given number of times, for any item chosen randomly from the total of 902 shown in Table VII, is taken as the number in that particular frequency class divided by the total of 902. This is the "expected" probability. If the

"observed" probability is taken to be one, then for each frequency class the weight should reflect the relationship between the observed and the expected probability, or 1/ expected probability. Thus, the weight for items reprinted only once would be 1 ÷ 850/902, the weight for items reprinted twice would be 1 ÷ 43/902, and so forth. Standardizing to permit the convenience of a weight of one to be assigned to items reprinted only once, the total computation for deriving the weight of items reprinted twice is: (1 ÷ 43/902) ÷ (1 ÷ 850/902)= 850/43 = 19.8

Smith, Adam, An inquiry into the nature and causes of the wealth of nations (London, 1776; new, 4th edit., 1789), NY: Modern Library, 1937, 976 p. 1

This first full exposition of a frame of reference now known as classical economics has been of the greatest intellectual and most lasting practical influence, and qualifies as the founding father publication of economics as an academic discipline. Many of the topical interests and categories of discourse used are still familiar--the divisions of labor, monopoly, protectionism, etc.--as are many of the arguments. The key presupposition of classical economics, and of much Western economic and political theory, is found here in Smith's "law of markets," by which each individual in seeking his own self-interest by working through a complex system of markets, "the invisible hand," is said to promote the interest of society as a whole"... more effectually than when he really intends to promote it." Book III, "Of the Different Progress of Opulence in Different Nations," contains what may be the earliest theory of development. Smith argues that the "natural course of things" is such that society in its growth ought to invest first in agriculture, then in manufacturing and, last, turn its attention to commerce.

-	6	-	182	-	-	-	-
Gei	cit	lis	rep	ant	eco	pol	soc

Malthus, Thomas R., An essay on the principle of population (London, 1798 and later years; 6th and last edit., 1826, 2 vols.), Homewood, Ill: Irwin, 1963, 290 p. 2

The Malthusian theory or "principle" of population states that population, when unchecked, grows in a geometrical ratio while the means of subsistence increase at best in arithmetic ratio, so that population tends to increase up to the limit provided by the means of subsistence. The theory addresses itself in familiar and simple terms to one of humanity's most cherished goals--the standard of living--and it provides a concise explanation, with clear political implications, of a most detested condition--poverty. It has elements in it which are not entirely scientific, and it also provides a convenient conservative answer to efforts to reform economic and political institutions. For these several reasons it has had one of the most lasting and successful careers in the history of ideas.

-	3	1	160	-	1	-	-
Gei	cit	lis	rep	ant	eco	pol	soc

43

Ricardo, David, On the principles of political economy and 'taxation' (London, 1817 and later years), NY: Dutton, 1960, 300 p. 3

In Ricardo's work, it is generally agreed, can be found the first consistent presentation of classical economic doctrine as well as a refinement and extension of the classical economic theory of development. The starting point is the conception that profits, rents and wages (to the extent that they exceed the level needed for subsistence), constitute the net revenue of the economy. When net revenue is employed for further accumulation of capital, development occurs. Of the three economically significant groups in the Ricardian model, capitalists are all-important for development, because it is only they who save; landlords and laborers do not. An important feature of the theory is the idea that the law of diminishing returns tends to reduce the rate of profit, and that this in turn lowers the rate of capital formation. Thus, unless inventions (or, to use the modern phrases--technological innovations and organizational progress) act powerfully as a counteractive agent, the rate of economic growth tends toward a stationary state. Development, consequently, is seen very much as a race between diminishing returns and inventions.

-	2	1	141	-	1	-	-
Gei	cit	lis	rep	ant	eco	pol	soc

Bolivar, Simon, "Address at Angostura, 1819" (Washington, D. C., 1819), p. 285-87 in L. L. Snyder (ed.) The dynamics of nationalism: readings in its meaning and development, Princeton: Van Nostrand, 1964. 4

In this speech, delivered at the opening of the Second National Congress of Venezuela on Feb. 15, 1819, El. Libertador relinquished his post of "Dictator Supreme Chief of the Republic" to the Congress. In it he warns against the machinations of the Spanish Crown, praises the people of the new nation of Venezuela, and charges the legislators to construct a government of righteousness, tolerance, peace, with equality and liberty "under the protection of inexorable laws."

-	-	-	143	-	-	-	-
Gei	cit	lis	rep	ant	eco	pol	soc

Malthus, Thomas R., Principles of political economy considered with a view to their practical application (London, 1820, and later years; 2nd. edit., 1836), NY: A.M. Kelley, 1951, 446 p. 5

"On the Progress of Wealth," pp. 309-437, contains
the logical complement to Malthus' population theory. The latter explains in terms of the "positive" and "preventive" checks
which act upon the death and birth rates respectively, why
population growth does not overleap the level of actual supplies.
Here is presented Malthus' theory of the causes of growth of
supplies or wealth. Among the causes are security of property,
law and its administration, "habits more favorable to regular
exertions" and the like, and the more immediate and proximate
causes or "effective stimulants." Among the latter, population
growth is, of course, excluded; included are capital accumulation, fertility of soil, and "inventions to save labor" on the supply side. On the demand side, heavily stressed, is value in
terms of high market prices, in turn accountable to effective
means of distribution and "the structure of the whole society,"
especially "a large proportion of the middle classes of society."

-	1	-	122	-	-	-	-
Gei	cit	lis	rep	ant	eco	pol	soc

Tocqueville, Alexis C. H. M. C. de, Democracy in
America (Brussels, 1840 and later years), revised, corrected
and edited by F. Bowen et al, NY: Knopf, 1945, 2 vols.   6
  Considered a masterpiece for more than a century,
this book was written about America and democracy primarily
for Europeans who were dubious or overly idealistic about both.
Included in vol. 1 are Constitution, Federal and local government, suffrage, the rule of law and that of the majority, parties, press, relations between citizen and national government,
between religion and democracy and among the three major
races. Vol. 2 deals with the influence of democracy upon social
and intellectual conditions, opinions, laws and feelings, all
leading in the end to the blunting of extremes, to a universality
and uniformity of character and action, to mild customs and
humane laws, to a general state of equality among all "perhaps less elevated, but... more just."

-	(2)	-	-	-	-	-	-
Gei	cit	lis	rep	ant	eco	pol	soc

Mill, John Stuart, Principles of political economy, with
some of their applications to social philosophy (London 1848
and later years), NY: Kelley, 1965, 1013 p.   7
  Part I of this classic is on production and its components and properties. Part II is on distribution, with chapters on
property, classes, competition and custom, slavery, etc. Part
III treats exchange--value, demand and supply, money, credit,
etc. Part IV sets forth Mill's views of the nature and sources
of progress; the last section of Ch. VII is synopsized as "Competition not pernicious, but useful and indispensable." The

last, Part V, concerns the role of government--taxation, national debt, protection of native industry, and conditions under which the laissez-faire principle ('the general rule") is most, and least effective.

-	2	1	114	-	1	-	-
Gei	cit	lis	rep	ant	eco	pol	soc

Marx, Karl, Capital: a critique of political economy. Book one: the process of capitalist production (Hamburg, 1867), transl. from the 3rd and 4th German editions, NY: Modern Library, 1936, 869 p.   8

In this chief work of a man whose ideas changed the course of history is outlined the central thesis of Marxism--that there exists a basic law of development of the capitalist economic system according to which it is inevitably replaced by social-ism. As simple commodity production changes into a capitalist form, the institutions of private ownership of productive prop-erty become increasingly maladaptive, economic contradictions develop along with two antagonistic social classes, the bour-geoisie and the proletariat. With this, class consciousness appears, the class struggle sharpens, and in a revolution the bourgeois ruling class is overthrown, permitting the social order to be reorganized from base to superstructure in a new, progressive socialist form. In spite of numerous shortcomings, theoretical and empirical, these ideas and this book wield tremendous influence in the contemporary world, in the less-developed countries (LDC's) as well as in the communist na-tions.

-	6	-	1860	-	-	-	-
Gei	cit	lis	rep	ant	eco	pol	soc

Jevons, William Stanley, The theory of political economy (London, 1871 and later years), 5th edit., NY: Kelley and Millman, 1957, 342 p.   9

The bulk of contributions to "pure" economic theory are to be found in this book. In it was presented, for the first time in English, the principle of marginal utility which the author (along with Gossen, Menger, Walras) developed, and which constituted the basis for the modern utility theory of value. Jevons also was one of the first to employ mathematical and statistical methods in economics, though he is perhaps equally well-remembered for some of his highly original but less suc-cessful ideas, such as his conclusion that business cycles could be attributed to agricultural crop fluctuations and ultimate-ly to sun spots.

-	(2)	-	-	-	-	-	-
Gei	cit	lis	rep	ant	eco	pol	soc

Marshall, Alfred, Principles of economics: an introductory volume (London, 1890 and later years), 8th edit., NY:
Macmillan, 1920, 858 p.   10

This is the most influential statement of the neoclassical school by the man generally considered the dean of English
economic theorists. Marshall saw development as necessarily gradual and continuous; his dedicatory slogan, natura non
facit saltum, was felt particularly to apply to economic growth.
For this reason he, like other neoclassical writers, saw good
reason for employing static partial equilibrium techniques of
analysis to the problems of development. At the same time,
influenced by Darwinian and Spencerian thought, he made liberal
use of organic analogy in conceiving of the economic system in
terms of progress or evolution. Marshall also introduced and
popularized a number of technical concepts of continuing importance, such as elasticity of demand, quasi-rent, external
economies.

-	3	-	-	-	-	-	-
Gei	cit	lis	rep	ant	eco	pol	soc

Lenin, (Ulianov) Vladimar I., The development of
capitalism in Russia: the process of the formation of a home
market for large-scale industry (St. Petersburg, 1899, 2nd
edit., 1908), Moscow: For. Lang. Pub. House, 1956, 751 p.
                                                                    11

Lenin's marxist classic was written largely in polemical
response to the interpretations of the Russian economic situation provided by Populist economists, especially Vorontsov and
Danielson. It is an analysis of the Imperial social and economic
system which traces in considerable detail the increase in the
"productive sources of social labor," as in the development of
large scale industry, and the "socialization" of such labor,
i. e., the transformation of small local markets into a large
national market, and the like. Lenin took special pains to
show, under the rubric of "disintegration," how the peasantry
were in the process of stratification, forming into a rural
bourgeoisie and proletariat. The general thesis is that this
and similar phenomena familiar in Marx's general model of
capitalist development were progressive in nature, and indeed
could in this respect be contrasted with a number of "ancient
institutions," or survivals, which retarded such development.

-	5	-	-	-	-	-	-
Gei	cit	lis	rep	ant	eco	pol	soc

Weber, Max, The Protestant ethic and the spirit of
capitalism (Archiv fur Sozialwissenschaft und Sozial-politik,
vols. 20-21, 1904-5), transl. by T. Parsons, NY: Scribner's,
1958, 292 p.   12

In this most famous of sociological contributions to the theory of social change Weber argues that the Calvinistic doctrine of predestination elevated asceticism--hard work, thrift, abstemiousness, etc.--to an ideal pattern of conduct which in turn constituted one of the basic sources of capitalist development in Europe. Specifically, the peculiar form the ascetic ideal took tended to identify success in a wordly calling as a sign of grace and eventual salvation. Thus was constructed the "spirit of capitalism," fathered by the Protestant ethic, and which has persisted as a work ethic even as the original source in religious devotion diminished in vitality.

-	(2)	1	-	-	-	-	1
Gei	cit	lis	rep	ant	eco	pol	soc

Thurston, Edgar and K. Rangachari, Castes and tribes of Southern India Madras: Government Press, 1909, 7 vols.
13
The seven volumes are part of the result of a systematic ethnographic survey commissioned by the Government in 1901. These describe more than 300 castes and tribes representing more than 40 million persons. Each is taken up in alphabetic order, and there are some good photos in addition to valuable anthropometric data gathered by Thurston. The quality of the information in the work ranges from a high level in the anthropometric field, through the ethnographic detail and historical interpretations to a low, defective level in the Sanskrit scholarship.

-	(2)	-	-	-	-	-	-
Gei	cit	lis	rep	ant	eco	pol	soc

Schumpeter, Joseph A. , The theory of economic development: an inquiry into profits, capital, credit, interest and the business cycle (Leipzig, 1912), transl. from the German by Redvers Opie, Cambridge, Mass.: Harvard University Press, 1934, 255 p.
14
This is one of the earliest expositions of dynamic economic theory, leading to a distinction between the capitalist and the technical expert on the one hand, and the entrepreneur on the other. Rejecting both the Marxian dialectic and the unilateral evolutionary approach, Schumpeter stresses the autonomy of the entrepreneur, and the irregularity of his appearance as well as his behavior, as manifested by the recurrent booms and crises of the business cycle. The entrepreneurial type, defined in sociological and psychological as well as economic terms, is held to be the crucial element in economic life. He makes the difference between a more or less stationary "circular flow" and actual economic development. A classic text in economic theory, originally published in 1912, when economics was not

yet clearly differentiated from sociology, this book has made a major impact on two generations of social scientists concerned with economic development.

Gei	cit	lis	rep	ant	eco	pol	soc
1	3	-	24	-	-	-	-

Luxemburg, Rosa, The accumulation of capital (Berlin, 1913), transl. from the German by A. Schwarzschild, New Haven: Yale University Press, 1951, 475 p.   15

In this modern anti-revisionist, quite technical, Marxist classic the thesis is developed that in capitalism the contradiction between productive capacity and outlets for products constantly increases. Thus, products must be sold to "third persons," in particular to the less developed countries. In pursuit of this "solution" to the capitalist contradiction, the backward countries become the victims of imperialism. The pattern is concretely expressed in the tendency of capitalist societies to expand and monopolize markets, and to make militaristic imperialism the major principle of their foreign policy.

Gei	cit	lis	rep	ant	eco	pol	soc
-	3	-	-	-	-	-	-

Farquhar, John N., Modern religious movements in India NY: Macmillan, 1915, 471 p.   16

Originally presented in 1913 at the Hartford Theological Seminary in the form of eight lectures, this work synthesizes a great amount of information in a dramatic narrative of the uprisings of the Indian spirit from 1800 to 1913. The great Awakening in India, which began about 1800 and is here described in terms of fresh religious movements, is attributed to two basic forces--the British Government and the Protestant Missions--and to a third factor appearing later on the scene-- the work of the great Orientalists. The conclusions point to both a steady advance of the ancient faiths and "increasing inner decay," much like the patterns of revival of the ancient religions of the Roman Empire in the early Christian centuries. It is stressed also that the spirit and norms of Christianity have been a guiding influence in undermining commitment to caste and to the more primitive features (widow-burning, etc.) of Hinduism and other of the old faiths.

Gei	cit	lis	rep	ant	eco	pol	soc
-	(2)	-	-	-	-	-	-

Marshall, Alfred, Industry and trade: a study of industrial technique and business organization, and of their influences on the conditions of various classes and nations London: Macmillan, 1919, 875 p.   17

This is both a description and a history of industry, trade and business organization. The subtitles of the various chapters suggest the main line of Marshall's arguments in Book I: "[England's]. . . drift toward massive production;" "[France's]. . . individuality and refinement in production;" "[Germany and]. . . science in the service of industry;" and "[USA and]. . . multiform standardization." Book II is on business organization--adjustment of production to demand, industrial standardization, marketing, speculation, management, etc. Book III is on monopolistic tendencies, trusts, cartels, etc. with much attention to specific examples in British, German and American economic history.

	(2)	-	-	-	-	-	-
Gei	cit	lis	rep	ant	eco	pol	soc

Pigou, Arthur C. , The economics of welfare (London, 1920 and later years), 4th edit. , London: Macmillan, 1952, 876 p.   18

Heir and successor to Alfred Marshall at Cambridge, Pigou's contribution is to bring theory closer to human reality, and to summarize the welfare implications of a variety of fiscal and social policies possible in a society without comprehensive national planning. He shows that it is incorrect to calculate the costs of production only in terms of the costs charged to the private producer, just as it is incorrect to measure the benefit of production solely in terms of private profit. In both cases there are costs and gains which are as much social as they are private--unemployment, injury to health, noise, smoke and, on the gain side, many public benefits which produce little or no private gain. Thus, contrary to the axiom of Adam Smith, the outcome of the competition under the aegis of the "invisible hand" does not necessarily maximize social welfare.

	(2)	-	-	-	-	-	-
Gei	cit	lis	rep	ant	eco	pol	soc

Marshall, Alfred, Money, credit and commerce London: Macmillan, 1923, 369 p.   19

This is Marshall's third and final major work. In it he continues to stress the implications of his basic positions, the notion that "economic evolution is gradual and continuous on each of its numberless routes," that economic activity is well-conceived as a set of self-adjusting, self-correcting forces (or as a system tending toward equilibrium), and that solid progress must in the end be in the form of improvements in human nature in terms of traits like industriousness, thrift, responsibility, etc. The four parts of the book treat money, business credit, international trade and fluctuations of industry, trade

and credit.
- (2) - - - - - -
Gei cit lis rep ant eco pol soc

Kulp, Daniel H. , Country life in South China: the
sociology of familism, vol. 1, Phenix Village, Kwangtung,
China (NY, 1952), Taipai (Taiwan): Ch'eng-Wen, 1966, 367 p.
20

A detailed descriptive study, with sketches, tables and
photographs, of a village in northern Kwangtung Province as of
1918-19, and based on summer field work, this report is offered as a healthy improvement over 'the danger of generaliz-
ing about wide areas of life in China" in the face of great differences among areas. Among the 71 findings summarized
in the introduction, some of the most interesting concern the
nature and fate of familism, a system whereby "whatever is
good for the family, however that good is conceived, is approved and developed; whatever is inimical to the interests of
the family, however they are formulated, is taboo and pro-
hibited. "

- (2) - - - - - -
Gei cit lis rep ant eco pol soc

Jenks, Leland H. , The migration of British capital to
1875 (NY, 1927), Camden, NJ: Nelson, 1963, 442 p. 21
This book tells how London became the business and
financial center of the world in the great commercial era
from 1815-1875. It also tells how Britain led the way in integrating the isolated and less developed regions and nations of
the world by exporting capital and the new patterns of machine
industry and capitalistic institutions. It reports how Britain
invested a good amount of its surplus wealth in railroads as
well as in extractive and manufacturing industries in South
America, Africa, India, the USA and other places, and derived
substantial benefit from it. This led to control from London,
leading to what the writer terms "economic imperialism. " It is
a solid, dispassionate and well-written history of the financial
substructure of the first international development experience.

- (2) - - - - - -
Gei cit lis rep ant eco pol soc

Young, Allyn, "Increasing returns and economic progress," Metal Indus 33:324-8, 1928. 22
The thesis of this article is that the chief vehicle of
progress is the size of the market. Large markets unim-
peded by tariff barriers produce large, highly differentiated
and specialized industries which, in turn, produce increasing
returns. Also, the growth rates of each industry are con-

ditioned by the rates of growth of other industries in a moving equilibrium of increasing returns and economic progress. Taking industrial differentiation as a form of the division of labor, it is correct to say that the extent of the division of labor is limited by the size of the market, but it is also true that the size of the market is limited by the division of labor.

-	(2)	-	-	-	-	-	-
Gei	cit	lis	rep	ant	eco	pol	soc

Tannenbaum, Frank, The Mexican agrarian revolution NY: Macmillan, 1929, 543 p.   23

This detailed compendium of Mexican agrarian statistics, laws and interpretations is based on official records and observations made by the author, who traveled in every Mexican state. It deals with the land problem, long a difficult matter in Mexico, toward which the Revolution of 1910 increasingly became oriented, and with the extent to which the policies and measures associated with it actually were implemented. Though falling below the highest scholarly standards in several ways, the book is useful for what it tries to do and for assorted small conclusions and facts, such as the author's point that there has been a continuing transfer of land to the free villages, to individual peasants and to the Mexican Government, and although he notes that 2,700 persons owned more than one-half of the privately-owned lands, he also asserts that the Revolution freed approximately one-half of the population from serfdom.

-	-	3	-	2	-	1	-
Gei	cit	lis	rep	ant	eco	pol	soc

Boeke, Julius H., "Dualistic economics," "Part I The Theory of Dualism" (Leiden, 1930), p. 165-92 in Koninklijk Institut voor de Tropen, Indonesian economics: the concept of dualism in theory and practice The Hague: van Hoeve, 1961.
                                                                      24

In this classic statement of the case, first presented as an inaugural lecture by Boeke when he took a post as professor of tropical-colonial economics at the University of Leiden, he informed his audience that where there is "a sharp, deep, broad cleavage dividing the society into two segments. . . Western economic theories lose their relation to reality--and hence their value." He further proposed that such a society be called "dualistic" and that new social sciences be nominated to study it--dualistic law, dualistic sociology, and dualistic economics. Defined succinctly, these are societies

> Where capitalism has not acted as a creative force exerting a strengthening and advancing influence on the technological and economic development of the masses, and where as a result a predominantly

agrarian population has stagnated economically and
Malthus' law still operates in its full vigor.
The dualistic society is described here in terms of six "antithe-
ses:" immobility of the factors of production, sharp distinction
between urban and rural, a money economy and a goods (subsistence) economy, increasing centralization vs. increasingly
less significant village localism, mechanical (Western, urban,
etc.) vs. organic (Eastern, nature-orientation, etc.), and a
producers' alongside a consumers' economy. In conclusion,
Boeke argues that the village cooperative and the Gandhian
ideal of the village cooperative deserve full support in such
societies, which they do not ordinarily receive in the rush to
see industrialization as a universal panacea.

Gei	cit	lis	rep	ant	eco	pol	soc
-	-	1	450	-	1	-	-

Redfield, Robert and Alfonso V. Rojas, Chan Kom: a
Maya village Washington, D. C.: Carnegie Institution of Washington, 1934, 387 p.   25
Chan Kom is a village in Yucatan of 250 persons, most-
ly Indian, but integrated with the state government. This work
is a detailed listing, in the manner of ethnographic description,
of factual information under such headings as housing, food,
clothing, agriculture, and so on. Two unusual features are an
autobiography of the village leader, and a diary kept by the
junior author which reveals the day-to-day events in the village
for a year. It is useful for data on the personal and interper-
sonal side of culture contact and change; the village was a
rather dynamic one, having doubled in population since 1918,
and it showed some of the "spontaneous progressiveness" of a
pioneer settlement.

Gei	cit	lis	rep	ant	eco	pol	soc
7	-	3	-	2	-	-	1

Clark, Colin, The conditions of economic progress
(London, 1940), 3rd, largely rewritten edit., NY: Macmillan,
1957, 720 p.   26
The main argument and contributions of this landmark
publication can be summed up in the desire of the author to
substitute for the speculative and theoretical reasoning of the
English university economists "a science based on the collection and examination of the actual facts of the economic
world." Of primary interest is the operational definition of
total income and sectoral data and comparisons of the nations
in terms of national income levels and rates of growth.
Crammed with statistical data and carefully constructed indicators of technical concepts, the main original theoretical

contribution is described as "the morphology of economic growth," by which is meant the tendency for the relative importance of the three types of production, grouped by Clark into primary, secondary and tertiary, to change in association with level of national income. With a rise in the latter the proportion of the labor force in primary industry (agriculture, fishing, etc.) declines; the proportion in secondary production (manufacturing, public works, etc.) first rises, then falls; and that engaged in the tertiary production (services, primarily) tends steadily to rise.

-	4	1	-	-	1	-	-
Gei	cit	lis	rep	ant	eco	pol	soc

Cleven, Nels A., The political organization of Bolivia Washington, DC: Carnegie Institution, 1940, 253 p.   27
The main focus here is upon the nature and organization of the constitutional system of Bolivia. Clevel believes that the political organization of Bolivia cannot be understood apart from its geography, peoples, and its entire history. He looks at Bolivia as a mediterranean country which consists of three physical regions, and argues that it is the geographic factor which explains many of the problems relating to the decentralization of the national government, the development of the means of communication and transportation, and the development of natural resources. The fact that Bolivia has always had a unified government is seen by Cleven as due to its size, location, topography, climate, and to the ethnic composition of the country. The study includes the years up to 1931. One basic interpretation which emerges is that the history of Bolivia is complex, and that its political organization must be considered in view of this fact.

-	-	3	-	2	-	1	-
Gei	cit	lis	rep	ant	eco	pol	soc

Fortes, Meyer and E. E. Evans-Pritchard (eds.), African political systems, NY: Oxford University Press, 1940, 301 p.   28
In their introduction to this volume of anthropological essays on political systems, the editors point out that "most of the forms described are variants of political organization found among contiguous or neighboring societies." Thus, the book covers a large part of Africa, and so provides an important reference work for social scientists. The political systems studied fall into two general groups. One consists of societies with a centralized form of administration, with distinctions in wealth, privilege and status. The other group is marked by a comparative absence of such structural details. The political systems investigated include the Kingdom of the

Zulu of South Africa, the political organization of Ngwato of Bechuanaland Protectorate, the Bemba Tribe of Northeastern Rhodesia, the Kingdom of Ankole in Uganda, the Kede (a Riverain State in Norther Nigeria), the Bantu of Kavirondo, the Tallensi of the Northern Territories of the Gold Coast and the Nuer of the Southern Sudan.

8	-	3	-	-	-	3	-
Gei	cit	lis	rep	ant	eco	pol	soc

Redfield, Robert, The folk culture of Yucatan Chicago: University of Chicago Press, 1941, 416 p.   29

This classic account of the "folk society," with a sharp distinction made between folk and urban cultures, has served as a frame of reference for many community studies and early accounts of modernization. Redfield studied four communities in Yucatan: Tusik, a tribal village of semi-independent Maya in Quintana Roo; Chan Kom, a peasant village; Dzitas, a town on a railroad; and Merida, a city of 96,660. The communities manifest in relative order the "folk features" of isolation and homogeneity and the "urban features" of disorganization of culture, secularization and industrialization. Durkheim's distinction between sacred and secular, however, is not entirely supported, nor is Linton's argument that one can distinguish between folk culture and modern civilization in terms of a ratio between "universals and specialties" on the one side and "alternatives" on the other.

7	-	5	-	5	-	-	-
Gei	cit	lis	rep	ant	eco	pol	soc

Rosenstein-Rodan, Paul N. , "Problems of industrialization of Eastern and South-Eastern Europe," Econ J 53: 202-11, 1943.   30

This is one of the earliest statements of the "balanced growth" approach to economic development. The concept used by the present author to support the thesis is "complementarity of different industries." Investment in, and transfer of agrarian excess population into, a whole set of different industries rather than into one or a few "basic industries" will create its own internal market, will produce in addition several important external economies, and will be profitable collectively even though taken one at a time they would be unprofitable. The author also stresses the beneficial effect for the world economy as a whole of the creation of productive employment for the agrarian excess population. The article was written during World War II and today the author's plan for an "Eastern European Industrial Trust" is out of style, but it still might serve as a plan for other "depressed areas."

1	2	2	320	-	1	-	1
Gei	cit	lis	rep	ant	eco	pol	soc

Wilson, Godfrey and Wilson, Monica, The analysis of social change Cambridge, England: Cambridge University Press, 1945, 177 p.   31

On the basis of experiences in Central Africa, the writers attempt to build a general model of social change. Departing from the assumption of a society as a system in equilibrium, the authors note a series of contradictions inherent in the social structures of Central Africa at the time of writing. The crucial one is the permanent conflict between races and the fact that Africans, whose education and customs Europeans are supposedly trying to improve, are discriminated against as inferior and primitive. This type of conflict is referred to as "radical" since it cannot be solved through the existing social-control mechanisms. Radical conflicts lead to social change as the only way to solve them and to restore a state of equilibrium. The book makes the interesting point that radical contradictions are solved and change effected once the existence of the contradiction becomes a conscious fact. Radical conflicts submit persons to contradictory demands, but when they understand these contradictions and their social character, the existing social arrangements will be changed. The European minority cannot preserve a system in which there is a growing disequilibrium between the advancement of such structural aspects as education, economic production, and industrialization in which Africans participate, and the preservation of cultural prejudices regarding them as inferior. Hence, social change is inevitable.

7	-	4	-	2	-	-	2
Gei	cit	lis	rep	ant	eco	pol	soc

Lorimer, Frank, The population of the Soviet Union: history and prospects Geneva: League of Nations, 1946, 289 p.   32

Based on the censuses of 1897, 1926 and 1939 and a good amount of careful estimation, this definitive analysis of Soviet population data provides an invaluable record of the demographic patterns and costs of the Soviet experience of rapid industrialization. For one example, the urban population increased by almost 30 million in the 1926-1939 period, producing a rate of growth substantially higher than that of the USA or the countries of Western Europe. Among the costs must be included the high mortality associated with the policy of forced collectivization and resettlement in the early 1930's. This resulted, among other things, in a loss of approximately 1.5 million persons from the nomadic Kazakhs of the steppes of Central Asia. On the whole, though, in addition to a detailed description of the Soviet peoples, the figures tell a story of "the most remarkable expansion of mechanical, tech-

nical and administrative activity ever achieved in any nation
in so short a time."

-	3	-	-	-	-	-	-
Gei	cit	lis	rep	ant	eco	pol	soc

Smith, T. Lynn, Brazil: people and institutions (Baton
Rouge, 1946), 3rd rev. edit. , Baton Rouge: Louisiana State
University Press, 1963, 667 p.   33
The characterization of Brazil as a total society is accomplished here in a fashion which conveys a great amount of
factual information without becoming a victim of encyclopedic
tediousness. The description of Brazilian institutions and
cultural patterns is enlivened with observations of the Brazilian
past contributed by foreign visitors as well as by such national
writers as Josúe de Castro, Gilberto Freyre and Teixeira de
Freitas. Among the interesting features stressed are the contrasts between Brazil and Spanish America, between the dynamism of the cities and the apathetic traditionalism of the
countryside, and between the intolerance of some other countries and the striking tolerance found in Brazil for alien religions, races and cultural patterns. Presumably this helps
account for the notable assimilation, successes and contributions of such minorities as the Japanese.

-	-	3	-	-	-	1	2
Gei	cit	lis	rep	ant	eco	pol	soc

Domar, Evsey D. , "Expansion and employment," Am
Econ R 37:34-55, 1947.   34
Domar's work is a landmark study of the interrelation
between the rate of growth of income, that of investment, and
the capital-output and the savings parameters. He reasons
that if unemployment and inflation are to be avoided during
the process of economic growth, the rate of growth of investment and of income must be equal to each other and to the
product of the multiplier and the capital-output ratio. The
analysis is not only descriptive and predictive but has political implications as well, for it lends itself to policy decision-
making. While the author studies some of the implications of
both income and capacity growth, his treatment of the parameters is superficial. Moreover, population growth is not
brought into the analysis; nor are changes in human capital.
Another crucial assumption that fails to accord with reality
is that of the simultaneity of investment and the growth of
capacity and income. While income is earned as investment
proceeds, capacity growth lags behind so that in this respect
as well, Domar's presentation is at least a slight distortion
of reality. Still, it is an important piece as one of the first

attempts to study the dual role of investment in generating both capacity and income and their consequences.

Gei	cit	lis	rep	ant	eco	pol	soc
1	2	1	120	-	1	-	-

Gillin, John, "Modern Latin American culture," Social Forces 25:243-248, 1947.   35

There is at hand in the Western hemisphere a variant of Western civilization which has distinctive traits, institutions and themes as well as subsidiary or subcultural variations. Among the important elements of this "Latin American culture" are Roman Catholicism (cult of the saints, public fiestas, parades, etc.), the Spanish language, the "plaza plan" in towns, male dominance in the family, etc. Ideologically, it is humanistic rather than puritanical; intellectually, it stresses logic and dialectics rather than empiricism and pragmatics; etc. In addition to distinctions based on historical, geographic and ethnic features, there is, in fact, in most countries a strong indigenous influence. These cultures have absorbed some Western civilization elements but do manifest patterns different enough to be termed "Republican Native culture." The penetration of the latter by Latin American culture and/or its incorporation into it, is an important process in Latin America, and has produced a number of movements with special goals relevant to it--indigenismo (preservation of "Republican Native Culture"), hispanismo (a return to classical Spanish culture), and modernismo (a conversion of Latin American culture into a Spanish-speaking version of the USA).

Gei	cit	lis	rep	ant	eco	pol	soc
-	-	3	-	3	-	-	-

Gluckman, Max, "Malinowski's contribution to social anthropology," African Stud 6:41-6, 1947.   36

Gluckman reviews Malinowski's posthumously published A scientific theory of culture and other essays, 1944, and finds it to be largely a restatement of ideas published earlier, but insofar as it varies from those, "he deals more with the processes by which the human organism is conditioned so that purely biological cannot be separated from cultural behavior . . ." In this Gluckman finds one of the major weaknesses of Malinowski's functional theory, for it caused him to retreat from considering the phenomena he discussed in cultural terms. The key to his difficulty lies in the fact that his major units, the institutions, cannot be broken up for analysis, and therefore do not permit the formulation of "comparative problems on the cultural plane."

Gei	cit	lis	rep	ant	eco	pol	soc
-	-	1	320	1	-	-	-

Tschopik, Harry, Jr., Highland communities of
Central Peru Washington, DC: Smithsonian Institution, Institute for Social Anthropology, Public. No. 5, 1947, 56 p.   37
This report, carried out in 2 months by the author and
3 Peruvian collaborators, records the findings of an ethnographic survey of 14 communities in the heretofore little
studied highland communities. These range in type from small
Quechua-speaking herding settlements high (some over 14,000
ft.) on the punas (treeless, bleak tableland in the higher
Andes) to agricultural towns in the valleys and progressive
mestizo communities. The highest concentration of Indians
and the greatest amount of cultural traditionalism is found in
the areas least inviting to the Spanish--the punas--except in
places where these contain minerals.

Gei	cit	lis	rep	ant	eco	pol	soc
-	-	3	-	2	1	-	-

Whetten, Nathan I., Rural Mexico Chicago: University
of Chicago Press, 1948, 671 p.   38
Based on three years of intensive work by a rural
sociologist at a time when Mexican-American ties were particularly close, this comprehensive study of Mexico gives
special attention to its most problematic features--problems
and patterns of agriculture, village life and integration of the
Indian masses into the modern era. Landholding patterns and
the problem of efficient agriculture are discussed. While the
diffusion of land tenure (1940) was considerable, in relation to
the previous situation (1910), agricultural productivity on the
ejidos remained law. Woven into the discussion are two interpretive motifs of particular interest. One is the comparison
of the active efforts of the rural cultural missions sponsored
by the Mexican Government to demonstrate the superiority
of the new ways with the disinterest of the rural priests in
the physical, social and moral welfare of their parishioners.
The other motif is the Mexican Revolution, which is treated
by Whetten as a continuing process, and, one would add today,
a powerful modernizing influence, which in spite of mistakes
and injustices, earns in his view "a net positive balance."

Gei	cit	lis	rep	ant	eco	pol	soc
-	-	4	-	2	-	1	1

Collier, John, Jr., and Anibal Buitron, The awakening
valley Chicago: University of Chicago Press, 1949, 199 p.
39
This beautifully photographed and poetically told story
of the Indians who live on the Andean mountain slopes surrounding the Ecuadorean town of Otavalo is an example of
first-rate interpretive ethnology. It also has an important

argument to make, namely, that these Indians have managed
to integrate commercial economic activity into their traditional
way of life without disruption. Quite the contrary, their
skillful adaptation of modern techniques of manufacturing wool
textiles has enabled them to reap "the advantages of the modern
age without crushing their spirit." In this, they are said to
contrast strongly with the white and mestizo townspeople, who
are "tired and discouraged."

	-	3	-	2	-	1	-
Gei	cit	lis	rep	ant	eco	pol	soc

Mannoni, D. Otare, <u>Prospero and Caliban: the psychology of colonization</u> (Paris, 1950), tr. from the French by
P. Powesland, NY: Praeger, 1956, 218 p.   40
This original and early contribution to what has now
become a major topic in societal development is based on the
unsystematic but extensive observations of a colonial official
who lived for many years in Madagascar. The main phenomenon which the writer reports on and seeks to explain is racial-
ism--the sense of white superiority and domineering behavior
exhibited by many colonial whites together with submissive
meekness, lack of initiative and a small sense of responsibility on the part of the natives. A central factor in the explanation is psychological dependency. According to Mannoni, the
Malagasy is born into a set of relationships in the joint family
where dependency is encouraged, finds a similar role under the
rule and guidance of Europeans and never is able to confront
and master the challenges of independence.

	1	3	-	-	-	3	-
Gei	cit	lis	rep	ant	eco	pol	soc

Redfield, Robert, <u>A village that chose progress: Chan
Kom revisited</u> Chicago: University of Chicago Press, 1950,
187p.   41
Chan Kom, in Yucatan, Mexico, was first studied by
Redfield in 1931 when he noted that the villagers had thoroughly "committed themselves to progress and civilization." He
returned in 1948, stayed 40 days, and reports his observations
here. The main conclusion is an important one: the village
has been remarkably successful in changing in the directions
planned for, and under traditional Mayan leadership. Furthermore, increments of material progress and welfare have left
the villagers in possession of a large portion of their traditional culture and a sense of satisfaction even while bringing them
into contact with new institutions and opportunities. For instance, there has not yet appeared a desire for conspicuous
consumption nor a class system based on wealth. However,

there is some disquiet about the future, with the increased un-
certainty brought by a higher level of participation in Mexican
society as a whole.

-	-	3	-	1	-	1	1
Gei	cit	lis	rep	ant	eco	pol	soc

Singer, Hans W. , "The distribution of gains between in-
vesting and borrowing countries," Am Econ R Pap & Proc,
40:473-85, 1950.   42
This article delineates the main aspects of the Singer
trade thesis in a modern form. The theory explains the maldistribution of international wealth in terms of unfavorable
price conditions on the international primary product market.
Foreign trade balances are more important to underdeveloped
countries and serious fluctuations are disastrous to the economy. Technology puts the advanced country in a position to
manipulate and control the fate of non-advanced countries. Investment flows out, and the backward technology resists new
technological advance because it must remain in primary
products. Singer changes from his earlier position in that,
in this article, foreign investment is welcomed on the condition that it is accompanied by native investments, and that
internal markets are expanded via the new technology.

2	1	2	200	-	1	-	1
Gei	cit	lis	rep	ant	eco	pol	soc

Balandier, Georges, "The colonial situation: a theoretical approach," Ch 3, p. 24-57 in I. Wallerstein (ed.),
Social change; the colonial situation NY: John Wiley, 1966.
                                                             43
One of the major events of recent history has been the
expansion throughout the entire world of most European peoples. Colonialism has been imposed on subject people and
has resulted in a special type of situation. The colonial situation causes problems for the new states just emerging from
colonialism. One of these problems is race relations.
Balandier looks at the colonial situation from the viewpoints of
the colonial historian, economist, politician and administrator,
sociologist, and psychologist concerned with race relations. An
approach to colonial studies, using each of these disciplines,
can give a standpoint from which to understand the evolution of
indigeneous social structures when placed in the colonial situation. The author also discusses the "crises" of the colonial
situation which enable the sociologist to achieve a more
comprehensive analysis of the colonies. (Orig. publ. in
Cahiers Internationaux de Sociologie, 11:44-79, 1951).

-	-	3	160	1	-	2	-
Gei	cit	lis	rep	ant	eco	pol	soc

Bauer, Peter T. and Basil S. Yamey, "Economic progress and occupational distribution" Econ J 61:741-55, 1951.

44

It is a widely accepted view that economic progress is associated with a relative increase in the proportion of individuals engaged in tertiary activities, after the theory proposed by Clark. This view, however, is both conceptually and statistically fallacious. Part of the error derives from the inability to classify individuals into distinct occupational categories in economies in which occupational specialization is imperfect. For example, in West Africa where trade constitutes only one of the activities of a vast proportion of the population, Africans frequently do not regard trade as an occupation, but, rather, as part of existence. Trade, most definitely tertiary, is a major activity in many economically underdeveloped nations. Entry into small-scale trade is easy, as at this level no technical or administrative skill is required and only very little capital. This article convincingly points out the severe limitations of the view that a high proportion of labor in tertiary activities is both a consequence and a measure of a high standard of living.

-	2	-	160	-	-	-	-
Gei	cit	lis	rep	ant	eco	pol	soc

Hoffer, Eric, The true believer: thoughts on the nature of mass movements NY: Harper, 1951, 160 p.   45

Included under the concept mass movement are religious movements such as Christianity and Islam, social revolutions such as the communist and fascist varieties, and genuine nationalist movements toward modernization such as occurred in Japan and Turkey. All of these share certain common properties--their birth takes place amidst misery and frustration; people are led to self-sacrifice by leaders who are masters of the art of "religiofication," the art of turning practical purposes into holy causes; large numbers of fanatics, the "true believers," are generated; individual creativity is destroyed during the movement's active phase; etc. The style is aphoristic and the author is often opinionated if not oracular, but the ideas are most important and, after all, there are good as well as bad mass movements.

-	-	3	-	-	-	2	1
Gei	cit	lis	rep	ant	eco	pol	soc

Lewis, Oscar, Life in a Mexican village: Tepoztlán restudied Urbana, Ill.: University of Illinois Press, 1951, 512 p.   46

Building upon the knowledge contributed by Redfield's pioneering study of the same town in 1926-27, benefitting from the accumulated substantial advances in research method and technology in the intervening years, using data from techniques novel for anthropological field studies, and enjoying the assistance of a dozen professional assistants, Lewis has contributed an unusually complete description of this village of 3,500 inhabitants. In fact, it is more than a "community study," for government and politics, the life cycle, indeed Mexican culture as a whole, are described, in words, sketches and photographs. One of the book's best-known features consists of the emphasis, contrasting with the "rousseauan" image of Redfield, upon the impersonal, uncooperative "individualism" of the villagers, upon their reserved, suspicious, fearful traits. It also has a detailed critique of Redfield's concept of the folk-urban continuum, and a good summary of the changes occurring since the earlier study, in which the school is assigned an important role as an agent of change.

-	-	3	-	2	-	1	-
Gei	cit	lis	rep	ant	eco	pol	soc

Moore, Wilbert E., <u>Industrialization and labor: social aspects of economic development</u> Ithaca: Cornell University Press, 1951, 410 p.   47

This book is a structural-functional comparative analysis in the Mertonian tradition, based on a vast amount of relevant literature, and on the author's study of two Mexican villages that are located near several modern factories. Part I, being a summary and evaluation of the many previous studies in this field, and buttressed by an extensive bibliography, is the most valuable part. The conclusions are general and theoretical rather than practical and specific, stressing "the recognition of functional interdependence of organizational and motivational elements," and always hedged with the important but debilitating qualification that prediction in any concrete case needs to take into account a great number of specific variables, those that apply to the particular situation being studied. If the subtitle had read "some social aspects . . . etc.," it would have been a more accurate description of the book's content. Actually, Moore is concerned mainly with "the relevance for economic development of labor supply in the qualitative, motivational sense."

1	1	4	-	1	1	-	2
Gei	cit	lis	rep	ant	eco	pol	soc

United Nations. Department of Economic Affairs. <u>Land reform: defects in agrarian structure as obstacles to economic development</u> (E/2003/Rev. 1 ST/ECA/11), NY: UN, 1951, 101 p.   48

The General Assembly on Nov. 20, 1950 adopted a
resolution recommending

> an analysis of the degree to which unsatisfactory
> forms of agrarian structure and, in particular,
> systems of land tenure, in the under-developed
> countries and territories impede economic develop-
> ment and thus depress the standards of living
> especially of agricultural workers and tenants and
> of small and medium-sized farmers.

The report succinctly documents and illustrates the fact that
certain features of agrarian structure do present serious obstacles to development. Among these are: farm size too
small, maldistribution of land ownership (under-utilized large
estates side by side with landlessness of a large part of the
rural population), fragmentation of land holdings, high rents
and insecure tenancy, indebtedness and lack of credit facilities
for small farmers, absence of settled title to land and water,
plantation economies which offer low wages and no share in
management to the cultivators, unfair taxation policies, and a
general absence of incentives for agricultural workers to raise
production. Though lack of precise information makes it im-
possible to give a full account of the situation, and although no
attempt is made to analyze in full any one country, the evidence suggests that these defects are widespread throughout
the less-developed world.

Gei	cit	lis	rep	ant	eco	pol	soc
-	-	-	1089	-	-	-	-

Baran, Paul A. , "On the political economy of backwardness," The Manchester School of Economic and Social Studies
20:66-84, 1950.   49

The middle classes can be considered a source of progressive change only in their beginnings. With the revolt of
the popular sector, middle class groups defend their vested
interests and make alliances with the upper classes. Development has to start in the industrial sector; agriculture cannot
furnish the basis for development. The needed capital for
industrialization may be offered only by upper classes but they
prefer short-run, easy, money-making investments. The
capitalist state cannot evolve a real development policy because
of the pressures of the upper classes. In this situation, social
upheavals are in order. This is an important polemical and
controversial point of view by the late Stanford professor.

Gei	cit	lis	rep	ant	eco	pol	soc
-	1	-	180	-	-	-	-

Comas, Juan, "Cultural anthropology and fundamental
education in Latin America," Int Soc Sci Bul 4:451-61, 1952

50

This article is about the "native problem"--the more than 30 million persons in America belonging to different ethnic groups and who have specific characteristics which differentiate them from "white" or "Western" civilization, who have the lowest standard of living, and who, being relatively unassimilated, do not constitute an active factor in national production and consumption. There is no such situation in Uruguay or Cuba, but it is very important in Bolivia, Ecuador, Guatemala, Mexico and Peru, and has been so recognized by conferences, congresses and authoritative writers such as Gamio and Villa Rojas for many years. The thesis of the author is that no solution to this problem is possible without the active participation of applied cultural anthropology. In support of his view he cites numerous resolutions and comments, and describes current cooperative educational and work projects in which an important role is played by anthropologists.

-	-	3	-	3	-	-	-
Gei	cit	lis	rep	ant	eco	pol	soc

Fanon, Frantz, "The ordeal of the black man," p. 75-87 in I. Wallerstein (ed.), Social change: the colonial situation, NY: Wiley, 1966.   51

What does it feel like to be a black man in a white world? To be rejected, to be refused recognition, to have one's self-concept structured from without, to act from an implicit position of inferiority. The black man is not only the slave of an "idea" which others have of him, he is the slave of his appearance. Color prejudice is the unreasoning hatred of one race for another, the contempt of the stronger and richer peoples for those whom they consider inferior to themselves, and creates bitter resentment among those kept in subjection and so frequently insulted. The black man withdraws into the irrational and fashions an anti-racist racism. The ethnic idea of negritude is transformed into the notion of the proletariat. The white symbolizes capital while the Negro symbolizes labor. That is why the most ardent poets of the black race are at the same time militant Marxists.

> The thesis is the theoretical and practical affirmation of the White Man's superiority; the position of Negritude, as antithetical value is the moment of negativity. . . . The synthesis [is] the fulfillment of the human potential in a society without racism.

As if to apologize to his black brothers for affirming a synthesis which denies the importance of negritude, Fanon salutes the historical opportunity that permits black men to utter "the great Negro cry with such intensity as to shake the foundations of the world." (Orig. pub. in Peau noire, masques blanca, Paris: Ed. du Seuil, 1952.)

2	-	1	14	-	-	1	-
Gei	cit	lis	rep	ant	eco	pol	soc

Frankel, S. Herbert, "Some aspects of technical change," Int Soc Sci Bull 4:263-9, 1952.   52

The author begins by noting that we readily tend to use the phrase "social consequences of technical change," but decline to use the phrase "technical change as a social consequence." He concludes that the verbal pattern shows "that we have formed the habit of regarding technical change in mechanistic terms--as an independent force, which, by impinging on society, sets in motion certain desirable, or undesirable reactions." And that these reactions "are then presumed to require study in the same fatalistic spirit in which one might try to cope with the destruction left in the wake of a battle or of an earthquake." The position taken by the author is that technical change not only affects, but depends upon, indeed is inseparable from, administrative, social and psychological arrangements, and that these latter are little understood and badly need detailed comparative study.

1	-	-	121	-	-	-	-
Gei	cit	lis	rep	ant	eco	pol	soc

Galbraith, John K. , American capitalism: the concept of countervailing power Boston: Houghton Mifflin, 1952, 217 p.   53

Here is, in effect if not in explicit form, a theory of development for American capitalism. In spite of structural change which has taken it far from the competitive ideal postulated by "liberal economics," the American economy has produced reasonably acceptable results. The rise of concentration of market power in the form of industrial oligopoly, with attendant decline of price competition, has not removed the incentives to technological progress but furnished a favorable climate for it. Galbraith's thesis is that the rise of oligopolistic power generates "countervailing" power which operates on the opposite (rather than the same) side of the market in the public interest, as, for example, in the case of chain stores acting as large, powerful, retail buying organizations. Similarly, particularly disadvantaged groups, such as farmers, take recourse to government intervention. Thus, the positive use of government power also becomes an essential element in the satisfactory performance of the economy.

-	3	-	-	-	-	-	-
Gei	cit	lis	rep	ant	eco	pol	soc

Goode, Richard, "Reconstruction of foreign tax systems," p. 212-22 in National Tax Association, Proceedings of the

Forty-Fourth Annual Conference on Taxation Dallas, Texas, 1951, Sacramento, Cal.: NTA, 1952.   54

This is a classic statement of the arguments against heavy reliance on income taxes in the LDC's, written by a man who is now head of the Fiscal Affairs Department of the International Monetary Fund. It is also a comprehensive and clear account of the specific problems likely to be encountered in the institution and administration of other types of taxes in such countries. These include export taxes, consumption taxes and real estate taxes. Export taxes are in fairly wide use in the LDC's because they are convenient to administer and because of the substantial degree to which companies for the exploitation of mineral and agricultural resources are foreign-owned. However, they are often short-sighted, and might well be substituted by a special tax on the net profits of such companies. Consumption taxes are in wide use, heavily regressive in effect but probably indispensable. It is in the realm of real estate taxation, argues the writer, that the LDC's are confronted with a promising source of revenue, and which would also have a general beneficial effect upon the performance of the economy.

1	-	1	210	-	-	-	1
Gei	cit	lis	rep	ant	eco	pol	soc

Hoselitz, Bert F. (ed.), The progress of underdeveloped areas Chicago: University of Chicago Press, 1952, 297 p.   55

Under the chairmanship of Bert F. Hoselitz, sixteen economists, anthropologists, political scientists, sociologists and governmental administrators were invited by the 27th Harris Institute on International Relations to consider the problems inherent in the various technical aid programs and the role in them of the social sciences. The result is this volume of essays. Implicit in these discussions is the query of what can the social sciences do to aid the development and implementation of technical aid programs. The book is comprised of three parts: (1) the historical approach, (2) the cultural aspects, and (3) the problems of economic policy. The introductory chapter discusses the developing field of scholarly interest in nonindustrialized areas, and presents a framework for an interdisciplinary approach.

8	1	3	-	1	1	1	-
Gei	cit	lis	rep	ant	eco	pol	soc

Lewis, Oscar "Urbanization without breakdown: a case study," Scientific Monthly 75: 31-41, 1952.   56

This is a preliminary report of Lewis's effort to follow migrants from Tepoztlan into Mexico City, to see what happened to them there. The results suggest a remarkable finding: quite contrary to the image long-established of maladjusted family life, decline of religious faith, delinquency, etc. , the Tepoztecan peasants in Mexico City adapted to city life with far greater ease than did American farm families. Little evidence was found of disorganization, culture conflict or serious differences between generations. Family life became even stronger in Mexico City--there were fewer cases of separation and divorce, no abandoned mothers or children, more extended families than in the village, religious life became more Catholic and more disciplined (although men play a smaller religious role in the city), and among it all ties to the village remained strong. Explanations offered include long-established contact between Mexico City and Indian villages, a city population which is racially and culturally quite homogeneous, the closeness of Tepoztlan to Mexico City, etc.

-	-	5	-	3	-	1	1
Gei	cit	lis	rep	ant	eco	pol	soc

Miner, Horace, "The folk-urban continuum," Am Social R 15: 529-37, 1952.   57

Research findings reported from Mexico, Guatemala and Africa have raised some question about the usefulness of Redfield's concept of the folk-urban continuum. The basic problem is that there are observed discrepancies between the type and specific social structures. However, because the concept itself is so diffuse these facts do not in themselves invalidate it. Another problem is the low reliability (Redfield vs Lewis on Tepoztlan) between observations made in the same community. To handle this, more precision in both nominal and operational definitions is needed. Finally, the author defends the concept on the ground that it at least provides a way of explicitly paying attention to processes of socio-cultural change.

-	-	3	-	1	-	-	2
Gei	cit	lis	rep	ant	eco	pol	soc

Nurkse, Ragnar, "Some international aspects of the problem of international development," Am Econ R 42: 571-83, 1952.   58

This is one of the best statements of the theory of balanced growth in economic development. The inducement to invest is limited by the size of the market and the general level of productivity. In backward areas the output of a new single industry will invariably meet with insufficient demand. This difficulty is not present where there is a synchronized application of capital to a wide range of different industries.

Such a set of new industries would ensure markets for each other's products--providing their production corresponds with the pattern of consumer's preferences. Because the capital demanded for such an investment package is very high and because the return on investment in this particular case is greater from the social point of view than from the private, government may frequently have to play the planning and/or entrepreneurial role. The author also comments on the increasing difficulty in generating savings in low-income countries. The already great and growing gaps between the income levels of different countries, combined with increasing awareness of these gaps, tends to expand consumption and thus reduce savings. It is also becoming politically more difficult to use taxation as a means of compulsory saving. Prosperity then, rather than spreading smoothly throughout the world, may generate disequilibrium and inflation in the poor countries. This essay, especially with respect to the concept of balanced growth, has generated a good deal of controversy. For more, see Celso Furtado, "Capital formation and economic development" and H. W. Singer, "Balanced growth in economic development."

2	2	1	140	-	1	-	-
Gei	cit	lis	rep	ant	eco	pol	soc

Rao, Vijendra K. R. V., "Investment, income and the multiplier in an underdeveloped economy," Ind Econ R 1: 55-67, 1952. 59

Keynes applied the principle of the multiplier to developed, industrialized economies on the assumptions of involuntary unemployment, an industrial economy with an output supply curve sloping upward, excess capacity in the consumer goods industries, and a comparatively elastic supply of working capital. With these assumptions he suggested cheap money, deficit financing, etc. as remedies. However, in an LDC economy, the principle works with reference to money income and not with reference to real income, employment and output. This is because of the presence of disguised unemployment--analogous to Keynes' full employment or near-full employment -- an agrarian economy with a steeply inelastic and backward rising supply curve, the absence of excess capacity in consumer goods industries, and a comparatively inelastic supply of working capital, with household enterprise, production for consumption rather than for the market, and various structural deficiencies and bottlenecks. Keynes was concerned with movements from low to full employment, but in the LDC's the problem is to move from one stage of development to the next higher one, from full employment at one level to full employment at the higher level.

1	-	-	180	-	-	-	-
Gei	cit	lis	rep	ant	eco	pol	soc

Seers, Dudley, "The role of national income estimates in the statistical policy of an underdeveloped area," R Econ Stud 20:159-68, 1952-3.
                                                                    60
Economists and administrators alike have frequently relied on national income estimates to set major policy in under developed areas. Although these estimates provide a reasonably adequate amount of information in more highly developed countries, they are often unrealistic and dangerously inadequate for providing a satisfactory picture of income estimation in underdeveloped areas. In these areas much of the time national income estimates serve purposes other than those for which they are used in developed areas. For example, although it is useful to know the total value of production in developed countries, we are more concerned, in underdeveloped areas, with the relations between various parts of the economy. Statistical estimates then have no real value unless they are used with adequate knowledge of their limitations and purposes.

-	-	3	8	-	3	-	-
Gei	cit	lis	rep	ant	eco	pol	soc

Singer, Hans W. , "The mechanics of economic development," Ind Econ R 1:1-18, 1952.
                                                                    61
The author aims to clarify some of the problems involved in development planning by use of a numerically described model community and a more general model of the kind made familiar by the work of Domar, Harrod and Hicks. The agricultural/nonagricultural ratio assumed in the community is 70/30, whereas in developed countries it is 20/80 or even 15/85. The task is to create structural change in this ratio, by maintaining a constant absolute size of agricultural population, and absorbing the increasing population (assumed to be 1. 25 percent per year in the model community) in the nonagricultural sector. With the assumptions made the author calculates estimated cost, magnitude of the deficit which can be met by foreign capital, variable amounts from increased per capita income which can be reinvested, and the number of years it will take development to be self-supporting.

-	-	-	180	-	-	-	-
Gei	cit	lis	rep	ant	eco	pol	soc

Spicer, Edward H. (ed.), Human problems in technological change: a case book, NY: Russell Sage Foundation, 1952, 301 p.
                                                                    62

This book aims to assist in teaching students how "to introduce new ideas and methods in agriculture, industry, and medicine to areas deficient in these technologies." Fifteen cases of successful and unsuccessful attempts to introduce change are presented, each with a statement of (1) problem, (2) course of events, (3) relevant factors, (4) outcome, and (5) analysis. A final chapter discusses "Conceptual Tools for Solving Problems." Six recurrent groups of problems are considered but no integrated conceptual scheme is presented. In general, the cases deal with "problems of cultural linkage," "problems of social structure," "problems of cultural bias," and "problems of buffer organization."

8	2	8	-	8	-	-	-
Gei	cit	lis	rep	ant	eco	pol	soc

Viner, Jacob, <u>International trade and economic development: lectures</u> Glencoe, Ill.: Free Press, 1952, 154 p.
63

Viner's work is most useful in the present context for its carefully reasoned though properly critical argument for retaining or, better, adapting a good part of the classical theory of international trade, and for its discussion in Ch. 6 of the conceptual and measurement difficulties in the notion of underdevelopment. The new circumstances of the world economic scene which require modification of, but do not invalidate, the classical doctrines of Ricardo and company include the decline of competition, the growth of central planning, the rise of new international institutions, the increase in trade barriers, etc. Viner makes many pertinent observations on trade theory, emergent factors and their relevance for national commercial policy.

1	-	2	1053	-	2	-	-
Gei	cit	lis	rep	ant	eco	pol	soc

Barnett, Homer G., <u>Innovation: the basis of cultural change</u> NY: McGraw-Hill, 1953, 462 p.
64

Innovation is defined as any thought, behavior or thing that is new because it is qualitatively different from existing forms," but the argument rests on the notion that the organization of elements, the idea (or configuration of ideas), which may or may not be transferable into tangible form, is central. The theory is built from and illustrated with data from six main sources: the Yurok, the Tsimshian, the Yakima, Palauans, Americans, and the Indian Shaker cultists of the Pacific Northwest. Topics discussed include cultural background, incentives to innovation, innovative processes, and acceptance and rejection. The emphasis is upon the social psychological processes at work. For example, wants, both social and personal, are linked with the phenomenon of self-definition. Wants can be sublimated, and these are especially important, because they are part of the process by which value systems are developed. For another example, Barnett classifies those likely to be acceptors of innovations as "dissidents," "indifferents," "disaffected," and "resentful." This is a detailed, pioneering study of one of the key patterns in development.

7	2	5	-	3	-	1	1
Gei	cit	lis	rep	ant	eco	pol	soc

Beals, Ralph, "Acculturation," p. 621-41, in A. L. Kroeber (ed.), Anthropology today: an encyclopedia inventory Chicago: University of Chicago Press, 1953.   65
This is a survey of the concept of acculturation as used by anthropologists of the British Commonwealth (The British equivalent is "culture contact"), the USA and Latin America. The concept came into use about a third of a century ago and has had a vexed history since then. There is little agreement about how precisely to define it, how to distinguish it from analogous or associated concepts such as diffusion and assimilation, whether it refers, or should refer, essentially to a two-way process of influence and change or only to a one-way process (in which indigenous cultures are modified by European cultures), and so on. As far as method goes, the author distinguishes and summarizes the situation for each of the following topics: use of historical data and approaches, the comparative approach, the "trait list" vs. the wholistic approach, the role of the individual and the psychological approach, linguistic acculturation studies, the major cultural processes (including "acceptant," "syncretism," and "reaction"), and quantification and indices.

-	-	5	-	4	-	-	1
Gei	cit	lis	rep	ant	eco	pol	soc

Beals, Ralph L., "Social stratification in Latin America," Am J Sociol 58: 327-39, 1953.   66
Increasingly, the system of social stratification in Latin America has been analyzed in terms of the theoretical concepts and empirical indicators currently useful in the analysis of European and North American social stratification. This is both an unrealistic and unfruitful approach to the understanding of Latin American social structure. The unique historical background and demographic characteristics of that region necessitate a reevaluation of present methodological techniques, coupled with an awareness of the basic structural differences between the North American and South American

regions. The present Latin American social structure clearly emerged from a basically Spanish and Portuguese feudal landholding system, evidence of which is still quite obvious, particularly in the rural sectors. Further complicating a generalized analysis of the region as a whole is the differential proportions of Europeans, Indo-mestizos, and Negro components varying from country to country within Latin America. There is, in consequence, great need for systematic analysis of the specific problems, institutions and cultural variations of the Latin American region.

| - | - | 3 | - | 1 | - | 2 | - |
| Gei | cit | lis | rep | ant | eco | pol | soc |

Blanksten, George I. , Peron's Argentina Chicago: University of Chicago Press, 1953, 439 p.   67
This book basically consists of a series of essays discussing Argentina before Peron, the rise of Peron to power, and the effects of the Peron regime on Argentinian culture and society. Blanksten also analyzes the effects of Peron's rule upon Argentina's foreign policy and relations, particularly with the USA. Of particular interest is the explanation given by Blanksten of the theory of justicialismo, the ideology of the Peronist government. In studying the Peronist rule, the author brings attention to many of its repressive aspects. He is also able to describe the forces and powers in Argentina which stood behind Peron and gave support to him. This feature does a great deal to aid the reader in understanding Peron's years in power.

| - | - | 5 | - | 2 | - | 3 | - |
| Gei | cit | lis | rep | ant | eco | pol | soc |

Chenery, Hollis B. , "The application of investment criteria," Q J Econ 67: 76-96, 1953.   68
Chenery develops a model for a social marginal product criterion for investment decisions. This is a measure of the value added in the domestic economy per unit of investment, the total operation cost per unit of investment, and the balance of payments premium per unit of investment. He utilises his empirical knowledge of Italian development programs to compare its application to that of other investment criteria, principally that of capital turnover, the balance of payments effect, and that of social costs. He claims that only by using all three of the components of the social marginal product criterion is it possible adequately to assess investment programs, because of the interplay of the various factors. Separate investment tests may be useful in establishing the priorities among sectors and major projects. The author notes that the SMP criterion, when properly applied, can indicate 'the direc-

tion in which an area's comparative advantage in international trade lies." The major difficulty with the approach is that it stresses the present over the future and has little to say about the dynamic, long-term utility of various projects which may well be more critical to development programs.

-	-	3	-	-	3	-	-
Gei	cit	lis	rep	ant	eco	pol	soc

Deane, Phyllis, Colonial social accounting National Institute of Economic and Social Research, Econ. and Soc. Study XI, Cambridge, England: Cambridge University Press, 1953, 347 p.   69
The National Institute of Economic and Social Research assigned Miss Deane the task of bringing modern economic research and measurement to bear upon two territories involved in economic and political change, Northern Rhodesia and Nyasaland. In the face of the great diversity of institutions and habits found in the two territories, and the formidable obstacle posed by the fact that the market economy encompasses only a small sector of the economy, the problem of measurement was extremely difficult. In spite of all, statistical data on income and consumption were prepared and can be inspected here. The data show, for example, that in both places the share of black Africans in national income rose significantly from 1938 to 1945, but subsequently tended to revert, especially in Northern Rhodesia, to the 1938 level. Some qualitative observations are useful, e. g., non-black Africans tend to invest their savings in their countries of origin, whereas black Africans, especially those in rural areas, save little.

-	-	3	-	-	3	-	-
Gei	cit	lis	rep	ant	eco	pol	soc

Deutsch, Karl W., Nationalism and social communication: an inquiry into the foundations of nationality NY: Wiley, 1953, 292 p.   70
In this stimulating though largely programmatic rather than finished discussion the author promotes several interests. First, what are the conditions and patterns of development of nationalism? Roughly, nationalism develops when a group of people who communicate among themselves but are shut off from communication with other peoples are thrown into economic or military contact with these peoples because of urbanization, industrialization, or military conquest. When this happens they become aware of their distinctive national characteristics, but precisely how nationalism develops depends upon many additional geographic, demographic, linguistic, etc. factors. A second theme in the book is the argument, not very successfully demonstrated, that the cybernetics model of com-

munication and change can and should be applied to the study of
human society, and that the concept of information useful in the
former can be translated into terms appropriate for the latter.
Finally, Deutsch provides many elegant and suggestive examples
of the creative merging of highly generalized concepts and specific, operationalizable variables, even for such unorthodox
notions as national "will" and "consciousness."

Gei	cit	lis	rep	ant	eco	pol	soc
-	1	5	-	-	-	4	1

Hoselitz, Bert F., "The role of cities in the economic
growth of underdeveloped countries," J Pol Econ 61:195-208,
1953.   71
This is a statement of acceptance of, but also dissatisfaction with, the broad, and widely held proposition that
industrialization and urbanization are closely and necessarily
related. It also is an analysis of the many conditions and
forces making for variations in the form taken by cities, and
a listing of important research tasks which would produce
clarification of the exact nature of the relationship. Urbanization can be studied in terms of the theory of location, in
terms of manpower requirements for economic development,
and as a vehicle for changing the values and beliefs of the people in a society. The author describes some of the patterns
manifested by cities as they developed in Western Europe in the
Middle Ages, suggesting many parallels likely to be found in the
LDC's, but cautioning that LDC cities are confronted with a new
factor--the impact made upon them by the country's integration
into the world economy. Urgently needed, to clarify the role of
urbanization in economic growth, are surveys of the institutions, and social and occupational composition of different
urban centers in the LDC's.

Gei	cit	lis	rep	ant	eco	pol	soc
1	1	3	1	1	-	-	2

Lewis, W. Arthur, Report on industrialization and the
Gold Coast Accra, Gold Coast (Ghana): Government Printing
Office, 1953, 23 p.   72
This is an early and succinct account of the economic
situation and potential for development of a very underdeveloped
country. Lewis, as a result of three week's worth of interview and visits, and by commission of the Gold Coast Ministry
of Commerce, contributed a primer of development economics
complete with recommendations. Separate sections treat the
genesis of industrialization, analysis of industries, ownership and management, initiative and aid, and government
agencies. Among the conclusions and recommendations: number one priority to be given to setting the development process

in motion by concentrating on more efficient food production; number two priority to be extended to improvement of public services, research, credit and banking facilities, etc.; and relatively low priority to manufacture for the home market.

-	-	-	180	-	-	-	-
Gei	cit	lis	rep	ant	eco	pol	soc

Mead, Margaret, (ed.), <u>Cultural patterns and technical change</u> Paris: UNESCO, 1952, 348 p.   73
This handbook describes the implications for mental health of technical change; presents examples of such change, along with effects, in agriculture, maternal and child care, nutrition, education, public health, etc.; and makes recommendations to guide personnel engaged in technical assistance programs so that the disruptive effects of change can be minimized. While not confined entirely to them, much of the reader's attention is directed toward five "whole" cultures--Burma, Greece, Palau, the Spanish Americans of New Mexico and the Tiv of Nigeria. This useful, readable and reasonable manual stresses the complexity and integrity of cultures, but is not recommended if one's interest is in mental health, for the concepts of personality structure and change needed to discuss such a matter are virtually absent. It is also possible that there is a tendency to overemphasize the disruptive effects of change, to the neglect of the beneficial effects.

8	1	5	-	4	-	-	1
Gei	cit	lis	rep	ant	eco	pol	soc

Nurkse, Ragnar, <u>Problems of capital formation in underdeveloped areas</u> (revised version of lectures presented to the Brazilian Institute of Economics in 1951), NY: Oxford University Press, 1953, 162 p.   74
This well written and important book is an attempt to apply some aspects of the economic theory of underdevelopment on a nontechnical but rigorous basis. It is a pioneer for its time for its postulation that capital is not the necessary and sufficient condition for the growth of less developed areas. Perhaps most important is the thesis of the "vicious circle of poverty," affecting the demand for and the supply of capital. The "low level of income, reflecting low productivity" in the LDC's, contributes to the lack of inducement to invest in capital goods formation. As to the capacity of the people themselves to encourage investment by their savings, Nurkse is pessimistic. Much of the reason for this seems to hinge upon the application to the international scene of the Duesenberry concept of "demonstration effect," namely, the idea that exposure to the higher standards of living and the "superior" products of the industrialized nations stimulates increased consumption,

and negates the desire for the postponement, or investment, of savings. A "self-help" scheme is presented to encourage the transfer of surplus or "underemployed" labor from the dominant agricultural sector into more "productive" employment, thereby raising the income levels of the population. Distinction is made between the relative degrees of population pressure among the LDC's and the effect of "overpopulation" or "underpopulation" on the feasibility of the withdrawal of labor from agriculture. Other areas are covered--external sources of capital, commercial policy and capital formation, and recent trends in the theory of international capital movements.

2	2	6	9	-	4	1	1
Gei	cit	lis	rep	ant	eco	pol	soc

Redfield, Robert, The primitive world and its transformations Ithaca, NY: Cornell University Press, 1953, 185 p.
75

The enlarged scope of Redfield's later comparative and historical interests is suggested by such chapter titles as "Human society before the urban revolution," "Civilization and the moral order," and "The transformation of ethical judgment." The main interest developed is in the way cities have produced changes in human life, including the production of great civilizations. As in other of his writings, Redfield sees society in terms of three ideal types--folk (pre-literate, primitive, pre-civilized), peasant and civilized--and is interested in the patterns of contrast, change and development manifested in all three of them. One of the most provocative chapters seeks to compare the "world view" of the folk society with that of modern civilization. In the former case God, man and nature are mutually involved and, perhaps, coordinated; in the latter they are separated and noticeably independent. Another interpretation of some interest which contradicts the stereotyped image of Redfield as a sentimental defender of folk societies, is the argument that conscious moral creativeness and reform occur only in, indeed are diagnostic of, civilizations.

-	-	6	-	5	-	1	-
Gei	cit	lis	rep	ant	eco	pol	soc

Tax, Sol, Penny capitalism: a Guatemalan Indian economy (first publ. as Smithsonian Institution Institute of Social Anthropology Publication No. 16, 1953), Chicago: University of Chicago Press, 1963, 230 p.
76

A detailed community study of Panajachel, a Guatemalan Indian community of some 800 Indians and 400 ladinos as of the late 1930's. The focus is on economic life and the goal is to lay bare "on a microscopic scale" a primitive, underdeveloped but "capitalist" society. There are no machines, no factories, no co-ops nor corporations, yet "every man is his own firm and works ruggedly for himself." Because of land scarcity, small population size, etc., Panajachel has no social classes and is not likely to develop them. Thus, though neither the mode of production nor the social structure would suggest it, a capitalist-type superstructure seems to have developed.

Gei	cit	lis	rep	ant	eco	pol	soc
7	-	4	-	2	-	-	2

Theodorson, George A., "Acceptance of industrialization and its attendant consequences for the social patterns of non-western societies," Am Sociol R 18: 477-84, 1953.   77

Industrialization of non-machine societies will eventually lead to the development of new societal patterns that will resemble certain dominant patterns of western industrialized society, which may not be rejected by any people who accept the machines of the West. Theodorson employs a structural-functionalist view of modernization to dispel the myth that the old culture can be integrated with the social patterns that are necessitated by industrialization. Technological development disrupts the old order by creating new roles, new facilities and new rewards. Also, previously unimportant resources and skills tend to place individuals in positions of power who have new attitudes, behavior, expectations and values. Moreover, technological development leads to the production of large quantities of cheap goods the distribution of which is likely to have a destabilizing effect. The reorganization of the social system, Theodorson analyzes in terms of Parsons' pattern variables. An increase in industrialization is accompanied by an increase in universalism, achievement, suppression of immediate emotional release, and specificity. The demands of the factory situation have wide repercussions in the social system because of functional interrelationships among different spheres and aspects of action. The only cultural continuity that may be possible after industrialization may be in music, art, religious beliefs about the non-empirical world, and folkways which do not in the long run conflict with the patterns of human relationships basic to a machine society.

Gei	cit	lis	rep	ant	eco	pol	soc
-	-	3	13	1	-	1	1

Wagley, Charles, Amazon Town: a study of man in the tropics NY: Macmillan, 1953, 305 p.   78

Ita, a small community and county seat in the Lower Amazon drainage area, was visited periodically from 1942 to 1948, when the author and three assistants spent four months there for UNESCO Amazon survey of the International Hylean Amazon Institute. This community study, complete with map and drawings, contains a vivid description of the houses, stores, community life, the relationship of the trader to the people, details of slash and burn agriculture, social events and festas, etc. Probably quite representative of the Amazonian culture pattern, the book is made even better by the author's efforts to put the community into the framework of Brazil as a whole, which affords good insight into the total picture of Brazilian culture.   Of particular relevance to those interested in development is Wagley's discussion of the great difficulties and complications which newly introduced programs of health, sanitation, and agriculture which fail to consider the context of local customs and beliefs will have in such a community. Relevant also is Ch. 1, where the author deals with the potential of the Amazon area under the heading of "The problem of man in the tropics."

7	-	4	-	3	-	-	1
Gei	cit	lis	rep	ant	eco	pol	soc

Coleman, James S. , "Nationalism in tropical Africa," Am Pol Sci R 48: 404-26, 1954.   79
        This excellent study of the roots, nature and probable outcome of African nationalism was written at a time when Western scholars were just beginning to realize its existence. Considered are the various forms of African nationalism-- traditionalist, syncretistic, and modernist movements--and how they differed spatially.   The importance of understanding the foundations of current African nationalist movements lies in the desirability of being able to predict their viability in the post-independence era.   Coleman is adept at comparing the similarities and differences of developments in both East and West Africa among people controlled by the various colonialist powers.   There is also a good review of the factors conditioning the development of nationalism, the various types of tensions that have resulted from colonialization, and the prospects they pose for success.   This is a valuable essay because of the questions it raises and the areas of needed research it suggests.

2	-	-	20	-	-	-	-
Gei	cit	lis	rep	ant	eco	pol	soc

Emerson, Rupert, "Paradoxes of Asian nationalism," in Far East Q 13: 131-42, 1954.   80
        The paradoxes of nationalism develop from its Western origins.   It was the Western colonial regimes who created the administrations and drew up the boundaries which today must serve all of the new states faced with the problem of integrating by and large diverse peoples with different languages and cultures into a single people.   It was the West which

drew attention to the traditions and culture that are the very basis of nationalism. It was the West which trained the leaders, supplied the basic ideas of nationalism, and provided the models which are being followed today by most new states. It is the West today which provides the newly developing nations with their goals of material progress. While nationalism developed most strongly where it mobilized the people against the colonial regimes most strongly entrenched, the coming of independence may provide a more divisive than integrating influence. New leaders are often less interested in the masses than in their own interests, the creation of nations is giving rise to minorities who feel themselves threatened, and the "unity" of authoritarian colonial regimes is yielding to the "separatism" of democratic rule or the "unity" of authoritarian independent regimes. Will nationalism help or impede the new nations? Are they indeed nations?

Gei	cit	lis	rep	ant	eco	pol	soc
1	1	3	12	2	-	1	-

Fitzgibbon, Russell H. , Uruguay: portrait of a democracy New Brunswick, NJ: Rutgers University Press, 1954, 301 p.   81

In many respects Uruguay is a paragon of virtue among nations. In striking contrast to much of the rest of Latin America it boasts a responsible and stable polity, honest and progressive social legislation, an effective semi-socialist economy, an unobtrusive church and military, and, according to this friendly portrait, a widespread sense of maturity, adjustment, pride and well-being among the people. Surely this "Switzerland of America" merits careful study as an example of successful development. The answer given here to what gives Uruguay such a happy position is that "Uruguay is an integrated country"--geographically, ethnically, socioeconomically (no extremes of wealth and poverty), sociosexually (women enjoy high status) and psychologically.

Gei	cit	lis	rep	ant	eco	pol	soc
-	-	3	-	2	-	1	-

Heller, Walter W. , "Fiscal policies for underdeveloped countries," p 1-22 in United Nations. Taxes and fiscal policy in underdeveloped countries NY: United Nations, 1954.   82

The tasks of tax and budgetary policies in the LDC's are basically similar to those of the MDC's; to make available for economic development a maximum of resources consistent with minimum current consumption requirements, maintain reasonable economic stability in the face of long-run inflationary pressure and short-run international price movements, and reduce inequalities in wealth, income and con-

sumption which undermine productive efficiency, offend
justice and endanger political stability. In pursuing these
tasks in the LDC, it is inescapable that the government will
have to play a large role in providing social overhead capital
both as a direct instrument of economic development and as a
prerequisite to the increased participation of private capital
in the development process. A crucial problem is how to make
the tax system more effective. Experience shows that the
less advanced the country the lower the ratio of tax payments
to national income. Finally, a most difficult matter is the
vulnerability of the LDC's economy to the ebb and flow of the
world market.

1	-	1	1275	-	-	-	1
Gei	cit	lis	rep	ant	eco	pol	soc

Hoselitz, Bert F. , "Recruitment of white-collar workers in underdeveloped countries," Int Soc Sci Bull 6:3-11,
1954.   83
In the advanced countries white collar employees are
the proletarianized masses of the working force, with salaries
usually lower than those of skilled manual workers. Their
jobs require little skill, and they can usually be replaced by
machines. The same does not hold for the LDC's where the
illiteracy rates are high and it is often considered demeaning
to dirty one's hands. As the level of literacy begins to improve, there is a run on white collar jobs. The primary
means of acquiring them is through relatives or friends.
Machines could probably be brought in, but this would not use
the available cheap labor and would cause adepletion of foreign exchange. Bureaucracies in LDC's suffer from poor administrative procedures. In many the prestige system has a
feudal appearance. For this reason the bureaucracy tends to
be conservative, but this creates a group of alienated intellectuals. Also, the universities still have a strong bias toward
a kind of training which does not prepare good administrators.
Then, since business can usually pay better, the most qualified do not take public office. Such are among the problems
faced in the creation and maintenance of the bureaucracies of
white collar workers in the LDC's.

2	-	-	20	-	-	-	-
Gei	cit	lis	rep	ant	eco	pol	soc

Lewis, W. Arthur, "Economic development with unlimited supplies of labour," The Manchester School of Economic and Social Studies 22:139-91, 1954.   84
In many capitalist economies an unlimited supply of
labor is available at a subsistence wage. In quite a few sectors of such countries, where there is overpopulation relative

to natural resources, the marginal productivity of labor is negligible, zero, or even negative. Capital accumulation can proceed faster than population can grow. When the surplus labor is
exhausted, wages begin to rise above the subsistence level. Ac-
cordingly, as soon as wages begin to rise, mass migration and
the export of capital operate to check the rise. Mass migration
of unskilled labor might even raise output per head, but its effect would be to keep wages in all countries near the subsistence
level of the poorest countries. The importation of foreign capital does not raise real wages in countries which have surplus
labor unless the capital results in increased productivity in the
commodities which they produce for their own consumption. The
main reason why tropical commercial produce is so cheap is the
inefficiency of tropical food production per man. The Law of
Comparative Costs is just as valid in countries with surplus
labor as it is in others. But whereas in the latter it is a valid
foundation of arguments for free trade, in the former it is an
equally valid foundation of arguments for protection.

1	3	4	641	-	3	1	-
Gei	cit	lis	rep	ant	eco	pol	soc

Nurkse, Ragnar, "International investment today in the
light of nineteenth-century experience," Econ J 64: 745-58, 1954.
85

The problem of international investment today is posed in
circumstances which have no real parallel in the 19th century.
Overseas, mainly British, investment in the last century was
quite exceptional. About two-thirds of it went to what were
called "regions of recent settlement," the spacious and fertile
plains of the USA, Argentina, Canada, Australia. Furthermore,
capital traveled to these promising lands and temperate latitudes
in the company of a huge migration of trained and enterprising
persons from the British Isles and continental European
countries. These conditions do not exist today, and are unlikely
to recur, with the possible exception of Soviet Siberia. In this
century capital exports from the USA go to a different type of
country and are generally viewed as a substitute for the movement of people. For this reason the impressive record and
brilliant reputation of 19th century international investment is
apt to build false hopes, and end by disappointing. However,
there are possibilities for international investment, and
specific needs to be attended to in the LDC's. Ranking very
high is investment in public utilities--transport, power, water
supply--which is probably to be accomplished, for a number of
reasons, by international grants-in-aid and low-interest loans
to the LDC's from the government funds of the MDS's.

-	-	-	80	-	-	-	-
Gei	cit	lis	rep	ant	eco	pol	soc

Scitovsky, Tibor, "Two concepts of external economies," J Pol Econ 62:143-51, 1954.   86

There is agreement about the general meaning of external economies--services (and disservices) rendered without compensation by one producer to another--and that they are a cause for divergence between private profit and social benefit, consequently, also serving as one way to account for the failure of perfect competition to lead to an optimum solution. However, there are many reasons for this latter, and it is not clear which of them qualify under the heading of "external economies." In this contribution, the author argues that the concept is used in two different contexts, and in terms of two distinct bodies of economic theory--equilibrium theory and the theory of industrialization of underdeveloped countries. Further, it is argued that external economies in the theory of industrialization include, but go far beyond, the external economies of equilibrium theory. The ways in which this occurs include both "technological external economies" of direct interdependence and "pecuniary external economies," that is, interdependence among producers through the market mechanism, a concept which has no place in equilibrium theory.

1	-	2	120	-	2	-	-
Gei	cit	lis	rep	ant	eco	pol	soc

Staley, Eugene, The future of underdeveloped countries (NY, 1954), 2nd ed, NY: Praeger, 1961, 483 p.   86a

This edition of the one first published in 1954 by the Council on Foreign Relations consists of a fourth part dealing with the 1960's rather than a complete revision, since the ". . . the book's central message is still valid and more relevant than ever." Part I defines successful development and Parts II and III analyze the communist and capitalist paths to development. The argument can be summarized as follows: a great economic, social, and political transformation is sweeping the LDCs; their future is a vital matter for the future of Western civilization, and therefore touches the security and way of life of the American people; material progress for the LDCs is a necessary but not a significant condition for peace, freedom and human dignity; better social institutions as well as opportunities for a fuller life must be developed and expanded; and the events of recent years point to the necessity of a world community approach to the development of LDCs rather than bilateral and individual programs. A good exposition of the liberal democratic view of development, this work reveals a perspective which involves as much interest in the future of the USA and Western civilization as in the future of the LDCs themselves.

2	2	1	-	-	-	1	-
Gei	cit	lis	rep	ant	eco	pol	soc

Apter, David E. , (Orig. pub. as The Gold Coast in transition, 1955), Ghana in transition NY: Atheneum, 1963, 432 p.   87

In addition to being a detailed geographical and histor- ical survey of the Gold Coast-Ghana, with special emphasis on political institutions, this is an important study because it deals with the process of institutional transfer. Can the norms, roles and governmental structures associated with Western democracy be fundamentally institutionalized in a newly in- dependent African nation? No conclusive answer is given, but rather a set of possible alternative outcomes is presented. One of these, presented in the first version, was the possibility of a "premature decline of charisma." This has indeed proved to be the case, with the result, among other things, that at the time of writing Nkrumah had taken a great amount of power into his hands and that considerable violence and alienation of key persons and elite groups had occurred. Thus, as of 1963, Apter concludes that Ghana has as yet taken no irreparable steps, that change is a slow process, and that "political institutional trans- fer" has as yet neither succeeded nor failed but remains, and will remain "in a kind of political limbo."

Gei	cit	lis	rep	ant	eco	pol	soc
7	1	6	-	-	1	5	-

Bronfenbrenner, Martin, "The appeal of confiscation in economic development," Econ Dev Cult Ch 3: 201-18, 1955. 88

The author argues that confiscation brings desired prag- matic results in the sense that it shifts income from capital- ists' consumption, transfers abroad and unproductive invest- ment to development investment. Three very simple hypo- thetical models of underdeveloped, over-populated economies are presented to demonstrate this argument, even when it is assumed that private enterprise is more efficient than public. In fact, the only argument against confiscation seems to be a non-economic one, something on the order of the "divine right of capital." Democratic alternatives to confiscation (tax- ation, increased savings, mobilization of savings etc.) are as- sumed to be too little and too late in order to analyze what might answer the appeal of confiscation. The author sees the West as trying to combat these revolutionary movements through military assistance to the status quo and/or through economic aid. However, attempts by the West to bribe or buy its way through simply increase the temptation to confiscate and, in- deed, Brofenbrenner sees the possibility that this may become the new "white man's burden." Instead of this course he recom- mends a neo-isolationism that would see aid as outright gifts rather than as ransom.

Gei	cit	lis	rep	ant	eco	pol	soc
2	1	-	762	-	-	-	-

Cairncross, Alec K. , "The place of capital in economic progress," Ch. 9, p. 235-48 in International Economic Association, Economic progress: papers and proceedings of a round table held by the I. E. A. , edited by L. H. Dupriez and D. C. Hague, Louvain: Institut de recherches economiques et sociales, 1955.   89

This writer doubts that capital accumulation is such an important influence in economic development as many economists and laymen assume it to be. Rather, technical innovation--the introduction of new and cheaper ways of doing things--is the factor dominating economic progress. And it is not likely that technical innovations make systematically heavy demands on capital; modest requirements are more likely, and many innovations can be introduced in the course of capital replacement out of depreciation allowances. Generally, in the LDC's the big problem is not one of capital but of organization--

> of training managements and men, of creating new
> attitudes towards industrial employment, and of
> taking advantage of innovations that need little
> capital and using the resulting gains to finance in-
> vestment elsewhere.

1	-	2	100	-	-	1	1
Gei	cit	lis	rep	ant	eco	pol	soc

Fallers, Lloyd, "The predicament of the modern African chief: an instance from Uganda," Am Anthrop 37: 290-305, 1955.   90

The modern African chief is caught between two worlds, occupying a role with many contradictory elements. As in the case of the Soga of Uganda he is the focus of the major elements of disharmony and conflict associated in the African and European institutions. "A chief may, for example, read a newspaper and have a good working knowledge of world politics, but he may still not be quite certain that Europeans are not cannibals or that witchcraft does not really work." As a result there is a high casualty rate among chiefs and considerable psychic cost. At the same time, these men, by taking into their own personalities the conflicts which might otherwise express themselves in open conflict between groups or individuals, are maintaining unity and stability in the society.

-	-	3	11	1	-	2	-
Gei	cit	lis	rep	ant	eco	pol	soc

Flemming, J. Marcus, "External economies and the doctrine of balanced growth," Econ J 65: 241-56, 1955.   91

The author presents a discussion and critique of the assumptions underlying the balanced growth doctrine of Young,

Rosenstein-Rodan and Nurkse. His main point is that this doctrine overemphasizes the repercussions on the demand for additional industries caused by the introduction of unprofitable though efficient large-scale production in one industry, and tends to ignore the repercussion on their costs. The latter are apt to rise steeply in an economy where the factors of production are in fixed supply, which is likely to be characteristic of the economies of the LDC's. On the other hand, the balanced growth theorem acquires validity to the extent that

> the necessary additional capital is obtainable on easy terms, when unions can be prevented from pushing up wages in industry, when reserves of underemployed agricultural labor are eagerly waiting to obtain industrial employment, when there are opportunities for economies of scale in the basic factor-- producing industries, and when, taken singly, the investments in question are only just not profitable.

1	1	-	80	-	-	-	-
Gei	cit	lis	rep	ant	eco	pol	soc

Galenson, Walter and Harvey Leibenstein, "Investment criteria, productivity, and economic development," Q J Econ 69:343-70, 1955.   92

The authors criticize the Kahn "social marginal productivity" investment criterion which stresses maximization of the capital-output ratio, labor use, and the export-investment ratio in deciding investment choices. They believe that such a criterion does not adequately balance the future against the present. It is the impact of current investment on future income and the need to maximize labor productivity which they stress in presenting an alternative criterion, the marginal per capita reinvestment quotient, or the extent to which investments yield returns that can be reinvested to expand capital. They analyze the implications of the criterion. Future employment is given as a function of the net return from investments that can be reinvested. The institutional barriers to modernization are considered along with the interrelation of industrialization, urbanization and population growth. Some attention is given to the pattern of industrialization. While the analysis represents one possible decision-making process, the authors ignore the need to take social welfare into account. Is it worthwhile for the present and succeeding generations to sacrifice some consumption so that some future group might enjoy a large increase in welfare? Some compromise is necessary; this is a political decision. If the choice should be to give more weight to the future than to the present, the Galenson-Leibenstein criterion is one way to select investment projects.

1	1	3	-	-	3	-	-
Gei	cit	lis	rep	ant	eco	pol	soc

Gluckman, Max, Custom and conflict in Africa   Oxford:
Basil Blackwell, 1955, 173 p.   93
    The theoretical importance of this contribution lies in
the notion of conflict as normal to the day-to-day operation of
society, not only "nonpathological" but necessary for social
stability. The thesis is pursued in the form of six lectures--
each approaching the matter differently--on feuding, witchcraft, familial estrangement, the "frailty of authority," the
"license in ritual," and African-European relations in South
Africa. In the African societies, which receive primary attention, conflict breeds rebellion but not revolution, for change
in the system is rarely even contemplated. In general, conflicts are engendered by customary allegiances, but open violence is typically avoided through the agency of other allegiances placed upon people which act upon them "over a wider
range of society or through a longer period of time."

-	-	3	-	1	-	2	-
Gei	cit	lis	rep	ant	eco	pol	soc

    Hoselitz, Bert F. , "Patterns of Economic Growth,"
Canad J Econ Pol Sci 21:416-31, 1955.   94
    There are three dimensions or variables which are of
particular importance in seeking an understanding of the role
of social, cultural and political, as well as economic factors,
in constructing a theory of growth. The first involves the relation between population and natural resources. Where the
latter are small or scarce relative to the former (Switzerland,
Holland), the resulting pattern of growth focuses upon optimum
combination with capital and labor and intensive application of
labor, and is termed "intrinsic." When the population is small
relative to resources (USA, Canada), the problem is to widen
the application of capital and labor, and the growth pattern is
"expansionist." A second distinction is the degree of depend-
ence of one country upon another, leading to "dominant" and
"satellitic" patterns of growth. Thirdly, the role of the government is crucial; active intervention produces "induced" development, and development without such intervention is termed
"autonomous." Combining the three sets of dichotomies leads
to eight ideal types of pattern, to which countries can be assigned, and which provide new insights into the conditions of
economic progress.

-	1	3	-	-	1	2	-
Gei	cit	lis	rep	ant	eco	pol	soc

    Hoselitz, Bert F. , "A sociological approach to econom-
ic development," Atti del congresso internazionale di studio
sul problema della aree arretrate 2:755-78, 1955.   95
    It has been generally assumed by Western theorists and

policy-makers that economic development in the LDC's would require the simultaneous transformation of the societies in question toward more correspondence with Western social institutions and values. There are, it appears, two theories which propose a general explanation of this--the Marxist theory of social and economic development, and the "theory of social deviance." In the latter, Schumpeter's analysis of the role of the innovating entrepreneur--the prototype of the social deviant--plays a crucial role. Such deviant-innovative behavior is typically introduced by individuals who are socially marginal, e. g., Jews and Greeks in the Middle Ages. However, over and above these two major theories, one must take into account additional features of a society, in order to include all the conditions for economic development--resources, geographical size, size of population, the structure of class relations and the nature of the government. Finally, close inspection of the development experience of Japan and the New Zealand Maori suggests that there may be a third general explanation of economic growth, namely, "a reinterpretation of social objectives by already existing elites."

-	-	-	60	-	-	-	-
Gei	cit	lis	rep	ant	eco	pol	soc

Kahin, George M., Guy Pauker, and Lucian W. Pye, "Comparative politics in non-Western countries," Am Pol Sci R 49:1022-41, 1955.   96
The purpose of this early and important article was to reorient the study of comparative politics, and to point out appropriate research strategies for analyzing the rapidly changing political systems of the developing areas. The authors above all indicate and urge sensitivity to the diversity and peculiarities of patterns existing in the new states. To foresee the general direction of development, they argue, it is important to evaluate the significance of particular elements in the total complex of political life. They suggest that these new states can provide a laboratory for analyzing patterns of political development, and they call for sustained field work on major political problems. They ultimately seek a general theory of politics, but believe this can only be built upon an extensive basis of empirical research.

-	2	3	-	-	-	3	-
Gei	cit	lis	rep	ant	eco	pol	soc

Kuznets, Simon, "Economic growth and income inequality," Am Econ R 45:1-28, 1955.   97
Kuznets describes and explains the character and causes of long-term changes in the distribution of personal incomes. Does inequality in income increase or decrease with

economic growth? After examining the cases of Great Britain, the USA, and Germany, the author concludes that in the early stages of development inequality increases while in the later stages it decreases. This article is valuable because it suggests that as a part of modernization the underdeveloped countries may have to pass through a stage of increased inequality in income distribution.

1	-	-	120	-	-	-	-
Gei	cit	lis	rep	ant	eco	pol	soc

Kuznets, Simon S., "Toward a theory of economic growth," Ch. 3. p. 12-103 (with discussion) in R. Lekachman (ed.), National policy for economic welfare at home and abroad (NY, 1955), NY: Russell and Russell, 1961.   98
Among the topics treated in this rich and provocative essay are the reasons for current interest in economic growth (concern over possible stagnation in the MDC's, interest in the prospects of the LDC's, the emergence of the authoritarian societies with command economies aimed at rapid growth and the significant link between growth and the chances of success in armed international conflict), trends over the past two centuries in population growth, trends in the growth of national product, shifts in industrial structure, trends in capital formation, trends in the movement of resources, aggression and warfare in relation to economic growth (rapid growth tends to produce disparities in the economic and social conditions among nations which often lead to aggression), theoretical prospects (at least five subtheories should eventually be united into one theory of economic growth--population growth, growth of the stock of knowledge, internal adaptation to growth potentials, external relations of national units in both cooperation and conflict, and theoretical interrelations among all these complexes), and ultimate uses of a theory of the economic growth of nations (which cannot be a purely "economic" theory of economic growth).

-	2	-	9	-	-	-	-
Gei	cit	lis	rep	ant	eco	pol	soc

Kuznets, Simon, "Underdeveloped countries and the pre-industrial phase in the advanced countries," Meeting No. 26, p. 947-69 in United Nations, World Population Conference, 1954: proceedings, papers NY: United Nations, 1955.   99
This paper expertly and concisely compares the present situation in underdeveloped countries with the earlier situation of the more developed countries. The most cogent finding seems to be that "there is no comparable earlier situation in the history of the economically developed countries of the New

World when their per capita incomes were so far behind the economic leaders or at such low levels as are those of most underdeveloped countries today." In the presently advanced countries, economic development appeared to have been the culmination of a long period of learning and intellectual growth accompanied by social change. No such development has yet been evidenced by the presently developing nations. The pre-industrial level in the developed countries was several times that of most underdeveloped countries today. This disparity is continually increasing, and is hypothesized to be correlated with the tremendous rate of population growth in underdeveloped countries today which never presented a problem to the advanced countries in their pre-industrial phase. In conclusion, the author asserts that the situation of the underdeveloped countries today defies comparison with that of the pre-industrial phase of the advanced countries.

	1	3	6	-	1	-	2
Gei	cit	lis	rep	ant	eco	pol	soc

Levy, Marion J., Jr., "Contrasting factors in the modernization of China and Japan," Ch. 17, p. 496-536, in S. Kuznets, W. E. Moore, and J. J. Spengler (eds.), Economic growth: Brazil, India, and Japan, Durham, NC: Duke University Press, 1955.   100
This excellent paper compares the process of industrialization and westernization in China and Japan. The main concern of the paper is to account for the difference in the way socio-economic changes occurred: While Japan's modernization proceeded at a very fast pace and with little internal violence, the introduction of Western forces in China led to a complete breakdown of the old order, to disorganization and violence. Levy's main thesis is that these differences were not due to variations in the way new Western elements were introduced or to differences in non-social factors such as raw material resources, but to differences in the traditional social structures of the two countries. While similar in many respects, the organization of Japanese society had some key advantages over that of China: the discipline and internalization of an ideology of absolute respect and obedience to one's superiors by all classes enabled the Tokugawa ruler and his successors to direct the process of change and to maintain effective social control over individual deviance. The closed-class system of traditional Japan propelled the merchant class to increasing efficiency and economic capability. They could not aspire to mobility status, as in China, and their only security was to do their job well. This merchant class was thus ready to take over the process of industrialization and economic change. Finally, the discipline of the ruled made it

relatively easy for the modernizing elite to eliminate from
key roles those individuals not adapted to carry on the required
changes.

2	1	4	-	-	-	2	2
Gei	cit	lis	rep	ant	eco	pol	soc

Lewis, W. Arthur, The theory of economic growth
Homewood, Ill: Richard D. Irwin, 1955, 453 p.   101
     Not only one of the first modern texts, and of continu-
ing influence, but well-written and forcefully argued, this book
has helped establish the field of development economics. In
its breadth of coverage, including many topics ordinarily dealt
with in other disciplines--family obligations, religion, land
tenure, etc.--Lewis writes in the tradition of 19th century
political economy. Though Lewis disclaims the goal of formu-
lating a general theory of development, he does in fact propose
a model of development, in places explicitly, in other places
implicitly. There are two sectors in the model of an economic system, capitalist and subsistence. In the former,
which may be private or state-owned, capital, income and
wages per head, proportion of income saved, and rate of technical progress are all much higher. The subsistence sector
is stagnant, and institutional arrangements maintain this
chronic disequilibrium between sectors. The process of
development is essentially the growth of the capitalist sector
at the expense of the subsistence sector, with anticipated
eventual absorption of the latter by the former. Thus, the
main thesis argued is that a private or state-owned capitalist
sector is a condition of economic development, because this
sector alone can generate the required savings and investment.

7	8	3	100	-	3	-	-
Gei	cit	lis	rep	ant	eco	pol	soc

Paul, Benjamin D., with the collaboration of Walter
B. Miller (eds.), Health, culture and community: case studies
of public reaction to health programs NY: Russell Sage Foundation, 1955, 493 p.   102
     Sixteen case studies reporting community reactions to
attempts at changing attitudes and practices regarding aspects
of health are presented in this volume. Contributors are for
the most part anthropologists and sociologists, although psy-
chologists, psychiatrists, and epidemiologists are present.
The papers generally follow the pattern of stating a problem,
giving detailed information about a proposed program, reporting community reactions to the program, and discussing cultural factors which influenced these reactions. The editor
provides an introduction to each paper. In a concluding chapter the major findings reported by the several contributors are

integrated, and a clear demonstration of the use of the conceptual tools of social science is provided. This book is a valuable reference for public health administrators as well as students in the fields of anthropology and sociology, for in the course of describing the impact of proposed new health programs on the groups studied the contributors tell us a great deal about culture and human society.

8	-	5	-	5	-	-	-
Gei	cit	lis	rep	ant	eco	pol	soc

Service, Elman R. , "Indian-European relations in colonial Latin America," Am Anthrop 57: 411-25, 1955.   103
Both the starting-point situations and the final consequences of relations between Indians and European colonists varied greatly from one region to the next. In between, the Spanish and Portuguese settlers exploited the Indians by encomienda tribute or forced labor projects, made agricultural slaves and household servants of them, drove them from areas of their own settlement, exterminated them, or, as in the highland areas, were able to take almost immediate control of the more highly organized political and religions institutions and thus control the population, but with little culture contact for some time. Among the variables discussed in this important survey are degree and rate of racial assimilation or amalgamation, degree and rate of acculturation, and--largely as the independent variable--aim, style and degree of control exercised over the Indians. Among other conclusions, Service reveals that Spanish and Portuguese had a practically identical pattern of aims in their relations with them.

-	-	3	-	3	-	-	-
Gei	cit	lis	rep	ant	eco	pol	soc

Steward, Julian H. , Theory of culture change: the methodology of multilinear evolution Urbana: University of Illinois Press, 1955, 244 p.   104
This book is composed of 12 essays written over a 20 year period. Their common purpose is, in reaction to the atomistic, idiographic bias of the Boas school (which rejected large generalizations and "systems"), "to develop a methodology for determining regularities of form, function, and process which occur cross-culturally." Such regularities, when they occur, are termed evidence for multilinear evolution, which Steward contrasts favorably with both "unilinear" and "universal" evolution. Steward's position is in favor of scientific generalization but opposed to the overly broad categories of the classical evolutionists. He affirms the existence of "cross-cultural regularities" but denies that they must

necessarily pertain to all societies. He is critical, for instance, of the notion that all cultures must pass through similar developmental stages. Among the important concepts proposed is "cultural ecology," a creative adaptation of human
groups to environment. Cross-cultural regularities arise out
of similar adaptive processes in similar environments.

7	-	4	-	4	-	-	-
Gei	cit	lis	rep	ant	eco	pol	soc

Wagley, Charles and Marvin Harris, "A typology of
Latin American subcultures," Am Anthrop 57: 428-51, 1955.

105

The authors propose nine significant types of subculture
with corresponding social groupings in Latin America: (1)
tribal, aboriginal Indian which is rare; (2) modern Indian, resulting from the fusion of aboriginal cultures and Iberian cultures of the 16th and 17th centuries; (3) peasant, to include
both relatively isolated agricultural peoples and the lower
class of small, isolated towns variously termed mestizos,
cholos, ladinos, etc.; (4) engenho plantation--workers on
family-owned estates; (5) usina plantation--large modern cor-
poration-owned establishments; (6) middle and upper classes
of towns serving as administrative, market and religious
centers; (7) metropolitan upper class; (8) metropolitan middle class, the emerging professional, business and white
collar workers; and (9) the urban proletariat.

-	-	5	-	3	-	1	1
Gei	cit	lis	rep	ant	eco	pol	soc

Wolf, Eric R. , "Types of Latin American peasantry: a
preliminary discussion," Am Anthrop 57: 452-71, 1955.   106
There are two major types of peasantry identified and
described in detail. In Type I, found in the upper highlands,
agricultural cultivation is extensive, and practiced both for
subsistence and cash received in local markets. These
peasants live in a corporate community with definite boundaries,
clear identity over time, and located on marginal land exploited by traditional technology. Stratification and religious
systems are closely integrated, endogamy is strongly pre-
ferred, and there is an institutionalized "cult of poverty" at
the same time that laziness, greed, etc. are denounced. Type
II is found in the humid low highlands and in tropical lowlands
where sugar cane, cocoa, coffee and bananas are raised. In
contrast with Type I, capital flows in from outside, and the
community is an open one, but in it the peasant is the most
important of the several subcultures. Here individual accumulation and display of wealth and concern with status are more
pronounced, and there are frequent and shifting socio-economic

and political alliances and alignments. There are, in addition,
still other types--foreign colonists, peasants living on the out-
skirts of the capitalist market, etc.

-	-	3	-	2	-	-	1
Gei	cit	lis	rep	ant	eco	pol	soc

Bendix, Reinhard, Work and authority in industry:
ideologies of management in the course of industrialization
NY: Wiley, 1956, 466 p.   107
    This study sheds light on the consequences of manageri-
al policies for patterns of labor-management relations and for
societal development in general. The focus is on manegerial
ideologies which try to justify mass subordination to factory
discipline and to managerial authority. Totalitarian and non-
totalitarian forms of subordination in economic enterprises are
compared--England in its early industrialization period with
tsarist Russia, and America in the modern period with contemporary East Germany. The two main conclusions are (1)
the great change in industrial social structure, bureaucratiza-
tion, leads to ideological shifts, at least in the West, from
idealization of the entrepreneur to a stress on labor-management cooperation; (2) the Western model differs from the
tsarist Russian and German communist model in regard to the
laborer's place in the ideologies of management. The scope
of analysis, the creative use of content analysis of speeches
and documents, and the comparison of communist and non-
communist patterns of industrialization make this an important contribution.

2	2	3	-	-	-	2	1
Gei	cit	lis	rep	ant	eco	pol	soc

Bloomfield, Arthur I. , ''Monetary policy in underdeveloped countries,'' Ch. 8, p. 232-74 in C. J. Friedrich and
S. E. Harris (eds.), Public policy: a yearbook of the Graduate School of Public Administration, Harvard University,
vol. 7, Cambridge, Mass.: GSPA, 1956.   108
    This is an informative survey of the practices and the
possibilities in the use of monetary policy as an instrument
for achieving more rapid economic development in the LDC's.
The fact serving as a point of departure is that since 1945
central banks have been newly established or thoroughly reorganized in 27 underdeveloped countries or areas, from the
Belgian Congo to Syria. The institutional setting within which
these banks and their governments must operate (large subsistence sector, underdeveloped capital markets, few facilities for the extension of credit, etc.), the objectives and
principles of monetary policy (i. e. how to maintain financial
stability), instruments of credit control, and the use of

monetary policy for development are all discussed, with
numerous references to the experience of particular countries.
In the final section specific measures recommended to central banks are listed.

| 1 | - | 3 | 4 | - | 3 | - | - |
| Gei | cit | lis | rep | ant | eco | pol | soc |

Kling, Merle, "Towards a theory of power and political
instability in Latin America," West Pol Q 9:21-35, 1956.   109
        Kling seeks to elucidate the relationship between po-
litical and economic power and political instability in Latin
America by generalization, inference, and pointed examples.
Kling argues that there is a clear relationship "between the
control of the economic bases of power and the real exercise
of political power." His main theorem is that "chronic instability is a function of the contradiction between the realities
of a colonial economy and the political requirement of legal
sovereignty" among the Latin American states. Because of
the static nature of the conventional economic bases of power,
landholding and mining, and because of the "colonial nature of
the Latin American economies," government office provides
the most readily accessible goal for the ambitious seekers of
wealth and power, hence the instability of politics in Latin
America. This article has significant implications not only for
theory and research on contemporary society, but also for
American foreign policy.

| 1 | - | 4 | 80 | - | - | 3 | 1 |
| Gei | cit | lis | rep | ant | eco | pol | soc |

Mead, Margaret, New lives for old: cultural transforma-
tion--Manus 1928-1963 NY: William Morrow, 1953, 548 p.
                                                        110
        This is the story of how a largely Stone Age people
living on Manus Island off the NE coast of New Guinea experienced rapid modernization. Decisive influences were a
casual exposure to Western technology, religion and law in
1928; interruption of Australian trusteeship by Japanese occupation and subsequent staging of a million American fighting
men through the island during WW II; and the talented, creative leadership of a native, Paliau, supported by the middle-
aged men of Manus in the New Way (democratic government,
money economy, schools, medical clinics, and a heretical
version of Catholicism). The general conclusions are that
"rapid change is not only possible, but may actually be very
desirable," and that "a people may want to change rather than
merely submit to being changed."

| 2 | 1 | 4 | - | 3 | - | 1 | - |
| Gei | cit | lis | rep | ant | eco | pol | soc |

Myrdal, Gunnar, An international economy: problems and prospects NY: Harper, 1956, 381 p. 111
The book is especially important because Myrdal synthesizes much of the thinking of the representatives of the LDC's and other critics of traditional international trade theory. Myrdal's main criterion of economic progress in the modern world is equality of opportunity on an international level. This pattern would have to go in a direction contrary to the trend actually at hand. The major thesis is the idea that the LDC's should be exempted from many of the fair trade practices outlined in most of the postwar agreements on international trade, and the idea that the USA ought to take unilateral action in liberalizing its trade position.

Gei	cit	lis	rep	ant	eco	pol	soc
-	5	3	-	-	2	-	1

Rostow, Walter W., "The take-off into self-sustained growth," Econ J 66:25-48, 1956. 112
The take-off may be characterized as an industrial revolution, then, in which various sectors of the economy serve to sustain the growth if the societal conditions are conducive to economic development. One very important factor in sustaining economic growth is the creation of a sufficient supply of entrepreneurs. In the final analysis, a society will continue to sustain economic growth only if it finds a way to apply effectively its own peculiar resources.

Gei	cit	lis	rep	ant	eco	pol	soc
1	2	3	2762	-	1	-	2

Wallace, Anthony F. C., "Revitalization movements: some theoretical considerations for their comparative study," Am. Anthrop. 58:264-81, 1956. 113
In this important theoretical contribution the author proposes a general concept, revitalization. This revitalization involves the "deliberate, organized, conscious effort by members of a society to construct a more satisfying culture," and in this respect the revitalization movement contrasts sharply with other forms of culture change. As part of the theory Wallace also proposes a model of psychological behavior centering on the idea of stress and the mental image of the society and its culture which the individual maintains-- "the mazeway" -- which can aid him in reducing stress. When a number of persons cooperate to change both mazeway and "real" system together so as to reduce stress, a revitalization movement is at hand.

Gei	cit	lis	rep	ant	eco	pol	soc
-	1	3	-	3	-	-	-

Zinkin, Maurice, Development for free Asia NY:
Essential Books, 1956, 263 p.   114
    The main thesis of this book is that the state will have
to play an active role in accelerating the process of change.
The process of economic development cannot take root without
a change in the social structure and in the values of the people,
or would proceed all too slowly. Emphasis is placed on the
exhortative role of the politician in inducing changes in habits,
attitudes and institutions to meet the needs of economic development. Recognition is given of the great significance of
both the maintenance by the nation's leaders of a consuming
passion for development and the charisma to communicate
this to the people. A great deal of optimistic idealism is
displayed over the possibilities for democracy in Asia to solve
all the problems. The appendix contains a thorough analysis of
the model country for the author--India and its central planning system.

1	-	-	80	-	-	-	-
Gei	cit	lis	rep	ant	eco	pol	soc

    Bailey, Frederick G. , Caste and the economic
frontier: a village in Highland Orissa (Manchester, Engl. ,
1957), NY: Humanities Press, 1958, 292 p.   115
    Here is an unusually well investigated and clear ac-
count of the results of contact between a relatively isolated,
agricultural-based village and the modern world. The village
of Bisipara in the hilly section of eastern India underwent substantial changes in the division of wealth and the distribution
of political power over the 100 year period dating from the
mid-19th century just before inclusion in the boundaries of
British India, and 1952-54 when the fieldwork was accomplished.
Earlier, land was the only source of wealth, and was controlled by a Warrior caste-group that was also politically
dominant. Later, new sources of wealth appeared, influenced
by the "economic frontier," the peculiarities of the caste
system, and the policies of the Indian Government. For example, after 1870 two Distiller caste-groups were able to
monopolize the liquor trade, which led to a spectacular increase in their wealth, much of which was used to buy land,
and ultimately to a rise in their ritual status and political
power. This report is especially good for its careful research and analysis of the patterns and sources of land tenure
and alienation.

-	3	-	-	-	-	-	-
Gei	cit	lis	rep	ant	eco	pol	soc

    Baran, Paul A. , The political economy of growth, NY:
Monthly Review P, 1957, 305 p.   116

This is a Marxist analysis of economic backwardness in underdeveloped countries and criticism of Western capitalism, colonization, aid and trade, which, according to Baran, have been the chief causes of such backwardness. He asserts that all the LDC's have a potential economic surplus which, through rational utilization, could be used for their development. However, Western colonialization and neocolonialization have siphoned off these surpluses or else have encouraged their use by Westernized domestic ruling groups for luxury consumption and for unnecessary military forces. The argument has some truth to it but also hinges on a series of shaky presuppositions and generalizations. For instance, the alleged disappearance of investment opportunities in capitalist countries is alleged to cause Western businessmen and governments to turn to the alleged exploitation of the LDC's. Also exaggerated is the ease with which development might occur once Western exploitation and local interest groups were eliminated and rational socialist planning instituted. Baran's prognosis, eagerly supported by most Marxist believers, is that the LDC's will make it only when the capitalist countries turn socialist, resolving basic conflict, and permitting all nations to develop amicably and peacefully.

| 2 | 1 | 5 | - | - | - | 2 | 3 |
| Gei | cit | lis | rep | ant | eco | pol | soc |

Bauer, Peter T. and Basil S. Yamey, The economics of under-developed countries Cambridge, England: Cambridge University Press, 1957, 271 p.   117
Many of the propositions and presuppositions found in the literature of development economics are critically analyzed and refuted here. Among these are the view that capital is the key to development and the position that the international demonstration effect has a significant influence on growth. In general, the authors take a consistent conservative position, opposing government entrepreneurial action, criticizing the argument that the terms of trade run against the LDC's, opposing the idea that economic diversification is an all-important virtue, and taking a vigorous "individualistic" approach. As one reviewer put it, "one-dollar-one-vote, without regard to the distribution of income, is assumed to be a desirable mechanism in determining the course of economic development. . . "

| 7 | - | 3 | - | - | 2 | 1 | - |
| Gei | cit | lis | rep | ant | eco | pol | soc |

Bellah, Robert N. , Tokugawa religion: the values of pre-industrial Japan Glencoe, Ill: Free Press, 1957, 249 p.
                                                                                118
Parsonian conceptions of society as a social system and

religious ideas as expressions of central Japanese values are
utilized to analyze the Tokugawa period, 1600-1868, with a
view to clarifying the extent to which Japanese religion offered
a "functional analogue to the Protestant Ethic," by which rational mastery of the world became a religious obligation.   The
conclusion is that in Japan development is not best explained in
strictly economic terms, but rather that the religious ethic
nurtured during the centuries preceding the Meiji Restoration
gave prominence to the polity rather than to economic considerations.   This, by mobilizing loyalty on all sides, and in con-
junction with the specific work-relevant normative content of
Japanese religious values made it possible for Japan to move
quickly toward modern socioeconomic development.   Moreover,
it was the samurai class, not merchants, peasants, etc.,
which led the nation in breaking new ground, because its locus
of strength was the polity, not the economy.   Bellah's book is
important for its interpretation of the most conspicuous non-
Western example of modernization, for its conceptual elegance
(especially that stressing the merging of political and religious
influences), for its empirically defensible measures of national
values, and for its central general argument, stated most forth-
rightly on p. 185: ". . . both the Restoration and the subsequent modernization of Japan must be seen first in political
terms and only secondarily in economic terms."

3	3	4	-	1	-	1	2
Gei	cit	lis	rep	ant	eco	pol	soc

Callard, Keith B., Pakistan: a political study NY: Macmillan, 1957, 355 p.   119
    The author presents an excellent study of politics in
Pakistan in which he examines the development of the country
since independence in 1947.   He focuses on the difficulty in
establishing democracy in the political institutions of the
country.   Pakistan has suffered from a failure of leadership,
economic problems, and the division of the nation, the last
being particularly evident in relation to the minorities.   Attempts made to establish new political parties have not been
fully successful.   The result is that the country has accepted
democracy in theory, but has had major difficulty in institu-
tionalizing it.   The author studies all the major political events
since independence, although it may be noted that he fails to
give the full background for many of them.

-	3	1	-	-	-	1	-
Gei	cit	lis	rep	ant	eco	pol	soc

Eckstein, Otto, "Investment criteria for economic
development and the theory of intertemporal welfare economics," Q J Econ 71: 56-85, 1957.   120

Eckstein adopts the Chenery social marginal productivity criterion for investments, but notes that it must be corrected for the divergence of market prices from social values in an imperfect market structure. He develops the role of the interest rate in this criterion as well as its import in development planning. While criticizing the Galenson-Leibenstein approach which stresses the maximization of growth and future consumption, Eckstein, too, sees the need for such criteria by developing the concept of marginal growth contribution as a test for project worthiness. This measures the project's direct contribution to consumption, i.e., its efficiency, and the present value of the future income made possible by increased capital growth, i.e. increased saving. In a sense it is a synthesis of both the efficiency-oriented and the growth-oriented criteria. The role of the government is stressed both in the area of fiscal policy to promote investment and as a stimulator of projects resulting in large amounts of reinvestment.

1	-	3	-	-	3	-	-
Gei	cit	lis	rep	ant	eco	pol	soc

Eisenstadt, S. N., "Sociological aspects of political development in underdeveloped countries," Econ Develop Cult Change 5: 289-307, 1957.   121

The main problem in the development of political institutions in new countries is that of gaining social support for different and often contradictory aspects of a modern type of institutional framework. The basis of this problem is the uneven change which was sponsored during colonial times. For example, the colonial powers gave rudiments of technical and educational training without changing the values and aspirations of the natives. Needed today are political entrepreneurs to sell the new institutional framework to the populace and to rectify unevenness in the society. This article is suggestive of some problems of political development in underdeveloped countries, but suffers from overly abstract conceptualization.

1	1	-	90	-	-	-	-
Gei	cit	lis	rep	ant	eco	pol	soc

Haberler, Gottfried, "Critical observations on some current notions in the theory of economic development," L'industria: rivista di economia politica No. 2, 1957, p. 373-83.   122

Four important ideas which have played a central role in recent writing on economic development are critically discussed (if not liquidated): the concept of disguised unemployment in LDC's, the notion of "balanced growth" or "big push," the demonstration effect, and the theory of the trend toward deterioration in the terms of trade for LDC's. The claims of proponents of the "disguised unemployment" theory are greatly exaggerated or, in the most blatant form, preposterous, for cases where the marginal productivity of labor is equal to zero or is negative are quite rare or inconsequential. The theory of balanced growth overstresses the role of the size of the market, and also overlooks the possibility of increasing said size through international trade. The demonstration effect is most useful in explaining, and as an excuse for, inflationary policies; it would probably cause no trouble at all if it were not for lax monetary policies. However, it is an important concept for explaining the eagerness of the LDC's to adopt social welfare policies (social security, labor regulations, etc.) which it took the MDC's decades or centuries to develop. Finally, the deteriorating terms of trade thesis of Prebisch and company lacks historical proof, is based on a faulty explanation and a reckless extrapolation, and leads to irresponsible policy conclusions. Among its several faults is the fact that it makes no allowance for changes over time in the quality of the products exported by the industrial countries.

-	-	-	80	-	-	-	-
Gei	cit	lis	rep	ant	eco	pol	soc

Hoselitz, Bert F. , "Urbanization and economic growth in Asia," Econ Dev Cult Ch 6: 42-54, 1957.   123
　　　Large cities in Asia are relatively new, in the midst of rapid growth, serving as leading centers for cultural change, highly stratified, and exhibiting considerable disorganization. In general, South Asian countries may be "over-urbanized," a good measure of which is the relation between percentage of urban population and percentage of the non-agricultural labor force. Western countries with 13% of the population urbanized (which is the South Asian rate) had 55% of the labor force in the non-agricultural sector whereas the corresponding figure for the South Asian countries is only 30%. Such a situation creates great pressure on public service systems, and keeps a large part of the population in poverty. Much needed are attempts to create smaller urban places, and to disperse non-agricultural occupations from the overly dominating private cities.

-	-	3	3	-	-	-	3
Gei	cit	lis	rep	ant	eco	pol	soc

Hutchinson, Harry W. , Village and plantation life in northeastern Brazil, Seattle: University of Washington Press, 1957, 199 p.   124
　　　Perhaps the greatest contribution of this study to our knowledge of development lies still in the future. From field work done in this sugar-producing area in 1950-51 and then

later, in 1956, the author is able to chart some of the starting points and initial patterns of change which emerged largely as a result of changes in the ownership pattern of the plantations. The older pattern was a plantation of face-to-face relations between owner-director and workers; the new pattern is a "factory-plantation" with owners frequently absent, strained labor relations, and the role of manager becoming even more powerful. New sources of change, with effects as yet unclear, are a new crop, cacao, and a new, government-operated industry, petroleum. Community organization, religion, family and class system are also described in this succinct contribution to the literature on the plantation and its role in the larger society.

-	-	3	-	3	-	-	-
Gei	cit	lis	rep	ant	eco	pol	soc

Leibenstein, Harvey, Economic backwardness and economic growth NY: Wiley, 1957, 205 p.   125
This is a clear and relatively early version of a major position taken by many in the debate over the path to economic development. An LDC's economy is in stationary or quasi equilibrium and will stay there unless changes in the relevant variables are large enough to disturb it and promote a dis-equilibrium state ensuring sustained growth. Particular magnitudes of such changes are recommended for particular kinds of countries; for instance, countries with high fertility require a net investment rate of 11 percent or more initially for priority capital projects, and much higher subsequent rates. The argument has acquired renown as the thesis of "critical minimum effort." While today the broad argument still seems valid, and the theoretical model offered by Leibenstein of growth and depressant agents is useful, it is open to criticism on several counts, one being its failure adequately to include resources of "human capital."

2	1	4	-	-	2	-	2
Gei	cit	lis	rep	ant	eco	pol	soc

Meier, Gerald M. and Robert E. Baldwin, Economic development: theory, history, policy NY: Wiley, 1957, 588 p.
126
This textbook combines economic theory and economic history and also covers relevant "non-economic" factors in some detail. Part I outlines the major theories of development from Smith and Ricardo through Domar and Hansen. Part II gives the outlines of the Industrial Revolution and the growth of an international economy in the 18th and 19th centuries dominated by Britain. Part III, "Accelerating Development in Poor Countries," tells of the characteristics of these countries,

obstacles to their development, requirements for development, domestic and international policy issues, and these nations' prospects for development. Part IV concerns rich countries and discusses economic development, trends and prospects from their point of view.

7	2	5	-	-	4	1	-
Gei	cit	lis	rep	ant	eco	pol	soc

Merton, Robert K. , <u>Social theory and social structure</u>, rev. and enl. edit. , Glencoe, Ill: Free Press, 1957, 645 p.
127

The 19 essays in this book range widely over many substantive and theoretical topics of continuing interest in the field--general patterns of deviant behavior, bureaucracy, propaganda, roles and role-sets, and the relationship between theory and research. Unusually complete codification of established knowledge on little-known or particularly controversial fields, e. g. the sociology of knowledge, reference group theory, make a good many of the individual chapters young classics. Merton's theoretical position, in favor of theories of the middle range, and his disciplined defense of functional theory also contribute to making this probably the single most influential book in contemporary American sociology.

-	2	4	-	1	-	2	1
Gei	cit	lis	rep	ant	eco	pol	soc

Myrdal, Gunnar, <u>Rich lands and poor: the road to world prosperity</u> (English edit: <u>Economic theory and under-developed regions</u>) NY: Harper, 1957, 168 p.   128

A brilliant, readable and moving account of the major institutional and intellectual lag facing the modern world, namely the common but mistaken idea that the (international and national) market system and established economic theories can adequately explain and predict contemporary economic trends. Thus, economic differentiation tends to increase between advanced and underdeveloped countries and between analogous regions within the poorer countries. This is the "backwash effect" of growth. On the other hand, the more developed an economy becomes the more prominently does it influence neighboring countries and (within a country) areas. This is the "spread effect." These facts offer a challenge to the governments and economists of the LDC's, to the first to engage in comprehensive economic planning, to the latter to describe, supervise and adjust planning and develop more adequate theory of development.

2	6	8	-	2	3	2	1
Gei	cit	lis	rep	ant	eco	pol	soc

Nash, Manning, "The multiple society in economic development: Mexico and Guatemala," Am Anthrop 59:825-33, 1957.
129

The purpose of this comparative analysis is to propose the concept of multiple society with plural cultures in order better to grasp the process of economic development, and also to identify the groups within a society that are capable of innovative behavior and could, therefore, successfully promote economic development. Discussed are various segments of the populations, both rural and urban, in terms of their tendencies toward economic conservatism or innovation, command over wealth, and degree of political influence. The segment identified as most interested in development and promising as a political one is the urban middle class, the masa media, but to fulfill its potential, political ascendancy and support are necessary from the other, larger population groups, especially the urban lower class, and the Indians. This analysis is couched largely in terms of Guatemala and its potential, but the case of Mexico is deemed corroborative of the notion that political control by the middle class leads to rapid development.

1	-	3	9	3	-	-	-
Gei	cit	lis	rep	ant	eco	pol	soc

Rosenstein-Rodan, Paul N., "Notes on the theory of the 'big push,'" in The objectives of U. S. economic assistance programs Washington, D. C., 1957.
130

The "big push" theory, now nearly twenty years old, is defended here in a modern form. It is suggested that it is simply a matter of lumpiness, i. e. underdevelopment can be explained in terms of size of aggregate investment. Due to indivisibilities in functions of production, demand and saving, small increments cancel each other out.

> Instead of putting a hundred previously unemployed workers in one shoe factory let us put ten thousand workers in one hundred shoe factories and farms which will between them produce the bulk of wage goods on which the newly employed workers will spend their wages. You thus create an additional market demand according to Say's law.

Not only is size important, but kind also. Social overhead capital must precede direct high return private investment and since these kinds of inputs are not attractive to small private investors, it must be done by large concerns. A look at the stagnation of certain nations in the post World War II period shows that failure to institute a "big push" has been a block to other small scale investment.

Wolf, Eric R. , "Closed corporate peasant communities in Mesoamerica and Central Java," SW J Anthrop 13:1-18, 1957.

131

In both of the areas referred to, one can find peasant groups with similar economic, religious and social characteristics. The communities are "closed" because some effort is made to prevent outsiders from becoming members and to place limits on the ability of members to communicate with the larger society. They are "corporate" because, among other things, they attempt to equalize the life chances and risks confronting individual members by redistributing surpluses, preferably through the operation of the religious system, and by inducing people to content themselves with the rewards of shared poverty. Such communities emerge because of conditions in the larger society--mainly, relegation of the peasants to the status of part-time laborer oriented toward subsistence on his own land, together with charges imposed and enforced by semi-autonomous local authorities. Though closed corporate peasant communities have a current function, in the long run they are incapable of preventing change.

-	1	4	-	3	-	-	1
Gei	cit	lis	rep	ant	eco	pol	soc

Wolf, Eric R. , and Sidney W. Mintz, "Haciendas and plantations in Middle America and the Antilles," Soc Econ Stud 6: 380-412, 1957.

132

Haciendas and plantations are both systems of agricultural work with a dependent labor force, and they are both oriented toward the production of profit on invested capital, but there are important differences between them. The former is typically operated by a dominant landowner, organized to supply a small-scale market by means of scarce capital, and the factors of production are employed not only for capital accumulation but also to support the status aspirations of the owner. The latter is usually operated by owners organized into a corporation, organized to supply a large-scale market by means of abundant capital, and in it the factors of production are employed primarily to further capital accumulation, without regard to the status needs of the owners. Distinctions between these two varieties of agricultural estates are made, their causes and consequences analyzed, and examples are given from field data gathered in Puerto Rico, Jamaica and Mexico as well as written accounts from the past century. The analysis is made in terms of the environing conditions at stake: general c--which must be present in the larger society if one or the other is to arise; initiating c--which must be met to establish a particular hacienda or plantation; operational c--those essential to the continued operation of the systems subsumed under each type; and the derived cultural c--social relations and cultural forms which make the specific combination of operational c effective.

Gei	cit	lis	rep	ant	eco	pol	soc
-	-	3	-	3	-	-	-

Worsley, Peter, The trumpet shall sound: a study of "cargo" cults in Melanesia, London: MacGibbon and Kee, 1957, 290 p.   133

Cargo cults are a type of social movement, occurring frequently in this area during the past 70 years, which exhibit belief in some imminent, supernatural intervention in the existing social order such that all the material goods people desire will be provided by a return to earth of God or the ancestors. The author treats these cults as millenarian movements, and his thesis is that they are a form of social protest on the part of persons in depressed groupings who are disenchanted with their lot but who lack the means to attain their goals. They characteristically involve abandonment of established native customs, and assumption of rituals and offices modelled on European practices but with an inversion in the "new order" of current black-white status relationships. These cults are of considerable relevance in themselves, but at times, they may also change from essentially religious movements into secular political organizations.

Gei	cit	lis	rep	ant	eco	pol	soc
-	-	3	-	-	-	2	1

Alexander, Robert J., The Bolivian national revolution New Brunswick, NJ: Rutgers University Press, 1958, 302 p.
                                                              134

A case study of a poor and underdeveloped country for which a strong argument can be made to the effect that a revolution was an indispensable step on the path toward modernization, this book traces the background and early consequences of the 1952 Revolution, including such post-revolutionary goals as agrarian reform, universal suffrage, nationalization of the mines, and disbanding of the army. The Revolution, which was a true "social revolution" as well as a political one, is presented by the author in a generally favorable light, as it probably should be in view of the fact that it was based on a large amount of popular support and led to the establishment of a stable and reasonably successful government, at least for the years covered.

Gei	cit	lis	rep	ant	eco	pol	soc
2	1	3	-	2	-	-	1

Banfield, Edward C. and Laura F. , The moral basis of
a backward society Glencoe, Ill: Free Press, 1958, 204 p.
135
Based on field work in Montegrano, a South Italian village, the authors propose a hypothesis to explain why the villagers are unable to act in concert to achieve their economic
and political ends or generally improve their lot. The explanation offered is "amoral familism," a culturally approved,
though self-defeating, state of affairs in which each person be-
haves as if he were following this rule: maximize the material
and short-run advantage of your own nuclear family, and assume
that others do likewise. A short book with a powerful punch, it
is important for its main thesis, a corollary implication--that
lack of organization and involvement in the larger community
is a general barrier to progress--and for various other virtues,
including creative use in field research of the Thematic Apper-
ception Test, and high readability.

3	1	6	-	2	-	3	1
Gei	cit	lis	rep	ant	eco	pol	soc

Bellah, Robert N. , "Religious aspects of modernization
in Turkey and Japan," Am J Sociol 64:1-5, 1958. 136
The process of modernization involves changes in values
as well as in polity and economy. One aspect of value change
is the shift from a "prescriptive" type of value system, one
characterized by comprehensive norms and consequent lack of
flexibility--where religion has ultimate control over all segments of life--to a "principle" type, one in which religion merely lays down the basic principles of social action and does not
regulate all aspects of life, and in which differentiation is
made between religion and ideology, affording greater flexibility. Thus, the function of religion changes as society
modernizes. The process of modernization is often effected
by a movement which adds a religious coloration to its essentially political and ideological nature. Even when such a
movement is successful in effecting major structural changes
in the society and in increasing flexibility in economic and
political life, the problems imposed by its own partly religious origin and its relation to the traditional religious
system may still be serious indeed. Turkey is an example
of a state where nationalistic reform became the popular "religion," and is described now as having difficulty separating
the claim of "ultimate legitimacy" from the party in power.
Also, Turkish Islam has not been able to redefine itself effectively within the new system. Japan illustrates the same
general process but with differing detail.

2	-	1	8	-	-	-	1
Gei	cit	lis	rep	ant	eco	pol	soc

Coale, Ansley J. , and Edgar M. Hoover, <u>Population growth and economic development in low-income countries: a case study of India's prospects</u> Princeton: Princeton University Press, 1958, 389 p.   137
    Though classical Malthusian theory has by now been generally replaced by a more optimistic 'transition'' theory of population growth, the authors argue that even this model may not be applicable to contemporary underdeveloped countries, since the social and economic factors that are supposed to bring about the eventual decline in fertility are not directly comparable to those in the West. Projecting three alternative estimates of population growth for India and Mexico, and their differential effects on per capita income and total national income, the general hypothesis is supported that the lower the fertility-rate, the better the economic prospects. However, the authors do not indulge in predictions; this is an exposition of a theory and a method of projection, not a blueprint for planners.

1	1	4	-	-	4	-	-
Gei	cit	lis	rep	ant	eco	pol	soc

    Davis, Harold E. (ed.), <u>Government and politics in Latin America</u>, NY: Ronald Press, 1958, 539 p.   138
    This collection grew out of a seminar at the American University. According to the editor the seminar was exploratory--concerned with finding some better way to introduce the student to a comparative survey of the political institutions of Latin America, their structure, operation, strengths and weaknesses. Participants in the seminar included political scientists, economists and historians. Twenty Latin American countries are analyzed in terms of their common problems and trends in political life. The contributions are presented in three parts: (1) ''The Dynamics of Politics and Power,'' (2) ''The Structure and Function of Political Power,'' and, (3) ''Expansion of Government.'' While the purpose of the contributors was to analyze politics and institutions objectively, they have also tried to take particular account of how the intelligent Latin American views his politics and to portray political behavior within its cultural context.

8	-	3	-	2	-	1	-
Gei	cit	lis	rep	ant	eco	pol	soc

    Eckstein, Alexander, ''Individualism and the role of the state in economic growth,''<u>Econ Dev Cult Ch</u> 6: 81-7, 1958.
                                                                139
    Eckstein seeks to demonstrate that there is a ''potentially positive correlation'' between individualism and economic development. He points out the crucial factors conditioning

the role the state will play in economic development, and its impact on the individual. The state will play a more dominant role depending on five variables: the hierarchy of goals, the time horizon in economic development, the means available, the social structure, and the relative backwardness of the economy. The concept of "optimum level and patterning of state intervention" would help to determine the most appropriate way of maximizing growth while preserving the scope of individualism. The author argues that if a state successfully handles the provision of social and economic overhead needed for development, it will have less tendency later to intervene massively in the economy through centralized planning and controls, thereby leaving more room for growth coupled with individual choice.

-	1	-	327	-	-	1	-
Gei	cit	lis	rep	ant	eco	pol	soc

Epstein, Arnold L. , Politics in an urban African community NY: Humanities Press, 1958, 254 p.   140
In this study of a multiracial, copper-mining town in Northern Rhodesia the author reports how various social groups and associations emerge which are quite divergent from the traditional political organization. On the basis of occupational interests, education, and length of residence in town, associations based on a cross-section of the different tribal groupings debated political issues, struggled for recognition from the mining authorities (who had more power than the civil authorities), and usurped leadership from the tribal elders. A union is seen as the major integrating force in the town, and as the most vital organization in the political system, and its structure and operation are examined in detail. In contrast, the nationalistic movement was weak, of loose structure and diffuse goals, traits linked by the author to a lack of stable relationships in the town and to the territorial basis of the movement. A final chapter discusses the concept of detribalization.

-	-	3	-	2	-	-	1
Gei	cit	lis	rep	ant	eco	pol	soc

Hirschman, Albert, The strategy of economic development New Haven: Yale University Press, 1958, 217 p.   141
This important book is an argument for unbalanced growth and the stimulus created by it. It was written when "balanced growth" or "big push" arguments were receiving increasing interest. In disagreeing with the feasibility of the method of the big push, Hirschman concentrates on the dynamic path to development instead of the usual comparative statics approach. The fundamental strategy is to build de-

stabilizers or disequilibria into the economy relying on backward and forward "linkages" to induce the desired development. Investment for development is split into two categories: social overhead capital (SOC) and directly productive activities (DPA). It is argued that imbalance between the two areas is a "spur" for growth. The response to imbalance is the "linkage." If SOC is relatively great enough to make investment in DPA profitable, a forward or permissive linkage is formed. If further investment in SOC is warranted because of demands for DPA, a backward linkage has formed. In each case, investment has been "induced" via other investment needs, not by consumer demand or solely by government edict. The underlying assumption for this strategy is that the most scarce factor in LDC's is the ability to make initiating decisions and to coordinate changing attitudes. Emphasis is placed, perhaps too much so, on investment in the manufacturing sector, rationalized by the statement that manufacturing has more linkage possibilities than does primary production.

2	5	12	-	-	7	1	4
Gei	cit	lis	rep	ant	eco	pol	soc

Johnson, John J., Political change in Latin America: the emergence of the middle sectors Stanford: Stanford University Press, 1958, 272 p.   142

An original, provocative, near-classic analysis of the emergence of a particular social stratum as a progressive political force in five major Latin American countries. Until about 1850 the dominant concern in these countries was political consolidation but leaders were drawn largely from landed, church and military elites. From 1850 to about 1915 economic development was a major concern and in the transition to modernity the middle sector emerged to prominence and has played, and will play, an increasingly important role in achieving political stability and encouraging economic development. "Middle sector" as a concept differs from the notion of "middle class." Persons in it are of heterogeneous background but unified by urban residence, above average public education, sentiments favoring industrialization, nationalism, political parties and state intervention. They contrast, for example, with the social elite's tendencies to favor agriculture and class and family loyalty over nationalism. The "middle sector" is treated as a variable, being strongest in Uruguay and declining in influence from Chile to Argentina to Mexico to Brazil. Criticism has focussed largely on the conceptual and operational-definitional inadequacies of the notion of "middle sector."

2	1	10	-	3	-	4	3
Gei	cit	lis	rep	ant	eco	pol	soc

Kindleberger, Charles P. , Economic development
(NY, 1958) 2nd edit. , NY: McGraw-Hill, 1965, 425 p.   143
        This is an excellent textbook for undergraduate as well
as graduate courses. A systematic presentation, it starts
with a chapter on definitions and measurement problems,
treats non-economic determinants of growth in Ch. 2, theories
in Ch. 3, and then goes on to the traditional topics of land,
capital, labor, organization, technology, scale and transformation. Part II concerns domestic policy problems (direct allocation vs. allocation by the price system, industrialization
vs. agriculture, etc.), and Part III international issues (foreign trade or autarchy, borrowing abroad, regional cooperation, etc.). In a concluding chapter, some modest generalizations and opinions are offered. For example, the author advises policy makers that even though the price system does not
work perfectly, they are well-advised "to salvage the most
that can be saved" of it, because "it is more economical of
administrative talent to rely on private incentives."

| 7 | 2 | 5 | - | 1 | 3 | 1 | - |
| Gei | cit | lis | rep | ant | eco | pol | soc |

        Lerner, Daniel with the collaboration of Lucille W.
Pevsner and an introduction by David Riesman, The passing of
traditional society: modernizing the Middle East Glencoe, Ill:
Free Press, 1958, 466 p.   144
        This book is one of the first, but of continuing influence,
in the field because of its theoretical scope, involving models
of both "societal" and "personal" development; because it is a
field study report of results obtained with the best modern research methods; because it focuses on the role of the mass
media of communication; and because it includes brief case
studies of six Middle Eastern countries which point up the
problems, patterns and sources of societal variations and
uniqueness. The basic data were gathered for the Voice of
America by the Bureau of Applied Social Research of Columbia
University in 1950-51 mainly to study mass communications
behavior. From the analysis comes a theory of steps or
scalar (or sequential) preconditions to the achievement of
modernity: urbanization leads to literacy which leads to mass
media exposure which leads to increasing participation in
economic and political affairs. Integrated with the account of
what happens on the societal level is a theory of the individual experience which accompanies modernization. The pattern
of change is from traditional to transitional to modern man,
whose salient trait is "psychic mobility" or "empathy." Finally, the book describes and characterizes the extent of
modernism, dynamism (tempo of change), and stability in

each of the six countries studied. Here, too, is one of the
first studies of "happiness" as a personal attribute; tradition-
als are least happy, moderns most.

3	8	18	-	6	-	8	4
Gei	cit	lis	rep	ant	eco	pol	soc

Matossian, Mary, "Ideologies of delayed industrialization: some tensions and ambiguities," Econ Dev Cult Ch 6: 217-
28, 1958.   145
Some seemingly diverse ideologies--Gandhism, Marx-
ism-Leninism, Kemalism, and Shintoism--have important
features in common. They are self-definition, description of
the current situation in terms of the past and the future, and
certain imperatives "deduced" from this description. These
ideologies arise when intellectuals in LDC's are "assaulted" by
contact with the West and try to understand this influence.
There is a tension between archaism and futurism--they may
return to the past or attempt to escape it. They may fight or
accept Western ideas. To understand the ideology of a society which is in contact with the West but is still backward, one
must know what is borrowed from the West, what is retained
from the historical past, and what national characteristics are
encouraged by the ideology. This article presents an interesting way of analyzing political, religious, or national ideologies
and belief systems, but does not explain why different ones
arise in different countries. Some ideologies contribute to a
country's development and others retard it. In studying
societal development, the important thing to know is why this
happens, or how "progressive" ideologies can be developed.

2	-	-	484	-	-	-	-
Gei	cit	lis	rep	ant	eco	pol	soc

Mayer, Albert et al, Pilot project, India: the story of
rural development at Etawah, Uttar Pradesh Berkeley: University of California Press, 1958, 367 p.   146
This journal of the organization and execution of rural
development pilot projects has the advantage of providing an
on-going account of a development program in the field, but
the disadvantage of a lack of focus upon specific issues of
development. The author was chief planner of experimental
projects begun in 64 villages in 1948. He states that the assets
of the pilot project method are "to accumulate experience, to
serve as models to be examined and to act as practical training centers," as well as to allow for concentration of efforts
which will establish a pattern of success. Although the
author stresses village development through democratic procedures, the goal of the projects is primarily material ac-
complishments--increases in agricultural production and im-

provement of living facilities. Social factors are seen in relation to the material goals. The eliciting of the felt needs of the people, their participation in decision-making, and their commitment to adult education are effective in so far as they produce changes in the level of living of the village people. (The values of Gandhian "constructive workers" and missionaries led to an emphasis on moral well-being without appreciable improvement in the village level of living.) The author's assumption is that economic gains realized through the assistance of the projects strengthens the will of the people to improve their physical environment. The work lacks systematic analysis of the social, economic and political variables at both societal and village levels, but the author does show intuitive awareness of these factors in comments interspersed with the exposition of his planning and organizational activities. Although overburdened with detail, this work is a good account of one man's efforts to organize an administrative program around the goal of instilling a desire for achievement in village people.

1	-	4	-	4	-	-	-
Gei	cit	lis	rep	ant	eco	pol	soc

Nash, Manning, Machine age Maya: the industrialization of a Guatemalan community Glencoe: Free Press, 1958, 118 p.
147

Here is the story and analysis of the adjustment of Cantel, a community of Mayan Indians, to a large textile mill in their midst. The surprising conclusion is that the industry had positive effects on the life of the nuclear family through a lessening of economic tensions, and also led to the development of friendships not linked with kinship, produced a higher tone in recreational gatherings and precipitated a coalescence of community power around a labor union. The methodology and reporting combine the lack of rigor of field work with the lively interest associated with concrete description. This community saw the advantages of a money economy, had a normative pattern of nuclear, neo-local families and valued hard work. Thus, the people of the community had values which readily meshed with the industrial way of life. However, the ethnic and cultural homogeneity of the Indians required accommodations on the side of the industrial operators. These factors indicate that this is really a study of the coming to the village of an industry, not of industrialization. Added to this is the fact that an alternate form of work was available, namely, farming. Farm laborers could earn more in the mill, whereas those independent farmers with less than 10 cuerdas (1.08 acres) were more inclined to work in the mill than were the owners of larger plots. The author concludes that the ability to choose industrial work makes the transition easier. An informative case study, this analysis, generally interpreted, contradicts the assumed negative effects of industrialization on traditional cultures.

2	-	3	-	2	-	-	1
Gei	cit	lis	rep	ant	eco	pol	soc

Pye, Lucian W. , "The non-Western political process," J Pol 20: 468-86, 1958. 148

Pye seeks to move away from particularistic institutional analysis, and to "outline some of the dominant and distinctive characteristics of the non-Western political process." This article is a forerunner of the major work edited by Almond and Coleman, The politics of the developing areas (1960). In it Pye develops middle range comparative hypotheses, postulating 17 general hypotheses--"rather bold and unqualified statements, generalized models of the political process common in non-Western societies." All are related to the structural-functional approach of Gabriel Almond, and each hypothesis is briefly analyzed and related to concrete cases in the developing areas.

-	2	3	-	-	-	3	-
Gei	cit	lis	rep	ant	eco	pol	soc

Tinbergen, Jan, The design of development Baltimore: Johns Hopkins University Press (for the Economic Development Institute, International Bank for Reconstruction and Development), 1958, 99 p. 149

A general "development policy" to further the process of economic development should include four objectives: create the general conditions favorable to development; acquaint the government, business community, and the public with the potentialities and advantages of development; make "basic" investments (others call it social overhead capital or infra-structure); take measures designed to facilitate and stimulate private activity and investment. These objectives are briefly defined in the introductory chapter; the rest of the work discusses various elements of development policy proper, such as the essence of programming, the appraisal of projects for investment, and appraising and stimulating private investment. The book summarizes basic problems and policies for administrators in developing countries, enunciating clearly and non-technically the experience in planning and programming development by the IBRD. Important concepts are introduced to the general reader which makes the work a rather painless introduction to such things as the capital coefficient, shadow pricing, consistency, project evaluation, and funda-

mental disequilibria. Most interesting to many readers will
be the non-dogmatic evaluation of internal versus external ef-
ficiency--the criterion of measurement for decisions concerning public versus private ownership and their boundaries.

7	-	3	-	-	2	1	-
Gei	cit	lis	rep	ant	eco	pol	soc

Watson, William, Tribal cohesion in a money economy:
a study of the Mambwe people of Northern Rhodesia, NY: Humanities Press, 1958, 246 p.   150
    This able study of labor migration in relation to the
social and political organization of the Mambwe has an important thesis. Entering the labor market in order to get the
money they have come to require, the Mambwe people find
themselves in a situation without protective legislation or
security institutions. For this reason they protect themselves
by retaining subsistence agriculture as a basic way of life,
and by strengthening, rather than allowing to decline, their
traditional social organization.

-	-	3	-	2	1	-	-
Gei	cit	lis	rep	ant	eco	pol	soc

Adams, Richard N. , A Community in the Andes:
problems and progress in Muquiyauyo, Seattle: University of
Washington Press, 1959, 251 p.   151
    Muquiyauyo, a town of over 2,000, situated 11,000 feet
high in Peru's central highlands, has come to be known as a
uniquely "progressive" town. It has an efficient power plant,
good schools, innovations in local government, a good cooperative work-project system, social planning and a degree
of economic soundness rarely encountered in such communities.
How to account for such a fact? Though this was the task he
set for himself, after a year of hard data collection relying to
an unusual degree on historical documents, the author was unable to find out why the people of Muquiyauyo are more progressive. Though the big question is unanswered, and perhaps
cannot be answered without a different, comparative research
design, a large amount of information about the community is
presented for the reader's inspection.

-	-	3	-	2	1	-	-
Gei	cit	lis	rep	ant	eco	pol	soc

Bauer, Peter T. and Basil S. Yamey, "A case study of
response to price in an underdeveloped country," Econ J 69:
800-5, 1959.   152
    How responsive are agricultural producers to changes
in the market prices and price structure relevant to their
range of alternatives? In 1947, the statutory marketing

authorities in Nigeria, who controlled all major agricultural exports, offered the peasant producers substantial price incentives in hopes of raising the quality of cocoa and oil palm products. Their explicitly formulated hypothesis, the introduction of the presumed causal measures, and the results, which could be observed and precisely measured, resemble the method of experimentation in science. The results were most impressive: high grade cocoa and palm proved so responsive to the premium prices offered that the Marketing Boards were soon receiving premium quality products in the desired proportions.

-	1	3	-	-	3	-	-
Gei	cit	lis	rep	ant	eco	pol	soc

Chenery, Hollis B., and Paul G. Clark, Interindustry economics, NY: Wiley, 1959, 345 p.   153
        The goal of these authors is to combine the theoretical and practical aspects of interindustry economics in a short volume. It is useful as a survey of technical knowledge current at the time about the relations between input-output models, linear programming and economic theory and as a report on attempts made to apply such models for estimates useful in policy formation. It is recommended as a text for policy-oriented economics courses and is also readable for those not specializing in this field or in econometrics.

-	-	5	-	-	5	-	-
Gei	cit	lis	rep	ant	eco	pol	soc

Higgins, Benjamin H., Economic development: principles, problems, and policies NY: Norton, 1959, 803 p.
                                                        154
        One of the best texts available, thoughtfully eclectic, good on analytic generalizations, attentive to psychological, sociological, and political aspects of the subject, Higgins' book has 13 chapters, with 343 pages of discussion on the major policy issues of the field. This is partly a result of the author's own decade of experience in four different underdeveloped countries. As argued in the final chapter, the major thesis of the book is that development economics and equilibrium economics are two different things, and that serious mistakes in policy recommendations can be made if this is not recognized.

7	3	4	-	-	3	1	-
Gei	cit	lis	rep	ant	eco	pol	soc

Kornhauser, William, The politics of mass society Glencoe, Ill: Free Press, 1959, 256 p.   155

Here is a systematization of historical and political
writing on the sources of extremist political mass movements.
Included for analysis are fascism, communism and such recent
varieties as Poujadism in France and McCarthyism in the USA.
The main thesis argued is that such movements typically rise
up and prosper in mass society, which is one of four principal
kinds of society identified. The other three are communal (de-
centralized, with members bound to local groups or inclusive
corporations, as in Medieval Europe), pluralist (numerous
intermediate and competing groups, with overlapping member-
ships), and totalitarian. The main feature of mass society
which makes it vulnerable to extremist movements is the absence of intermediate groups (such as unions, neighborhood
organizations, voluntary organizations with political goals,
etc.), which in pluralist society mediate between the masses
of the people and their rulers. Part II of the book discusses
the conditions under which these groups break down; such
conditions include major military defeats, severe economic
crises, and rapid rates of urbanization or development. When
such secondary groups and associations are uprooted, the most
unintegrated (alienated, isolated) members of society become
available for mobilization in mass movements, and the ruling
elites become highly accessible to their protests and demands.

7	1	4	-	-	-	4	-
Gei	cit	lis	rep	ant	eco	pol	soc

Kuznets, Simon S., "The meaning and measurement of
economic growth," Lecture I, p. 13-19 in S. Kuznets, Six
lectures on economic growth NY: Free Press, 1961.   156
The concept economic growth means increase in volume of output which is sustained for a period long enough to
reflect more than a cyclical expansion, a post-calamity recovery, etc. In contrast to the distant past, the distinctive
feature of modern economic growth is the (usual) combination
of high rates of growth of the population and of per capita
product, thus implying an even higher rate of growth of total
product. This latter is possible only through major innovations, and these in turn typically require massive structural
changes in society and a corresponding increase in the
adaptive capacity of society. The fact of continuous structural
change is one reason why it is so difficult to measure economic growth, and a number of arbitrary assumptions have to be
made. Several of these are discussed, and Kuznets concludes
that whatever the difficulties of conceptualization and other
features of measurement "much can be learned by a determined scrutiny of the data."

1	-	-	20	-	-	-	-
Gei	cit	lis	rep	ant	eco	pol	soc

Lewis, Oscar, Five families: Mexican case studies in the culture of poverty, NY: Basic Books, 1959, 351 p.   157
    A collection of detailed descriptions of the life-style of five different Mexican families, in each case in the form of one day's recorded participant observations. While the ecological settings of these families range from a rural highland village, through an urban slum, to the aristocratic residential section of Mexico City, the common element in these case studies is the "culture of poverty" in which these families live, or from which they have more or less recently escaped. The book is an attempt to provide an account of a contemporary urban culture that has the same degree of conscientious and minutely detailed reporting as the traditional anthropological studies of small and isolated primitive cultures, in spite of the obvious handicaps involved in the sheer size of the culture studied. It is therefore a contribution to the methodology of the social sciences, as much as to the substantive knowledge of different cultures.

7	-	5	-	4	-	-	1
Gei	cit	lis	rep	ant	eco	pol	soc

    Lipset, Seymour Martin, "Some social requisites of democracy: economic development and political legitimacy" (Am Pol Sci R 53: 69-105, 1959). Reprinted in revised form as Ch. 2, "Economic development and democracy," p. 45-72 in S. M. Lipset, Political man: the social bases of politics, NY: Doubleday, 1960.)   158
    Lipset suggests and supports with data the idea that political democracy has been associated, historically, with a cluster of social factors, including an open class system, a degree of economic wealth, an equalitarian value system, capitalistic economy, high literacy, and high participation in voluntary organization. These factors may not always be associated with democracy, but Lipset proposes that political democracy is unlikely to develop in their absence. Yet man's will has some influence and can promote democracy. "To aid men's actions in furthering democracy. . . remains perhaps the most important substantive intellectual task which students of politics can still set before themselves." This approach, along with similar efforts by Shannon, Coleman and others, has produced one of modern social science's most important contributions to both substantive knowledge and method.

2	2	4	-	-	-	3	1
Gei	cit	lis	rep	ant	eco	pol	soc

    Morgan, Theodore, "The long run terms of trade be-

116

tween agriculture and manufacturing," <u>Econ Dev Cult Ch</u> 8:1-23, 1959.   159

A "must read" article for those interested in the role of foreign trade and the Prebisch-ECLA view of the declining terms of trade. Essentially what Morgan does is take Prebisch's data, which showed a decline in the terms of trade from 1870 onward, and extend these data backward to 1800. He finds that the 1870's were a time of most favorable relationships for the products of the LDC's, and that what has happened since then can be conceived as a return to normalcy. British trade data have two built-in biases which Prebisch forgot to consider: qualitative improvements, the greater productivity embodied in the manufactured goods; and the decline in transportation costs, from 30 to 70 percent of the value of world trade in very early times to just over 10 percent prior to WW II. Morgan also finds favorable terms of trade to agriculture in the USA. He also refutes Prebisch's claim that the workers in the LDC's, being unorganized, cannot increase their wages or share in boom times.

2	-	4	-	-	4	-	-
Gei	cit	lis	rep	ant	eco	pol	soc

Prebisch, Raúl, "Commercial policy in the underdeveloped countries," <u>Am Econ R Pap Proc</u> 49:251-73, 1959.
160

This is a clear statement of one of the most influential arguments ever penned about the relevance of international trade and payments to the process of development in the Latin American (and, by inference, other) countries. Prebisch divides the world economy into industrial centers and peripheral countries engaged in primary production. He then argues that because of disparities in the income elasticity of demand-- low in the centers for imports of Latin American primary commodities, and high in the periphery for imports of industrial goods from the centers--there occurs an inevitable transfer of the fruits of technological process, as long as market forces are permitted unrestricted play, from periphery countries to center countries. The disparity can be corrected by commercial policy designed to bring about import substitution, an increase in the proportion of goods supplied in the peripheral countries from domestic sources. Thus, the classic mechanism of the free play of market forces not only retards the industrialization of the periphery countries but, through the deterioration of their position in the terms of trade in the international market, induces a one-sided flow of the results of progress to the more developed countries. In consequence, the countries of the periphery need to engage in protection, subsidies, import duties, an export tax, or other forms of interference in the center-periphery trade relation, and to form and participate in a Latin American common market.

-	1	5	-	-	4	-	1
Gei	cit	lis	rep	ant	eco	pol	soc

Rostow, Walt W. , "The stages of economic growth,"
Econ Hist R 12:1-16, 1959.   161
    In this article is summarized Rostow's view of modern
economic history. The five stages are the traditional society,
the preconditions for take-off, the take-off, the drive to
maturity, and the age of high mass consumption. These
descriptive categories are rooted in certain dynamic propositions about supply, demand, and the pattern of production.
Sectoral optimum positions are determined on the side of
demand by the levels of income and of population, and by the
character of tastes; on the side of supply by the state of
technology and the quality of entrepreneurship, and the latter
determines the proportion of technology available and potentially profitable innovations actually incorporated in the capital
stock. Each stage is then described in terms of its main
characteristics and causal conditions. For example, the preconditions for the take-off include the build-up of social overhead capital, a technological revolution in agriculture, and
the expansion of exports. The final stage--the age of high
mass consumption--represents a direction of development a
society may choose when it has achieved both technological
maturity and a certain level of real income per head.

1	-	-	20	-	-	-	-
Gei	cit	lis	rep	ant	eco	pol	soc

Smelser, Neil J. , Social change in the industrial
revolution: an application of theory to the British cotton industry, Chicago: University of Chicago Press, 1959, 440 p.
                                                            162
    Using Parsons' model of social systems--value and
institutional emphases and interrelated roles organized to
contribute to four systematic functional tasks--an all-important
period is analyzed in detail. The setting is Britain during
the height of the Industrial Revolution, from 1770 to 1840, and
the chief interest is in the cotton industry and family of its
working class. A seven-step general model is proposed , beginning with dissatisfaction with the goal achievements of the
social system and a sense of opportunity for change, and ending with the institutionalization of new patterns. The main
observed fact in this process is structural differentiation, and
it is illustrated both in the factory and in the working class

family. In the latter case, for instance, after the Industrial
Revolution children were increasingly socialized for occupational roles by the school rather than by their parents. An especially interesting but problematic aspect of the entire treatment
is the nature and source of the initial, impelling dissatisfaction.

| (2) | | - | 2 | - | - | - | - | 2 |
| Gei | cit | lis | rep | ant | eco | pol | soc |

Spindler, Louise S. and George D. Spindler, "Culture
change," Ch. 2, p. 37-66 in P. J. Siegel (ed.), Biennial review of anthropology, 1959, Stanford: Stanford University
Press, 1959.   163
        The authors review studies on growth, disintegration,
reintegration and acculturation, all contributed in the 1955-58
period. Brief comments are made on 132 different publications
under the categories: theory and method, historical-descriptive
studies, culture change and social structure, urbanization,
technological development and cultural change, controlled acculturation, nativistic movements, values and culture change,
psychological processes and culture change, and special
problems. It is concluded that most of the studies reviewed
are problem-oriented, that "schools" and exclusive theories do
not predominate. Rather, anthropologists are flexible and
eclectic, and they also avoid "overresponding to the demands
for immediate applicability of their work to problems stemming
from... rapid and frequently disjunctive urbanization and westernization."

| - | - | 3 | - | 3 | - | - | - |
| Gei | cit | lis | rep | ant | eco | pol | soc |

Adams, Richard N. (ed.), Social change in Latin
America: its implications for United States policy, NY:
Harper (for the Council of Foreign Relations), 1960, 535 p.
                                                      164
        Six revised papers which were originally presented by
a study group at the Council of Foreign Relations comprise
this volume. In these essays, sociologists and anthropologists examine the effects of social change in international relations. Specifically, the recent developments in several
Latin American countries are analyzed in a societal context
and their effects are discussed in terms of relations between
the USA and each of these countries.

| 8 | 3 | 6 | - | 2 | - | 3 | 1 |
| Gei | cit | lis | rep | ant | eco | pol | soc |

Almond, Gabriel A., "A functional approach to com-

parative politics," 'Introduction," p. 3-64 in G. A. Almond and
J. S. Coleman (eds.), The politics of the developing areas,
Princeton: Princeton University Press, 1960.   165
    The premise of this influential theoretical statement
is that the comparative study of politics must discard concepts
and models of political affairs which are no longer useful and
take up new ones which serve to probe deeper and afford richer
comparisons among many different kinds of political systems
from the most primitive to the most modern. The categories
of description and analysis are structural and functional ones
phrased on a high level of generality and with properties derived from or amicably related to general sociological theory
of the kind associated in that field with Parsons, Levy and
Smelser. Almond's work is most useful, perhaps, for the
major "input functions" proposed--political socialization and
recruitment, interest articulation, interest aggregation, and
political communication--but contains a wealth of otherwise
provocative and controversial thoughts on the scientific approach to politics. It is indispensable reading for the serious
scholar.

2	1	6	-	1	-	5	-
Gei	cit	lis	rep	ant	eco	pol	soc

    Almond, Gabriel A. and James S. Coleman (eds.),
The politics of the developing areas, Princeton: Princeton
University Press, 1960, 591 p.   166
    Utilizing the structural-functional approach, this col-
lection of case studies of Southeast Asia, South Asia, Sub-
Sahara Africa, the Near East, and Latin America, provides
cumulative data as well as a theoretical framework for the
comparative study of political systems. The theoretical model,
which includes four input and three output functions, is derived
from the empirical and formal analysis of Western politics, and
applied as a basis for comparisons with political systems in
developing areas. Each contributor in his area study follows
closely the pattern of analysis explained in Almond's introduction: (1) background, (2) process of change, (3) political
groups and political functions, (4) governmental structures
and authoritative functions, and (5) political integration. In
his concluding chapter, Coleman emphasizes the general assumption of the book that political development is well conceived as a process in which developing nations move in the
direction of the "modern" polities of the western democracies.

8	6	5	-	1	-	4	-
Gei	cit	lis	rep	ant	eco	pol	soc

    Apter, David E., "The role of traditionalism in the
political modernization of Ghana and Uganda," World Pol

Political modernization poses sharply the issue of the nature and role of traditionalism. Here the author distinguishes two distinct types. The first is set in a context of hierarchical authority and instrumental values. In such a system change can occur by a simple extension of the notion of tradition, whereby innovations are integrated into long-established patterns, which reduces their novelty. The result is a localistic modernism, in which the tribal group can be the key vehicle, and the idea is illustrated by the Ganda of Uganda. In contrast is a culture where the traditionalism is loaded with "consummatory" values which are heavily religious, and in which the authority system is pyramidal. In the latter case authority is linked directly to kinship and other organizational structures with basic functions which are not authoritative. Change is much more difficult here, and typically requires a fundamental repudiation of traditionalism before it can occur. It is likely to lead to the emergence of political groups or parties which repudiate localism and separatism. Consummatory-pyramidal traditional is said to be characteristic of the Ashanti in Ghana.

1	-	3	-	-	-	3	-
Gei	cit	lis	rep	ant	eco	pol	soc

Benda, Harry J. , "Non-Western intelligensias as political elites," Austral J Pol Hist 6: 205-18, 1960.   168
The non-Western intelligensia in this essay consists of Western-trained intellectuals and military leaders who have assumed political power, usually as a result of social and/or political revolutions, and who constitute a relatively independent ruling class in their countries. There are three subgroups identified: intellectuals-rulers such as Nehru, Bourguiba, Nkrumah, Madero (of Mexico); military intelligensia such as Nasser, al-Kassem (in Iraq), Ne Win (in Burma), Peron; and communist elites in China, USSR, etc. They are a relatively new phenomenon, and exhibit several important characteristics: they are social revolutionaries who use coercive power to obtain ideologically-conceived social ends contrary to the status quo; they are frequently an isolated social group vis-a-vis the indigenous society; though small in number, the supply of them exceeds the demand (few are engineers, physicians or scientists); and they are strongly "ideological"--influenced by socialist and communist doctrines. Within this context, the author discusses the appearance of charismatic leaders, the trend toward the replacement of civilian or "pure" intellectuals by military ones, and the good possibility that although such ruling intelligensias probably constitute an intermediate stage in a society's historical de-

velopment, they may be expected to retain their virtual
monopoly of power in the LDC's for some time.

-	2	2	20	-	-	1	1
Gei	cit	lis	rep	ant	eco	pol	soc

Blanksten, George I. , "The politics of Latin America,"
Ch. 5, p. 455-531 in G. A. Almond and J. S. Coleman (eds.),
The politics of the developing areas, Princeton: Princeton University Press, 1960.   169
This is a comprehensive, elegantly composed survey
packed with information and with a presentation closely following the categories of classification and analysis set forth in the
introductory theoretical essay by Almond. For generalizations
about trends, patterns and problems common to all 20 of the
Latin American republics, along with specific note of exceptions and idiosyncracies, it is outstanding. For example,
ideological movements are classified into three groups, Marxist, native (Apristas in Peru, PRI in Mexico), and spurious
(those of Vargas in Brazil and Peron in Argentina), and Blanksten states that the first is holding its own, the second decreas-
ing in strength, except in Mexico, and the third is growing
stronger. In general, the amount and power of information
conveyed in this essay under such headings as "interest articulation," "interest aggregation," "political recruitment,"
etc. suggests that the functional approach to comparative
politics is most useful.

-	-	3	-	2	-	1	-
Gei	cit	lis	rep	ant	eco	pol	soc

Cancian, Francesca, "Functional analysis of change,"
Am Sociol R 25:818-827, 1960.   170
Functional analysis is generally thought of as being
useful in terms of static description rather than dynamic prediction. This need no longer be the case, argues the
author, and briefly describes the dynamic aspects and applications of functional analysis. Cited and outlined in the
article are four ways in which change is incorporated in functional analysis. Their justification lies in the definition of
functional systems and in the consequent possibility of order-
ing systems hierarchically and of treating subsystems as
problematic variables or "state coordinates" maintaining a set
of stable properties in a larger, more inclusive system. The
four methods can be used under the following conditions:
first, if it can be assumed that a set of phenomena form a
functional system; second, if information about an initial
change in a state coordinate can be obtained; and, third, if
there is information about whether this change is within or

outside of the limits governing the possibility of compensating changes in the values of other state coordinates. The approach is illustrated in terms of E. R. Leach's analysis of changing political systems in Burma, and Parsons and Smelser's analysis of the differentiation of control from ownership in the American economy.

7	-	3	-	1	-	2	1
Gei	cit	lis	rep	ant	eco	pol	soc

Chenery, Hollis B. , "Patterns of industrial growth," Am Econ R 50: 624-54, 1961.   171
        This is an econometric study of the causes, nature and consequences of industrialization in developing societies. Acknowledging the diversity of factors influencing industrialization, Chenery believes that five "universal factors"--common technical knowledge, similar human wants, access to similar markets for imports and exports, the accumulation of capital, and the accumulation of human skills--have a great deal to do with the causes and time path of industrialization in all developing countries. He develops models covering the cases of similar and differing resource endowment. Using cross sectional data from over 50 countries, both developed and developing, he carries out regression analyses of the impact of income and scale growth on industrialization. The finding is that while primary production declines in importance in the modernizing society, industry and transportation and communication become more prominent. The service sector remains at about the same level. In the industrial sector consumer goods lose ground to investment and related products. An attempt is then made to determine the causes of the variations in industrial growth left unexplained by the preceding analysis, by turning to some of the "particular" as opposed to "universal factors." Finally the implications for resource allocation are briefly explored. The analysis is a careful one, and the author does not fail to point out the relevant weaknesses and biases in his theory, analysis and data.

-	1	3	-	-	3	-	-
Gei	cit	lis	rep	ant	eco	pol	soc

Clairmonte, Frederick F. , Economic liberalism and underdevelopment: studies in the disintegration of an idea, NY: Asia Publishing House, 1960, 344 p.   172
        This book has two parts. The first part consists of a discussion of the origins of liberal economic doctrine, a critique of its adequacy for the underdeveloped world, and a series of specific comments on key aspects of underdevelopment. The doctrine of liberalism is seen as a direct consequence of the economic and social forces brought about by

the emergence of capitalism. Smithsian and Ricardian views
were initially progressive for England and other advanced nations. However, for new nations with weak economies, the
postulates of free trade and no government intervention have
proven to be inadequate. This was seen by List whose work
forms, in the author's view, the basis for an adequate theory
of development. List's main postulates are still correct. Industrialization is essential for development and protectionism
is necessary in its early stages. Growth should be balanced.
The doctrine of international specialization leads to abnormali-
ties and poverty in weak economies. State intervention is
necessary to guide economic growth. The second part, packed
with some most interesting statistical data, demonstrates the
accuracy of List's propositions stated above. Two points are
emphasized by the author. First, the inelasticity of food supplies generated by an inequalitarian and inefficient agricultural
organization creates structural bottlenecks preventing industrialization. Hence, the need for a radical agrarian reform.
Second, a total change in the internal power distribution of
underdeveloped nations is necessary for effective action. As
long as individuals who profit by the existing order hold the
reins of power, implementation of needed measures is impos-
sible.

(2)	1	1	-	-	-	-	1
Gei	cit	lis	rep	ant	eco	pol	soc

Coleman, James S., "The political systems of the
developing areas," "Conclusion," p. 532-576 in G. A. Almond
and J. S. Coleman (eds.), The politics of the developing areas,
Princeton: Princeton University Press, 1960.   173
In this essay several important points are made. In
contrast to modern society and polities with their highly differentiated and explicit structures and functions, the developing nations manifest economic, political and social processes
which are "mixed," a lack of political integration, and a wide
gap between the more modern elites and the traditional masses.
The underdeveloped countries' political systems are classified
according to several properties, leading to categories such as
"modernizing oligarchy," "terminal colonial democracy,"
"colonial and racial oligarchy." The road to modernity is seen
as one which leads to convergence in a shared modern pattern,
much like that now manifested by the Western democracies.
Finally, Coleman continues the analysis initiated by Shannon
and Lipset of the association between economic development
and "political competitiveness" among the LDC's, concluding
that it is impressively positive.

2	-	6	-	1	1	4	-
Gei	cit	lis	rep	ant	eco	pol	soc

Doob, Leonard W. , Becoming more civilized: a psychological exploration, New Haven: Yale University Press, 1960, 333 p. 174

The author makes use of published material on the psychological experience of being acculturated and some of his own results from research done in Africa and the West Indies to identify 27 hypotheses and corollaries about what happens to people as they come into contact with, and are influenced by, the way of life of modern Europe and America. The main index of acculturation used was education. Among the results: in comparison with those unchanged or already changed, persons who are "becoming more civilized" are more discontented, more aggressive, more tolerant of delay in achieving goals, ambivalent towards Europeans and Americans, more sensitive to other people, and less dogmatic. Other hypotheses deal with factors linked with the acceptance or rejection of innovation. Sometimes this study is tedious reading, and the generalizations or hypotheses are often only weakly supported by the data, but it is still a valuable and timely effort to identify the recurrent inner dimensions of the experience of modernization.

3	1	2	-	-	-	1	1
Gei	cit	lis	rep	ant	eco	pol	soc

Emerson, Rupert, From empire to nation: the rise to self-assertion of Asian and African peoples, Cambridge, Mass: Harvard University Press, 1960, 466 p. 175

Emerson's work is a detailed analysis of the historical and political processes that have shaped the rise of nationalism in non-Western countries since World War II. The author argues that, in the mid-20th century world, the attractions, virtues and dangers of nationalism are different for Western than for non-Western nations. While Western nations look towards internationalism for human progress, and establish international organizations to further this trend, non-Western nations see their chances for development in increased nationalism, and tend to utilize international organizations to that end.

23	3	4	2	-	-	3	1
Gei	cit	lis	rep	ant	eco	pol	soc

Emerson, Rupert, "Nationalism and political development," J Pol 22:3-28, 1960. 176

The thesis of this article is that nationalism is "the most important single force behind the revolutionary drive of the rising peoples of Asia and Africa," taking precedence even over the widely shared desire for an improved standard of living. In spite of its great importance, for which there is more than ample evidence, it is not easy to identify the content of nationalism, for it rarely consists of a coherent and positive body of doctrines and beliefs. However, one prominent feature of it is its predominantly negative or "anti" characteristic. Nationalism has a major role to play in laying the foundations for further political development, by uniting diverse peoples behind an active elite through providing them with shared experience and goals. Does nationalism tend to produce a particular type of polity? The answer to this is no, but in fact nationalism has in it a number of features which are productive of democracy; not least among which are the intangibles of the spirit--the restoration of self-respect, the building up of morale, and the stimulation of social solidarity.

1	-	-	80	-	-	-	-
Gei	cit	lis	rep	ant	eco	pol	soc

Foster, George M. , Culture and conquest: America's Spanish heritage, Viking Fund Pub in Anthropology No. 27, NY: Wenner-Gren Foundation for Anthropological Research, 1960. 272 p.   177

Here is a notably systematic effort to uncover the sources of and extent to which Spanish American culture derives from Spanish culture. On a chapter by chapter basis, for city, town, and village plans; agricultural practices; domestic animals; fishing techniques; etc. , etc. the American patterns are compared with their Spanish analogues. It is shown that both, as a matter of state and church policy and through informal processes a selection was made from Spanish culture for export to the New World. This is termed the "conquest culture." Over the centuries these patterns intermingled with the native Indian cultures and produced certain new forms and configurations of their own, a process called "cultural crystallization." Andalusia and Extremadura contributed most to this, partly because their emigrants predominated during the early colonization period.

-	-	3	-	3	-	-	-
Gei	cit	lis	rep	ant	eco	pol	soc

Gillin, John P. , "Some signposts for policy," Ch. 1, p. 14-62 in R. Adams, et al (eds.), Social change in Latin America today: its implications for United States policy, NY: Harper, 1960.   178

Gillin's lengthy article outlines the underlying values of the emerging "middle mass" in Latin America. He analyzes the general political and social changes occurring there, and stresses that they must be comprehended by American policymakers if our foreign policy is to be effective. Unless we understand the value orientation of the increasingly influential middle masses we will not be able to facilitate the develop-

ment of a Latin democratic political order. Gillin discusses
the way the Latin middle strata differ from the American middle classes, the forces acting upon them, and the way they will
probably influence Latin American development. The Latin
American middle masses differ from the North American in
their stress on nine core values; these include kinship,
hierarchy, transcendentalism, etc. Although Gillin doubts
that Western style democracy will develop in Latin America,
he suggests seven ways by which American foreign policy can
foster the development of Latin democracy and prevent communist take-overs.

Gei	cit	lis	rep	ant	eco	pol	soc
-	-	3	-	1	-	1	1

Gluckman, Max,"Tribalism in modern British Central
Africa," Cahiers d'etudes africaines 1: 55-70, 1960.   179
       Based primarily on case studies of Northern Rhodesia
and Nyasaland under British rule, Gluckman's article compares
the differential nature and effect of tribalism on the African
way of life in town and rural areas. In the countryside tribalism persisted because of governmental support and because of
the crucial nature of the tie to the land. Due to this tie the
individual accepts the tribal political system and culture.
While a form of tribalism persists in the towns, it does not
produce the same kind of organized system of political and
social relations existing in rural areas. Although tribalism
in the towns is important in grouping people into "categories"
and in producing mutual aid associations, class linkages develop which often overshadow the influence of tribalism. In
crisis, common interests arising from industrial association
often overcome the effects of tribalism. Gluckman concludes
that in the later stages of colonialism, the town dwelling
African's personality and activity were shaped both by his ties
to his village, which he preserved for his security, and by
his social and economic relationships in the town where he
worked.

Gei	cit	lis	rep	ant	eco	pol	soc
-	-	1	100	1	-	-	-

•

Hirschman, Albert O. , "Ideologies of economic development in Latin America," p. 3-42, in A. O. Hirschman (ed.),
Latin American issues, essays and comments, NY: Twentieth
Century Fund, 1960.   180
       What are the principal ideas about development pro-
posed by Latin American writers? From independence to
World War I was the age of self-incrimination, in which most
writers focussed attention on defects of social structure (too
many caciques, etc.) and intrinsic shortcomings of national

character (laziness, arrogance, etc.). In the interwar period
Latin American writing concentrated more on finding fault with
the outer world, the main theme being anti-imperialism. At
present the dominant body of ideas comes from the UN's Economic Commission for Latin America, organized in 1948 with
its seat in Santiago. ECLA doctrine stresses asymmetry in the
relations between industrialized countries and LDC's in terms
of the distribution of productivity gains, and the income elasticity of demand for imports, and supports the idea of differential
function and need for protection and import restrictions in
these two groups of countries. It also favors development programming techniques and a Latin American Common Market.
ECLA's critics, both Latin American and others, are in dis-
agreement with the basic diagnosis and emphasis of its ideology,
and also are skeptical of the capacity of the state in most Latin
American countries to conduct competent policy formation and
planning. Hirschman's personal recommendation in all this is
to cast off the chains of rigid ideological positions, relinquish
the search for perfect "systems," and actually investigate,
analyze, and learn from the growth which has already occurred,
especially in Brazil and Mexico.

	-	-	3	-	2	-	1	-
	Gei	cit	lis	rep	ant	eco	pol	soc

Holmberg, Allan R. , "Changing community attitudes and
values in Peru: a case study in guided change," Ch. 2, p. 63-
107 in Council on Foreign Relations, Social change in Latin
America today: its implications for United States policy, NY:
Random House, 1960.   181
The story of Vicos, a hacienda community of some 1,850
Quechua-speaking Indians located in an inter-Andean valley 250
miles NE of Lima, and at an elevation of 9,000-14,000 feet, is
surely eligible for inclusion among the rare cases of inspira-
tional literature of social science. In 1952, Cornell University, with the support of the Peruvian Government and in collaboration with the Indigenous Institute of Peru, undertook a
systematic program of research and development to determine
how an impoverished, isolated, exploited, and ignorant Indian
community would respond to a concerted effort to introduce it
to a more modern way of life. The results were extremely
impressive, even electrifying. At the end of five years agricultural production had greatly increased; sanitation, nutrition and modern medical services had become established;
education had become an important value and the children were
in school; community leadership had developed; and in general
". . . after 400 years of peonage under the hacienda system,
the Vicosinos have now become the masters of their own
destiny and of their own land."

		3	-	3	-	-	-
Gei	cit	lis	rep	ant	eco	pol	soc

Hoselitz, Bert F. , <u>Sociological aspects of economic growth</u>, Glencoe, Ill: Free Press, 1960.   182
        Seeing the need for a theory relating economic growth to cultural change, Hoselitz attempts to pursue a more limited objective, the development of models for different types of societies and different types of transitions from traditional to more modern forms of economic organization. To do this he seeks to identify the variables most significant in measuring economic advancement, classify countries as developed or underdeveloped, and investigate the interrelationships of those economic and social variables which describe the transition from an economically underdeveloped to an advanced society. Among the topics touched upon are cultural patterns (in terms of Parsons' pattern variables) and economic growth, the role of deviant groups (e. g. , Jews in Medieval Europe) in initiating departures from traditional economic patterns, types of businessmen (entrepreneurs, managers, speculators), and the relation between urbanization and economic growth.

8	5	6	-	-	-	2	4
Gei	cit	lis	rep	ant	eco	pol	soc

Kerr, Clark, et al, <u>Industrialism and industrial man: the problems of labor and management in economic growth,</u> Cambridge, Mass: Harvard University Press, 1960, 331 p.
                                                                183
        Based on studies of the Inter-University Study of Labor Problems in Economic Development, this book by four labor economists draws conclusions concerning the process of industrialization and especially of the role of leadership. In formulating a general theory of labor-management relations, they take into account differences among countries in different stages of industrial development, and project the industrialization process into the future. Many factors play a role in determining the nature of industrialism: the logic of industrialism, the stage of development of industrialism, the cultural inheritance, and the types of elites directing the process. The logic of industrialism leads to a convergence in all countries toward the pattern of "pluralistic industrialism," because it tends to create similar forms of communities, education, and "webs of rules" governing labor-management relationships. However, in the short-run, differences will remain. The process varies partly because of differences between five types of directing elites: dynastic, middle class, revolutionary-intellectual, colonial and nationalist. Their different "strategic concepts" lead to differences in the sources of capital,

priorities in production, nuances of labor-management relations, etc.

Gei	cit	lis	rep	ant	eco	pol	soc
2	-	6	-	1	2	3	-

Lieuwen, Edwin, Arms and politics in Latin America (1960), rev. edit. , NY: Praeger, 1961, 296 p.   184

The aim of this ambitious but uneven book is to analyze the role and relative political influence of the military forces of 20 Latin American republics in the years since independence, and to assess the military aid program of the USA in more recent years. In the former task, most of Lieuwen's attention is occupied by Mexico, which is treated as a case study in the curbing of militarism. Arguments against military aid by the USA are presented; in its place the author recommends more trade, and economic and technical assistance. Noting that the USA's fear of communism, concern for stability, and stress on military security have often identified it closely with unrepresentative military governments and given the impression that it is opposed to social reform movements, Lieuwen urges basic policy changes in the USA which would place it clearly on the side of much needed Latin American economic development and social reform.

Gei	cit	lis	rep	ant	eco	pol	soc
-	-	5	-	2	-	2	1

Malenbaum, Wilfred and Wolfgang Stolper, "Political ideology and economic progress: the basic question," World Pol 12: 413-21, 1960.   185

In 1960, these two economists contributed to the vigorous debate between capitalism and communism as to the best means for rapid economic growth. In this brief article, they highlight the main differences in economic results between two communist states (East Germany and China) and two non-communist states (West Germany and India). They conclude that there is no systematic relationship between ideology and the rate of economic progress. They stress that inflexible attachment to doctrines which run counter to indigenous economic and social relationships is detrimental to growth. "It is not an ideology or an economic theory that will bring growth; it is more energetic and imaginative responses to the record as revealed by intensive study." They advocate joint research and experimentation to eliminate pragmatically the bottlenecks hindering growth and to foster democratic development.

Gei	cit	lis	rep	ant	eco	pol	soc
-	-	-	80	-	-	-	-

Miner, Horace, "Culture change under pressure: a Hausa case," Hum Org 19:164-7, 1960.   186
The Anchau Development Scheme in Northern Nigeria was initiated to control an epidemic of sleeping sickness. Although the Hausa believed the disease was caused by spirits inhabiting the brush alongside streams, the British correctly attributed it to the tsetse flies in the brush. They introduced the control method of cutting down the brush by annual slashing.   Sleeping sickness was eliminated by this method, but even after 20 years of successful control Hausa village headmen maintained (1957-58) that they would not clear the stream banks unless they were forced to do so.   They never accepted the British explanation of the cause of the disease; consequently, coercion produced compliant behavior but did not produce fundamental culture change.

-	-	-	100	-	-	-	-
Gei	cit	lis	rep	ant	eco	pol	soc

Moore, Wilbert E. and Arnold S. Feldman (eds.), Labor commitment and social change in developing areas, NY: Social Science Research Council, 1960, 378 p.   187
This collection of essays is concerned with labor and the industrialization problems of developing nations.   The approach is both theoretical and inductive.   The articles deal with the many-faceted aspects of the involvement or "commitment" of people who have had little or no experience in industrial society.   The collection as a whole points up the difficulties involved in framing all-embracing generalities about the process of commitment, and suggests the danger inherent in producing generalizations that could lead to a closed conception of what a modernized society "should be like."   The problems discussed are for the most part treated as general social problems rather than as problems limited and defined by a single academic discipline.   In their final essay, Feldman and Moore attempt to tie together the more abstract theoretical notions and generalizations of the contributions.

8	2	4	-	1	-	3	-
Gei	cit	lis	rep	ant	eco	pol	soc

Parsons, Talcott, Structure and process in modern societies, Glencoe, Ill: Free Press, 1960, 344 p.   188
In this book of essays, some published previously, Parsons discusses a number of features of modern society. The first two chapters treat formal organizations--business firms, government bureaus, hospitals.   The next two deal with the context of economic development, largely as it occurred in the West, but with some preliminary comparisons with the non-Western world's experiences.   The next section concerns

politics--a general analysis, a critique of Mills' The power
elite, and a discussion of the social sources of McCarthyism.
Included in the last section are papers on medical education,
religion in the USA and on the "principal structures of community." A review of the features of modern society presumably lends clarity by contrast to one's picture of those societies which are not modern, as well as suggesting directions
in the press of these latter toward the goal of modernization.

	2	4	-	1	-	1	2
Gei	cit	lis	rep	ant	eco	pol	soc

Rostow, Walter W. , The stages of economic growth:
a non-communist manifesto, NY: Cambridge University Press,
1960, 178 p.   189

Rostow's work is a bold and extremely influential
effort to "make sense out of economic history" in the manner
of sociology by identifying five stages through which a society
must pass before it has reached economic maturity. The
stages are (1) traditional society, (2) appearance of the preconditions for the take-off into sustained economic growth,
(3) the take-off, (4) the drive toward maturity, and (5) the
society of high mass consumption. The main characteristics
of society are described for each stage, as are the conditions
which produce the transition from one stage to the next. This
book is notable also for its claim to have corrected and improved upon Marx, and for the fame, in some places notori-
ety, which several of its concepts--"take-off," "high mass
consumption" stage, reactive nationalism--have achieved. It
is one of the most important books in the field for its generality, sharp posing of questions, and for the continuing creative
controversy it has engendered. Is societal development well-
conceived in terms of stages? Whatever the proper answer,
we may be sure that the ideas in this book have themselves
been an active force in the course of history.

3	6	9	20	2	3	2	2
Gei	cit	lis	rep	ant	eco	pol	soc

Shils, Edward A. , "The intellectuals in the political
development of the new states." World Pol 12:329-68, 1960.
                                                           190
What part do "modern intellectuals" play in the political development of the new states? Their roles include that
of "instigator," the "leader," and the "executant" of political
life. Shils delineates social origins, psychic tensions, and
occupational status; shows the intellectuals' bias toward
nationalism, socialism, populism, oppositionalism, and in-
civility; and traces their contributions during three main
stages: constitutional liberalism, politicized nationalism, and

the assumption of power. While the intellectuals presented
a united front against the colonial regime, after independence
there is usually a split between the "ins" and "outs." The latter usually turn either to "anti-political passivity" or to a
form of activistic extremism, traditionalist or leninist.

Gei	cit	lis	rep	ant	eco	pol	soc
-	1	5	40	-	-	4	1

Apter, David E. , The political kingdom in Uganda:
a study in bureaucratic nationalism, Princeton: Princeton
University Press, 1961, 498 p.   191
This book focuses on one major section of Uganda, the
Kingdom of Buganda. Separatist feelings, as well as an anti-
colonialist sentiment, are strong in this area. The Kingdom
thus finds itself in opposition to the attempts of the British
Foreign Office and Uganda to establish a unified government
in preparation for independence. Apter describes the social,
economic, and religious factors at work which influence the
development of political parties, economic nationalism, and a
unified national government. By using historical, sociological
and political viewpoints, the author is able to demonstrate the
conflict between the interests of Buganda and the more nationalistic influences found in the other areas of Uganda.

Gei	cit	lis	rep	ant	eco	pol	soc
-	-	4	-	-	-	4	-

Ashford, Douglas E. , Political change in Morocco,
Princeton: Princeton University Press, 1961, 432 p.   192
This book is an excellent description of the national
politics of Morocco from 1955 to 1959. The author includes
studies of problems relating to government , citizenship, and
efforts made to bring about representative government in
Morocco. Ashford believes that there are four "general
relationships" which serve as a basis for political development.
These are charisma, coercion, institutions, and tradition.
For Ashford, it is the charismatic relationship between the
King and the people which serves as the basic factor of
Moroccan political life. The author claims that the complexity of Morocco has led to the development of specialized
interests and thus the beginnings of fragmentation.

Gei	cit	lis	rep	ant	eco	pol	soc
-	1	3	-	-	-	3	-

Bennis, Warren G. , Kenneth B. Benne and Robert
Chin (eds.), The planning of change: readings in the applied
behavioral sciences, NY: Holt, Rinehart and Winston, 1961,
781 p.   193
Divided into four major sections, this volume of

eighty-four items covers the following areas: "The Roots of Planned Change," "Conceptual Tools for the Change Agent: Social Systems and Change Models," "Dynamics of the Influence Process," and "Programs and Technologies of Planned Change." The first part, essentially an introduction, covers the philosophical, historical and social bases of planned change. In the second part, a critical review of some basic concepts in the social sciences is presented. The third part includes a discussion of the basic elements of all types of change. Finally, in the fourth part, some specific programs of planned change are explored. The editors provide an elaborate introduction at the beginning of the book and explanatory material before each major chapter. The result is a logical, well-organized book of readings.

8	-	3	-	3	-	-	-
Gei	cit	lis	rep	ant	eco	pol	soc

Braibanti, Ralph J. D. , and Joseph J. Spengler (eds.), Tradition, values and socio-economic development, Durham, NC: Duke University Press, 1961, 305 p.   194

The topics examined here are rate and direction of development with respect to the emotional and intellectual predispositions of the elites and the masses; political development in emerging nations; socio-economic variables in economic development; forms of tradition-oriented behavior; the impact of cultural influences in enhancing and deferring social innovation; effects of Islamic tradition on the ideological sources in Pakistan; technical assistance and its effect on the internal policies of the recipients; and analysis of social change in French Canada. The essays in this volume are not integrated into a continuing thread of thought. Nevertheless, there seems to exist a largely implicit agreement among the contributors that economic development may be achieved through the subordination of it to higher goals whose realization necessitates economic development.

8	2	4	-	2	-	2	-
Gei	cit	lis	rep	ant	eco	pol	soc

Chenery, Hollis B. , "Comparative advantage and development policy," Am Econ R 51:18-51, 1961.   195

This piece discusses the analysis of resource allocation in LDC economies from three points of view, by: ascertaining the extent to which the allocation principles derived from trade theory and from growth theory can be reconciled with each other without losing their operational significance; by comparing various approaches to the measurement of optimal resource allocation in terms of their logical consistency and their applicability to different conditions; and by examining some of the practical procedures followed in setting investment policy in underdeveloped countries in the light of the earlier discussion. Here development policy is considered from the standpoint of economic theory, as a problem in operation research, and as it is actually carried on by governments. For all these reasons the article is recommendable to policy makers also.

1	-	4	-1	-	4	-	-
Gei	cit	lis	rep	ant	eco	pol	soc

Deutsch, Karl W. , "Social mobilization and political development," Am Pol Sci R 55:493-514, 1961.   196
Social mobilization is defined as the process in which old social, economic and psychological commitments are broken and people become available for new patterns of socialization and behavior. The major hypothesis is that the degree of social mobilization affects the performance of the political system. Exposure to modern life, to the mass media, change of residence, urbanization, change from agricultural occupation, literacy and per capita income are seven indicators of social mobilization. It is hypothesized that social mobilization brings with it an expansion of the politically relevant strata of the population, and an expansion of the number and functions of the governing elites. Increasing social mobilization can be expected to encourage solidarity where there is linguistic and racial homogeneity and to produce disunity where people do not share the same language, culture, etc. The model is tested for 19 countries. This article is strongly recommended.

2	2	8	5	-	-	5	3
Gei	cit	lis	rep	ant	eco	pol	soc

Eisenstadt, Shmuel N. , Essays on sociological aspects of political and economic development, The Hague: Mouton, 1961, 88 p.   197
The essays included here, with minor additions and some references to literature published later, first appeared in 1956 and 1957. The first is "Sociological aspects of political development in new states" and is a long, general essay intended to identify the sociological factors at work in the LDC's, and to identify recurrent patterns (uneven change in colonial societies, new patterns of political motivation and participation after independence, etc.). The other two essays deal with Israel--traditional and modern social values in relation to economic development, and the conditions affecting the adaptation of Oriental immigrants in Israeli agricultural settlements.

8	1	4	-	-	-	2	2
Gei	cit	lis	rep	ant	eco	pol	soc

Erasmus, Charles J. , Man takes control: cultural
development and American aid, Minn: University of Minnesota
Press, 1961, 365 p.   198
      In this book man is cast into an active role in socio-
cultural change. Reacting against cultural determinism, the
tendency to see man as largely a product of his environment,
the author stresses motivation and cognition as agents of
change. Key concepts are motivation to gain prestige and a
cognitive process termed "frequency interpretations. . . a
probability estimate based on inductive inference from experience." These psychological variables are linked with social
stratification, property and types of societies at three different levels of "cultural development." In primitive subsistence
societies prestige is gained by "conspicuous giving" or sharing;
as society becomes more open to opportunities to possess
goods, "conspicuous ownership" becomes dominant; and in open
societies where the demand for goods is either restricted or
saturated, "conspicuous production" is found, and prestige is
gained from creative, productive or manipulative activity.
This scheme is applied and illustrated within the developing
society, where the author emphasizes that "conspicuous giving"
is a barrier to development, and that elites and/or the middle
classes are the most likely candidates for aid, because innovations have more chance of success at that level. Good illustrative material, especially a case study of part of Mexico, and
critical suggestions about USA foreign aid policy lend added
interest to an approach with rich implications and considerable
promise.

3	2	7	-		6	-	-	1
Gei	cit	lis	rep		ant	eco	pol	soc

      Erlich, Alexander, The Soviet industrialization debate,
1924-1928, Cambridge, Mass: Harvard University Press, 1961,
214 p.   199
      Narration and analysis of the famous debate over the
path to rapid development, which covered, 40 years ago, many
of the problems so eagerly debated today. Also, the reasons
conjectured for the final decision made by Stalin, which was
more radical (in respect to investment in heavy industry and
the forced collectivization of agriculture) than had been the
path proposed by such leftist protagonists as Trotsky and
Preobrazhenski. Erlich argues that Stalin's decision was a
political one, oriented to the dictator's unwillingness to tolerate
economic independence on the part of the peasants, either in
the market or in making decisions about production goals.
An engrossing and important story of the economic, social and
intellectual background from which Stalinist totalitarianism
emerged.

3	-	1	-		-	-	-	1
Gei	cit	lis	rep		ant	eco	pol	soc

Fanon, Frantz, <u>The wretched of the earth</u> (Paris, 1961), transl. from the French by C. Farrington, NY: Grove Press, 1966, 255 p. 200

An eloquent, intellectually respectable and very moving statement of the conditions and aspirations of the peoples of formerly colonial countries, this has already become an important document, and may prove to be our century's successor to the Manifesto of 1846. Fanon, a Negro, was born on Martinique, studied medicine in France, became a psychiatrist in Algeria, and joined in the national liberation war against the French. His thoughts, like those of Marx, are many things: an indictment of the exploitation and degradation brought about by colonialism, an analysis and justification of the creative role of violence in producing self-respect, a characterization of the forces and processes involved in nation-building, and a theory of the role of various social strata and groups (including the intellectuals) in the political struggles of the times. Violent revolution, it is urged, is the only way in which the rural peasant masses of the LDC's can be mobilized to form a national community, the latter being seen as a precondition of development.

3	2	6	-		-	-	4	2
Gei	cit	lis	rep		ant	eco	pol	soc

Furtado, Celso, <u>Development and underdevelopment</u> (Rio de Janeiro, 1961), transl. by Ricardo W. de Aginar and Eric Charles Drysdale, Berkeley & Los Angeles: University of California Press, 1964, 181 p. 201

Furtado's work is a rather technical exposition, with good attention to intellectual forbears--Adam Smith, Ricardo, Marx, Schumpeter, Keynes, etc.--and proposals for a general theory of development, one couched in "structural" terms. In addition to useful contributions toward a defining theory, the book is noteworthy for acceptance and creative use of the Marxist concept of surplus, for the author's insistence upon both a general or abstract theory of development and attention to the unique conditions in any particular historical society, and for the argument that "underdevelopment" today is not a mere recapitulation of experience already passed through by the advanced countries, but a special new phenomenon.

2	2	3	-		-	-	1	2
Gei	cit	lis	rep		ant	eco	pol	soc

Germani, Gino and Kalman Silvert, "Politics, social structure, and military intervention in Latin America," <u>Arch</u>

Europ Sociol 2: 62-81, 1961.   202
    The premise of this article is that political intervention
on the part of the military implies a weak and sick social
system. This being the case, the problem which faces Latin
American nations is political modernization. The Military will
be restricted to its professional functions when Latin American
societies develop a more complex power structure, the masses
are incorporated into the national body, and economic and social
conflicts find institutionalized expression. The authors see
this happening when these nations pass into the sixth historical
stage, its two forms being Total Participation Through Democracy or National-Popular Revolution. At this stage, or any of
the preceding, the nature of military-civilian relations may
take any of ten forms: 1) Classical Military Garrison State,
2) Modern Totalitarian Garrison State, 3) Totalitarian Politico-
Military Relations, 4) Military as Institutionalized Governor,
5) Military as Trustee Governor, 6) Military as Orienters of
National Policy, 7) Military as Pressure Group with Veto Power, 8) Military as Simple Pressure Group, 9) Military as a
Simple Police Force in Complete Subordination to the Government, 10) Military as a Political Arm of the State. In each of
these cases, military intervention does not imply an ideational
vacuum, but is invariably associated with wider social interests
and ideologies. This study is a good attempt to create functional
categories of military-civilian relations.

1	3	2	-		-	-	1	1
Gei	cit	lis	rep		ant	eco	pol	soc

    Echevarria, J. Medina and Philip M. Hauser, "Part one:
summary and conclusions. I. rapporteurs' report," p. 19-74
in Seminar on Urbanization Problems in Latin America,
Santiago de Chile, 1959. Urbanization in Latin America, edited by P. Hauser, Paris: UNESCO, 1961.   203
    In this authoritative and very general survey many of
the central trends and issues of development are discussed.
Urbanization is the focus of primary interest, however, and
the Latin American scene is described in terms of current
structure (hypertrophy of capital cities, etc.), historic trends
(some degree of urbanization without corresponding development, or "over-urbanization, etc. ,") and likely future patterns
(for example, exodus from the mountains toward the valleys,
and a tendency to movement away from seacoast areas toward
the center of the continent, where most of the raw materials
needed for industrialization are to be found). Many other
features shared by most Latin American societies--highly
skewed income distribution, inequitable and unproductive patterns of land tenure, patterns of rural-urban migration, etc.

--are treated, and the authors provide also a good summary of the current state of knowledge about what typically happens to people and institutions when a society develops. Finally, practical problems and recommended courses of action to deal with the situation are discussed under the heading of "planning" and "administration."

-	-	3	-	-	-	1	2
Gei	cit	lis	rep	ant	eco	pol	soc

Hirschmann, Albert O. (ed.), Latin American issues: essays and comments, NY: Twentieth Century Fund, 1961, 201 p.   204

In this collection of articles, some of Latin America's pressing problems, such as inflation, land reform and free trade zone are examined. All but one essay, that of Thomas F. Carroll on land reform, emerged from a study group set by the Twentieth Century Fund to promote a better understanding between the North and South Americas. A good portion of the book is devoted to discussions between "monetarists," and "structuralists." The main theme of the discussions is the usefulness of monetary and fiscal policy in checking inflation and the relation between structural factors and inflationary process. There are also articles on tax and land reforms, free trade zone, and historical evaluation of Latin American economics. No index.

8	-	3	-	-	-	-	3
Gei	cit	lis	rep	ant	eco	pol	soc

Johnson, Bruce and John W. Mellor, "The role of agriculture in economic development," Am Econ R 51:566-93, 1961.   205

In this key article five contributions which agriculture can make to development are identified: provide increased food supplies to feed the increasing urban population; enlarge agricultural exports to earn foreign exchange; supply labor to the non-industrial sector; contribute to capital formation directly by savings and indirectly by lowering the cost of foodstuffs; and serve as a market for the expanding industrial sector. The growing demand for food in the LDC's is not only a function of increasing populations, but also a function of income elasticity of demand for food, quite high in these countries (their average is around .6 as compared with .16 in the USA.) The latter part of the article deals with the re-source requirements and priorities for agricultural development, stressing the complementary nature of inputs such as technology, education and the institutional characteristics of agriculture. As most articles have, in the period before the Punta del Este Conference of 1967, the need for yield increas-

ing and labor intensive methods of increasing production is
urged, as is an emphasis upon agricultural research and extension programs conducted by qualified personnel.

-	-	4	-		-	4	-	-
Gei	cit	lis	rep		ant	eco	pol	soc

Lewis, Oscar, The children of Sánchez: autobiography
of a Mexican family, NY: Random House, 1961, 499 p.   206
    Jesús Sánchez, 50, and his 3 grown children comprise a
poor family living in a Mexico City slum which is described
Rashomon-like through the eyes of each member in the form of
tape-recorded, edited and re-arranged autobiographies. The
main purpose is to reveal what it means to live in poverty in a
large city undergoing rapid change; the main contribution is a
poignant, even dramatic, depiction of the culture of poverty,
which enables such families to survive the tremendous hard-
ships and defeats life brings them. A rare and revealing opportunity for the affluent reader to share, from a distance and
for awhile, the life and feelings of the very poor, which will
help him realize why economic development is such an important goal in the modern world.

-	1	4	-		3	-	1	-
Gei	cit	lis	rep		ant	eco	pol	soc

McClelland, David C. , The achieving society, NY:
Van Nostrand, 1961, 512 p.   207
    A broad range of data from a variety of contemporary
and historical societies and gathered with several different
methods are interpreted as support for the theory that need
achievement is the reason for differing rates of national economic development. The most significant of the many findings reported is that achievement themes in imaginative
literature increase in frequency prior to instances of economic
growth and decrease prior to economic decline. This result
appears, according to data ingeniously collected, for ancient
Greece, medieval Spain, medieval and early modern England,
the USA from 1800-1950, and with reasonable substitute
indicators, in preliterate societies. Another important result,
less convincingly demonstrated, is that entrepreneurship,
particularly in the role of businessman, is the crucial link
between achievement and economic growth. The study is also
important for its carefully reported negative findings. Not
confirmed were such hypotheses as: achieved status predomi-
nates in developed countries while ascribed status predomi-
nates in LDC's; asceticism, saving and renunciation of world-
ly pleasures are vital to economic development; and faith in
one's ability to conquer nature pervades the ethos of development. Weighty criticisms can be made of this book--

theoretical: Why is n achievement to be expressed in economic entrepreneurship rather than in some other direction, perhaps more strongly supported in the national value system? methodological: To what do themes of n achievement in folk tales really refer? interpretive: Do the data presented actually support the hypotheses? and so on. Nevertheless, it is one of the richest and most important books in the field.

3	2	5	-		-	1	3	1
Gei	cit	lis	rep		ant	eco	pol	soc

Millikan, Max F. et al, "The disruption of traditional societies," Ch. 2, p. 7-17 in M. F. Millikan (ed.), The emerging nations: their growth and United States policy, Boston: Little, Brown, 1961.   208

This is a statement jointly authored by ten members of an M. I. T. working seminar concerned with the reasons for and manner of disruption of traditional society. Through such a society is on the whole static, and it was the contact with the West, and attendant shock from this, that was most important in changing it, there were also cases in which the traditional mold was cracked by a more endogenous process. One such example is the traditional society faced by a war, which set changes in motion which led to modernization. Another is the general pattern whereby some articulate group or category of men have reason to become disaffected with the social order at hand, and are ready, when suitable opportunity permits, to take the lead against the rulers of the traditional in striving for modernization. Of course, the central vehicle of contact with the West was that of colonialism, and this specific pattern itself led to certain widespread and potent forces opposing traditionalism--frustration, nationalism and the quest for independence; population growth and land scarcity; and new conceptions of equity and procedure in the division of responsibilities and rewards.

-	-	3	-		2	-	1	-
Gei	cit	lis	rep		ant	eco	pol	soc

Millikan, Max F. and Donald L. M. Blackmer (eds.), The emerging nations: their growth and United States policy, Boston: Little, Brown, 1961, 171 p.   209

A group of articles based on a study prepared for the Senate Committee on Foreign Relations are put together in two parts in this volume. In the first part, in the manner of a group study, the contributors analyze the nature and dynamics of societies in transition, emphasizing the many-sided nature of the process and the range of differences among societies with varying histories, cultures, resources, and geography. At times attempts are made to reach a synthesis in terms of

common features of the transitional process and strategic
factors susceptible to external influences. The second part
of the collection deals with the implications of development
for United States policy.

8	3	4	-		1	1	2	-
Gei	cit	lis	rep		ant	eco	pol	soc

Nair, Kusum, Blossoms in the dust: the human factor
in Indian development, NY: Praeger, 1961, 201 p.   210
A Western educated Indian journalist provides here a
useful description of Indian village attitudes toward development, stressing how the human factor impedes development.
The author visited several villages in each of India's fifteen
states in 1958. While her research doesn't meet rigorous
social science canons, she sought to make her study convincing in numerous ways (e. g. , she visited several villages in the
same area to check her impressions). She interviewed villagers to determine their attitude toward major governmental
programs such as land reform and irrigation projects. Most
villagers were uncooperative, skeptical, pessimistic, and re-
sistant to change. This was due, partly, to factionalism
which often grew out of land reforms. Many villagers not only did not want more land, but also had low aspirations for a
higher standard of living. Government plans often yield
meagre and unintended results, for many "essentials," such
as the power pattern, deep economic cleavages, and the
"traditional hierarchical nature of intergroup relationships
which govern the economic life of village society" remain
virtually unchanged. It is argued that unless greater planning for social change is undertaken, economic development
will not succeed.

2	3	-	-		-	-	-	-
Gei	cit	lis	rep		ant	eco	pol	soc

Needler, Martin C. , "The political development of
Mexico," Am Pol Sci R 55: 308-12, 1961.   211
In spite of being a one-party political system, Mexico
has evolved toward greater consensus and stability, a fact
which is suggested by changes in political techniques and in the
typical skills manifested by Mexican presidents. The fact is
that a wide variety of organized interests, especially those
with fighting capabilities, have been incorporated into the
PRI through being given a stake in an ever-changing status
quo. The basis of allocating benefits among the various sectors in the party has changed over time from fighting potential
to number, which has meant increasing dominance by moder-
ate bourgeois elements. Although peaceful succession and civil
liberties are also among the achievements of this one-party

system, the author nevertheless judges it a transitional form which, by fostering development, will probably make itself obsolete.

	-	-	3	-		-	-	3	-
Gei	cit	lis	rep		ant	eco	pol	soc	

Nurkse, Ragnar, Patterns of trade and development (Lectures presented to the Wicksell Lecture Society in Stockholm, 1959), NY: Oxford University Press, 1961, 55p.   212
This short but informative work compares past and present patterns of development in the non-industrialized nations of the world. The 19th century pattern of economic growth through international trade was one in which outlying areas of the world economy were able to raise their incomes via a rapidly expanding demand for their primary exports in the developed, industrialized nations. However, in the 20th century so far, there has been a relative lag in the exports from the underdeveloped nations, leading Nurkse to hypothesize that the 19th century pattern of "exports as the engine of growth" is not entirely realistic for the present. Reasons include the low elasticity of consumer demand for agricultural products, the substitution of many raw materials by synthetics, the protectionism which the developed nations are not willing to relinquish on their manufactured products, the increased efficiency in the use of raw materials, and the dominant role which the developed nations play in trade flow patterns. Three means of growth for the LDC's are increased exports of primary products, growth through exports of manufactured consumer goods, and expansion of output for domestic markets. The weight given to each will differ from country to country in accordance with specific conditions, such as natural resources and external demand, but in general the first two need more emphasis.

	2	1	3	20		-	2	1	-
Gei	cit	lis	rep		ant	eco	pol	soc	

Patel, Surendra J., "Rates of industrial growth in the last century, 1860-1958," Econ Dev Cult Ch 9:316-330, 1961.
213
In answer to the increasingly important question of whether or not underdeveloped countries will ever be able to close the growing modernization gap between themselves and presently industrialized nations, the author provides an interesting and provocative, if not entirely convincing, argument. The major hypothesis, with which an ample presentation of data seems to concur, is that new entrants into the process of industrialization will be able to close the gap because they modernize at a much faster rate of growth than

their predecessors. This is due primarily to the great wealth of technological advance upon which they can draw, whereas the rate of development in the initially industrialized countries was determined by the constraining pace of independent technological innovation. Once underdeveloped countries embark on the road to modernization, closing the gap between industrialized and non-industrialized nations is an arithmetically inevitable consequence.

-	1	1	20		-	-	-	1
Gei	cit	lis	rep		ant	eco	pol	soc

Pearse, Andrew, "Part two: selected seminar papers. VII. Some characteristics of urbanization in the city of Rio de Janeiro," p. 191-202 in Seminar in Urbanization Problems in Latin America, Santiago de Chile, 1959. Urbanization in Latin America, edited by P. Hauser, Paris: UNESCO, 1961.   214
    In this contribution attention is focussed upon the favela or urban slum as found in Rio, its history, causes, and characteristics, including the patterns by which its residents become assimilated. There was a very rapid growth from about 1930, when the fall in prices of agricultural products lowered the rural standard of living, and raised the rate of immigration to the point where housing and transportation systems could not accommodate the flood of newcomers searching for jobs and independence. The physical conformation of Rio plays a role in the rise of the favela, but more generally it is a functional response to the huge gap between the richer, urban, industrial part of the country and the poor, rural agricultural portion. In the favela, though the house type is rural and conditions are primitive, other opportunities and welfare services are urban, and its dwellers count themselves fortunate in being able to enjoy the city's advantages.

-	1	3	-		2	-	-	1
Gei	cit	lis	rep		ant	eco	pol	soc

Rosenstein-Rodan, Paul N., "International aid for underdeveloped countries," R Econ Stat 43:107-38, 1961.   215
    Foreign aid should accelerate development to the point where a satisfactory rate of growth is achieved on a self-sustaining basis. This goal cannot be reached unless the aid is assuredly continuous and contributes to the increase in the rate of domestic capital formation. The best amount of aid is a marginal rate which is much higher than the average rate of savings as long as there is an absorptive capacity for such aid within the receiving country. The author continues by outlining various forms of foreign aid and suggests some principles for sharing the burden of aid. He then provides a method for determining the annual growth rate per person and an index of

absorptive capacity for an LDC. The rest of the article presents development statistics for a large number of aid-receiv-
ing countries and a formula for computing their capital inflow
requirements.

1	1	4	-		-	4	-	-
Gei	cit	lis	rep		ant	eco	pol	soc

Shils, Edward A. The intellectual between tradition and
modernity: the Indian situation, Comparative Studies in Society
and History, Supplement, The Hague: Mouton, 1961, 120 p.
216

Although described as a "preliminary report," this is
quite a detailed and convincing characterization of the history
and current problems of the Indian intelligentsia. The main
thesis is that Indian intellectuals are strongly attracted by the
tasks and accomplishments of the modern intellectual's role,
but are also very much influenced by the pressure of tradition.
When the latter is compounded by the lacklustre quality of
Indian intellectual institutions, job shortages and poverty there
results a widespread sense of alienation, a sense of being "half
an Englishman, half an Indian." Shils estimates that India may
have 160,000 persons who could qualify as "intellectuals" and
that among them are a score or so of outstanding accomplish-
ment. This is due to the indigenous intellectual tradition (which
also, however, exerts a substantial inhibitory effect because of
its indifference toward the empirical and the concrete), an
apparatus (universities, libraries, newspapers, etc.) such as
no other new state of Asia or Africa possesses, and the
English language, which makes Indian intellectuals citizens of
the world's English-speaking intellectual community. It is
concluded that a large part of India's chances for continuing
modernization lie in the hands of India's intellectuals.

-	3	1	-		1	-	-	-
Gei	cit	lis	rep		ant	eco	pol	soc

Silvert, Kalman H., The conflict society: reaction and
revolution in Latin America (New Orleans, 1961), NY: Am Univ
Field Staff, Inc., rev ed, 1966, 289 p.   217
The most significant contribution of this revised edition
of an earlier work is the analysis of nationalism. As the larg-
est developing area of the world with a strong feudal tradition,
Latin America contains countries with emerging middle classes.
Nationalism functions to maintain the equilibrium of societies
whose class structures are being split and expanded in the
middle. Also valuable is the view of the peculiar form of
underdevelopment existing in Latin America. Because it is
part of Western culture, its "social underdevelopment" is less
pronounced than its "economic underdevelopment," and there is

less resistance than usual to European norms for modernizing economic affairs. The ill-fated Camelot Project is discussed, and broadens into a treatment of the ethics of the U.S. overseas social science research. Limitations of this work include paucity of empirical data, too many generalizations made without support, and unevenness of quality from one section to the next.

1	2	5	-		-	-	4	1
Gei	cit	lis	rep		ant	eco	pol	soc

Stein, William W. , Hualcan: life in the highlands of Peru, Ithaca, NY: Cornell University Press, 1961, 383 p.

218

The study upon which this report is based was part of the Cornell-Vicos project, and was carried out largely in 1951-1952. It is an unusual contribution to ethnographic literature, for, in contrast to the usual custom among ethnographers, this writer aspires not only to describe Hualcan and the Hualcainos as they actually are but as they could become. Thus, the conclusion lends itself particularly well to the pool of knowledge about the potential for development and the obstacles thereto. The judgment reached is that the community is "underachieving or failing in a number of important respects", and that the main reasons for this are to be found in the strongly established kinship basis for cooperation, the salience of the fiesta in the lives of these people and their employment of surplus wealth for ceremonial and prestige rather than productive purposes. The study along with its conclusion, poses sharply a central dilemma in the field of development: if a society prefers its "non-productive values" to the production of more food, clothing, shelter, etc. one wonders if the words "underachieving or failing.....etc." are being properly used. Does a society or a community "fail" when it does not aspire to a goal its people do not desire?

-	-	4	-		2	1	-	1
Gei	cit	lis	rep		ant	eco	pol	soc

United Nations. Population Branch. Bureau of Social Affairs. "Part two: selected seminar papers. III. Demographic aspects of urbanization in Latin America," p. 91-117 in Seminar on Urbanization Problems in Latin America, Santiago de Chile, 1959. Urbanization in Latin America, edited by P. Hauser, Paris: UNESCO, 1961.   219

The purpose of this paper is to provide an overall statistical picture of urbanization and rural-urban differences in the 20 Latin American countries. Data refer mainly to censuses taken around 1950. Among the patterns revealed and discussed are the low sex ratios and low fertility, the under-

representation of children and older persons, the higher
literacy rates of the large cities; the differences among
countries in level of urbanization; comparison with other
parts of the world; historical growth rates by country and
size of locality; and other assorted topics of interest.

Gei	cit	3 lis	rep		ant	eco	pol	3 soc

United Nations. Secretariat of the Economic Commission
for Latin America. "Part two: selected seminar papers. IV.
Creation of employment opportunities in relation to labor supply," p. 118-48 in Seminar on Urbanization Problems in Latin
America, Santiago de Chile, 1959. Urbanization in Latin America, edited by P. Hauser, Paris: UNESCO, 1961.   220
Latin America, with its high rate of population growth
and its even higher rate of urban growth, has produced two
major deficiencies in the composition of urban employment:
there is imbalance in the level of distribution of workers in
services (too high) and in the manufacturing and construction
industries (too low), and there is a high proportion of marginal and sub-marginal labor. A good part of this article is devoted to listing and analyzing the components which govern
labor-absorption capacity within various sectors of activity.
At the end recommendations are given: small and medium-
sized towns should be developed, small enterprises with low
ratio of capital to personnel should be encouraged, level of
construction activity should be stabilized, etc.

Gei	cit	3 lis	rep		ant	eco	1 pol	2 soc

Vries, Egbert de, Man in rapid social change, NY:
Doubleday (for the World Council of Churches), 1961, 140 p.
                                                        221
In 1954 at Evanston, Ill., the second Assembly of the
World Council of Churches authorized a study of "areas of
rapid social change" to be conducted during the three years
following, with particular attention to be paid to the challenge
and responsibility brought about by rapid social change to
Christians and to the Christian churches. The present volume
is the result; it is a wide-ranging, informed, sophisticated
survey of current knowledge, with interspersed comment and
conclusions considered relevant for those whose views are
based on the Christian faith. Part I is a 100 page review of
the large picture--the approach of philosophers, sociologists,
historians, anthropologists; how traditional social changes
create ferment in the human personality, etc. Part II discusses more specific issues--family life, food supply and population, rural development, international cooperation, etc. Part

147

III is entitled "The Common Responsibility" and the main
thesis is the view that all Christians have as a primary responsibility the strengthening of ties with peoples (of Africa,
Asia, etc.) in areas of rapid social change and "the need to
share with others any material wealth accumulating in industrial society," to include social organization and natural resources
as well as personal possessions.

7	-	3	-		2	-	1	-
Gei	cit	lis	rep		ant	eco	pol	soc

Binder, Leonard, Iran: political development in a
changing society, Berkeley and Los Angeles: University of
California Press, 1962, 362 p.   222
This book is an examination of the contemporary political and social structure of Iran and is based upon research
done by the author in 1958-1959. The aim is to achieve a comprehensive understanding of political life in Iran. The author
concentrates on peculiar aspects of Iranian politics and attempts to explain the transitory and eccentric nature of the
contemporary political system. He describes his framework
of political analysis, develops its application to Iran, and explains the relevance of economic planning and international
relations. Binder belives that the Iranian political system is
in a period of transition from an eccentric, traditional system
to a modern, rational system. He also attempts to demonstrate how inaccurate and oversimplified are the assumptions
concerning economic aid and mutual security upon which USA
policy toward Iran is based.

-	-	3	-		-	-	3	-
Gei	cit	lis	rep		ant	eco	pol	soc

Chenery, Hollis B. and Michael Bruno, "Development
alternatives in an open economy: the case of Israel," Econ J
72:79-103, 1962.   223
Based on the theoretical work of Tinbergen and Theil,
four types of variables are considered necessary in order to
formulate a policy-model for a developing society: pre-
determined exogenous variables, instrument variables (those
variables that are given to governmental manipulation), objective variables (policy aims and goals), and other endogenous
variables (variables that are irrelevant for policy analysis).
The authors assert that too often only one or two types of
variables are considered in policy-making, which results in
an incomplete policy program. All four types have to be taken
into account. Taking Israel's economic development from
1950-1959, as an example, a policy model is developed and
demonstrated, resulting in basically two alternative programs.
The authors claim that similar models can be constructed for

other countries with equal usefulness. The introductory section is fairly straightforward, even for the layman. But the body of the article and its conclusions are strictly for the professional economist. Social scientists from other disciplines may want to question the practicability of a policy-model that ignores cultural, social and psychological factors entirely.

-	1	3	-		-	3	-	-
Gei	cit	lis	rep		ant	eco	pol	soc

Denison, Edward F. , The sources of economic growth in the United States and the alternatives before us, CED Supplem, paper no. 13, NY: Committee for Economic Development, 1962, 308 p.   224

This is a technical and clearly presented portrait of trends in USA output growth, sources to which such growth can be traced, and the implications for national policy of the findings.   Output is measured by the aggregated value of net or gross national product; inputs are expressed in terms of labor and capital; and an index of productivity is obtained by dividing national product by total factor input.   The most provocative, and controversial, portion of the presentation lies in the author's efforts, not entirely convincing, to assign numerical estimates to express the importance in output growth of such input elements as labor intensity, labor education, advances in knowledge of techniques, economies of scale, and advances in organization.

-	4	1	-		-	1	-	-
Gei	cit	lis	rep		ant	eco	pol	soc

Epstein, T. Scarlett, Economic development and social change in South India, NY: Humanities Press, 1962, 353 p.
                                                                    225
This study reveals the social effects of the introduction of improved irrigation into two proximate villages in South India. One village switched from dry to wet agriculture while the other did not receive water from the canal and remained dry. The village which changed its irrigation techniques retained its traditional power structure based on caste relations while many members of the other village turned to small business--a flour mill, grocery store, transportation of farm produce, etc.--as a result of the increased wealth made available in the area by irrigation. Some people in the dry town sought employment in factories in nearby villages. Thus, the dry village developed the roles of "entrepreneur" and "commuter." The economic changes in the dry village led to the formation of a progressive political grouping where earlier all were traditional, as people in the wet village con-

tinued to be. This is an important book because it shows how economic change spurs change in other institutions only if the economic opportunities are at variance with existing social patterns.

	2	2	3	-		3	-	-	-
	Gei	cit	lis	rep		ant	eco	pol	soc

Foster, George M. , Traditional cultures: and the impact of technological change, NY: Harper, 1962, 292 p.   226
A concise analysis, Foster's study gives effective examples of the factors affecting success and failure in development programs, especially in traditional rural communities. The factors are treated as "barriers" or "stimulants" to change and considerable attention is given to the roles of technical and scholarly experts. The book is also valuable as an introduction to the conceptual tools of social anthropology, to some of this discipline's contributions to general knowledge (e. g. , the importance of "culture," the experience of "culture shock," etc.), and to some of the ethical problems involved in intervening in a traditional culture in quest of development.

	2	-	10	-		7	-	2	1
	Gei	cit	lis	rep		ant	eco	pol	soc

Galbraith, John, Economic development in perspective, Cambridge, Mass: Harvard University Press, 1962.   227
These essays, based on lectures given while the author was ambassador to India, deal with many aspects of the problems of development. A wide-ranging eclectic approach is taken. For example, the Marxist and Western "explanations" of poverty and prescriptions for growth are both oversimplified, but also serve as complementary contributions toward a general formula of "conditions essential for development." On the other hand, it is emphasized that development is very much a process and that at certain points good public administration, hope for and/or confidence in social justice, etc. , are as important as rational planning and investment to increase capitalization. Galbraith also does not hesitate to give informed judgments about often controversial institutional forms. Private agriculture, autonomous industrial corporations, national planning and attending to the consumer needs of the many rather than the few are all strongly commended.

	2	3	1	-		-	1	-	-
	Gei	cit	lis	rep		ant	eco	pol	soc

Gerschenkron, Alexander, Economic backwardness in historical perspective: a book of essays, NY: Praeger, 1962, 456 p.   228
The essays reprinted here were originally published

between 1951 and 1961, and revised for this volume. The first
eight essays deal with problems of European industrial development in the 19th century, and the last six concern problems of
economic and social change in Soviet Russia.   The guiding
thesis is presented in the first essay and is a result of the
author's grasp of economic history and his reflections upon a
generalization by Marx in the preface to Capital--"The indus-
trially more developed country presents to the less developed
country a picture of the latter's future." For Gerschenkron this
is only a half-truth; differences between the patterns of development of the LDC's and the more advanced countries include rates of industrial growth, productive and organizational
structures of industry which emerge from such growth, application of distinctive institutional instruments, and the intellectual climate ("spirit" or "ideology"). Moreover, "the extent
to which these attributes of backwardness occurred...appears
to have varied directly with the degree of backwardness and the
natural industrial potentialities of the countries concerned."
Thus, "relative backwardness" is crucial; many features, for
example, of the Soviet experience can be traced to the great
opportunity for development--alongside great obstacles--pre-
sented by its backwardness relative to the West European,
Japanese, etc. situation.

8	2	6	-		1	2	1	2
Gei	cit	lis	rep		ant	eco	pol	soc

Hagen, Everett E. , On the theory of social change: how
economic growth begins, Homewood, Ill: Dorsey Press, 1962,
557 p.   229
Hagen believes that a single general theory of growth
and development can be constructed.   An economist by early
training and a government official by experience he has constructed a comprehensive, interdisciplinary, highly controversial theory of the social and psychological events and experiences leading to economic growth. The crucial starting
point is "withdrawal of status respect" from some (vaguely
specified) group through displacement by force, denigration of
valued symbols, inconsistency of status symbols or nonac-
ceptance in a new society. This sets in motion a chain of
events, focussed largely on the parental status and role of the
father and its consequences for the personality formation of
his son, which culminates in the replacement of the "authoritarian personality" of traditional society by a creative, innovative personality. Such a person actively approaches and
solves problems and overcomes the barriers to development.
The thesis is illustrated if not tested (some critics assert it
is not testable as stated) with materials from Japan, Indonesia,
Columbia and other societies.

3	5	24	-		5	7	7	5
Gei	cit	lis	rep		ant	eco	pol	soc

Hammel, Eugene A. , Wealth, authority and prestige in the Ica Valley, Peru, University of New Mexico Publications in Anthropology, no. 10, Albuquerque: University of New Mexico Press, 1962, 110 p.   230

Sixteen photos lend interest to this description of status groupings--Creole upper class, middle class and lower class Mestizos--and other patterns of coastal culture in Peru. The book is useful for its effort to show how social change has occurred by treating each topic in terms of historical periods, and also for its detailed attention to the dimensions of social stratification. In one chapter social class differences are conveyed in the form of descriptions of male representatives of each of the strata. One of the conclusions reached is that the dimensions of wealth, authority, and prestige are not highly correlated.

-	-	3	-		2	1	-	-
Gei	cit	lis	rep		ant	eco	pol	soc

Kautsky, John H. (ed.), Political change in underdeveloped countries: nationalism and communism, NY: Wiley, 1967, 347 p.   231

In his leading essay the editor sets the tone and framework for the twelve articles which comprise this volume. Kautsky analyzes the roles of various groups in politics--particularly the intellectuals--and formulates a number of broad generalizations concerning the political effects of industrialization in underdeveloped countries. He explores the nature of and relationship between nationalism and communism in this light, and projects the possible trends toward totalitarianism and democracy. The twelve articles enlarge upon and reinforce various points raised by the leading essay. The book lacks an index.

8	1	5	-		-	-	4	1
Gei	cit	lis	rep		ant	eco	pol	soc

Kuhn, Thomas S. , The structure of scientific revolutions, Chicago: University of Chicago Press, 1962, 172 p.
232

The word revolution probably is a suitable one in this case to dramatize the usual consequence of the strong sense of malaise experienced by the scientific community when "new facts" appear which do not fit established concepts, viewpoints, theoretical systems, or what Kuhn terms "paradigms." When such facts are uncovered, someone (generally several workers together) conceives a new paradigm which gradually becomes accepted. This is the "structure of the scientific revolution," a recurrent phenomenon, for the newly accepted paradigm will also in time have to be discarded. In Kuhn's view this process, occurring in the realm of culture, is analogous to the Darwinian process of natural selection in organic life. One of its important, controversial, implications is to cast some doubt upon the validity or meaning of what has long been deemed a general property of science--the property of cumulativity of scientific knowledge.

Gei	cit	3 lis	rep	ant	1 eco	2 pol	soc
-	-	3	-	-	1	2	-

Lewis, John P. , Quiet crisis in India, economic development and American policy, Washington, DC: Brookings Institute, 1962 , 350 p.   233

This book discusses in general terms the Indian development effort. The fate of India is important for the USA because it is the most important nation in the underdeveloped world, and most immediately because of the menace of China and the inevitable comparison by other nations between the paths of development of India and China. China's ruthless effort has been far more effective, but the Indian way has a unique asset--its respect for human dignity and its commitment to orderly, economic change. A second point is that the Indian effort entered its decisive stage in the sixties. All resources painfully accumulated in the past have been committed to the Third and Fourth Five-Year Plans. India starts its "take-off" in the sixties and after a certain speed has been reached and part of the runway used up, there is no turning back. Whether development can be attained within a democratic regime or not is a question to be decided, for India and many other countries, in this decade. Three conditions must be observed, if USA aid is going to be really helpful: worry about its own balance of payments should not lead it to aid reductions in this crucial stage; the USA should overcome its resistance to allowing Indian manufactures to enter its market on favorable terms; and USA private firms, as the most effective vehicles for carrying American industrial know-how, should be effectively encouraged to step up activities in India.

Gei	cit	lis	rep	ant	eco	pol	soc
2	2	-	-	-	-	-	-

Lipton, Michael, "Balanced and unbalanced growth in under-developed countries," Econ J 72: 641-57, 1962.   234

In this article the author takes to task the assumptions of both sides in the controversy over balanced versus unbalanced growth, and asserts that the argument confuses two separate problems--the optimum ratio of investment to in-

come and the allocation criteria for given values of investment.
The role of state intervention is assumed to be discontinuous
in an unrealistic way, and the whole controversy tends to support vested, anti-growth interests in the LDC's. Other criticisms include the tendency of the extreme form of the balanced
growth position to ignore variable returns, and the blurring in
Hirschman's unbalanced growth approach of distinctions
between sectors in which the state can compel and those in
which it can only induce, between privately-profitable projects
and those which are no more than socially profitable, and
between the producers goods and consumer goods sectors of
the economy.

		3	-		-	3	-	-
Gei	cit	lis	rep		ant	eco	pol	soc

Moore, Clement H. , "The Neo-Destour party of
Tunisia: a structure for democracy?" World Pol 14: 461-82,
1962.   235
Moore argues that the Tunisian one-party system, the
Neo-Destour, while authoritarian in structure, may ultimately
create a democratic society. In addition to a thorough
analysis of its structure, Moore indicates how this "national
party" mobilizes the population to implement state projects and
inculcates national feeling. The party has also proven able to
provide a political mechanism that can "maintain the cohesion
of a growing elite more effectively" than either an authoritarian
clique or totalitarian party. While there are some structural
similarities, the Neo-Destour deviates from both totalitarian
and constitutional mass parties. While real competition does
not exist, the party may further democracy in the future to
the degree that it encourages rational discussion of problems,
it maintains its representative character, etc. A major factor
affecting the nature of the Neo-Destour has been the ideology
and personality of President Bourguiba, who is strongly committed to freedom and human rights as well as modernization.
The author concludes optimistically that this powerful "national party," by creating a more developed and integrated
nation, may be a "training ground for possible democracy in
the future."

		3	5		-	-	3	-
Gei	cit	lis	rep		ant	eco	pol	soc

Morse, Richard M. , "Latin American cities: aspects
of function and structure," Comp Stud Soc Hist 4: 473-93,
1962.   236
In general, the development of cities in Latin America
follows the ancient Roman model more closely than that of
medieval Europe. Settlement patterns had a municipal point

of origin. Yet, during the centuries of colonial rule, rural institutions developed beyond the reach of municipal control, and rural social organization tended to revert to a form dominated by the extended family and small neighborhood units. However, in the 19th century, Latin American cities passed from a centrifugal to a centripetal phase, and in the process migrants from rural areas drew heavily upon established primary group patterns in accommodating to urban life. Thus, the Latin American city imparted an individualistic, exploitative spirit to the settling of the land, but it itself exhibits strong traces of an agrarian, familistic type of social system.

-	1	5	-	2	-	1	2
Gei	cit	lis	rep	ant	eco	pol	soc

Prest, Alan R. , Public finance in underdeveloped countries (London, 1962), NY: Praeger, 1963, 164 p.   237

This is a succinct, clearly organized, occasionally technical survey of the patterns and problems of taxation in the LDC's within the British Commonwealth (or otherwise having close ties with the UK). Chapters treat direct and indirect taxation; grants, subsidies and other allowances; debt policy; legislative and administrative procedure; and problems of federal finance. The discussion is based on actual practices currently found, with good exemplification and a sensitive eye to the potential dysfunctions always ready to attend upon ostensibly effective taxation measures, such as the tendency for individuals to evade tax payments by a "retreat into the subsistence sector" where valuation and collection is much more difficult.

-	1	3	-	-	3	-	-
Gei	cit	lis	rep	ant	eco	pol	soc

Pye, Lucian W. , Politics, personality and nation-building: Burma's search for identity, New Haven: Yale University Press, 1962, 307 p.   238

Pye's work represents the application of psychological, anthropological and political science knowledge to an examination of the development of traits and identity among leaders of a developing nation. He deals with personal restraints inhibiting modernization, the tendency toward ideological agitation, and the roles of colonialism and nationalism in the process of transformation. Pye contends that, as transitional people, the Burmese in his study lack the stable and more impersonal institutional forms which can harness man's more irrational compulsions and aggressions for national political and social progress. He predicts that consistent, efficient national modernization will come as the people develop new collective and individual identities. Pye may have over-emphasized

155

personal psychological inhibitions derived from traditional
family relationships while underplaying other important factors,
such as Burmese internal insecurity. But any criticisms are
not likely to detract from the over-all importance of this
study.

2	1	10	-		2	-	8	-
Gei	cit	lis	rep		ant	eco	pol	soc

Rogers, Everett, The diffusion of innovations, NY:
Free Press of Glencoe, 1962, 367 p.   239
The purpose of this work is to synthesize and evaluate
research findings and theories on the diffusion of innovations.
Rogers finds a general lack of agreement on the sociological
concepts involved in adoption behavior and the absence of a
synthesis of those concepts into a general theory testable by
empirical research. He concludes by positing five categories
of persons in a social system relative to the adoption of innovations: innovators, early adopters, early majority, late
majority and laggards. Rogers says the dominant value of
innovators is venturesomeness, through which they gain inter-
personal security. Innovativeness is related to a modern
rather than traditional orientation. Impersonal information
sources are most important at the awareness stage, and personal sources are most important at the evaluation stage.
Cosmopolite information sources are most important at the
awareness stage, while localite sources are most important
at the evaluation stage. Innovators are perceived as deviants
both by themselves and others in the social system. This
book is correctly judged a landmark in an expanding field of
social investigation, namely, diffusion research.

7	2	4	-		2	1	-	1
Gei	cit	lis	rep		ant	eco	pol	soc

Rotberg, Robert I., "The rise of African nationalism:
the case of East and Central Africa," World Pol 15:75-90,
1962.   240
Rotberg provides a social historical account of how post-
war nationalist parties in East and Central Africa emerged out
of a network of voluntary associations and religious movements.
These institutions provided the intermediary link in the causal
chain from colonialism to independence. The triumph of
African nationalism after World War II, Rotberg demonstrates,
was "but the final coordination and intensification of all the
tangled strands of an earlier, usually unrecognized disaffec-
tion." Especially after 1920, many natives in this region
organized themselves into "associations" (clubs, societies,
etc.) and schismatic sectarian and chiliastic movements.
These associations provided channels for mutual support and

protest, and a means for developing self-esteem within the racially oppressive colonial system. Although, Rotberg points out, these institutions were on the whole "ineffectual avenues of protest," they provided the bases for the more radical nationalist parties which sought independence after the War.

	-	-	4	4		1	-	3	-
	Gei	cit	lis	rep		ant	eco	pol	soc

Salisbury, Richard F. , From stone to steel: economic consequences of a technological change in New Guinea, NY: Cambridge University Press, 1962, 237 p.   241

The author investigates the effects of substitution of steel for stone axes among the Siane, a linguistic group of 15,000 in northeastern New Guinea who were unknown to Europeans until 1930. Theories of economic development based upon the concept of capital investment are examined, but the determining factors in Siane economic development are said to originate in the differential and changing demands for products and services of the Siane economic system. Salisbury's account of the latter is important in itself, for he found 3 relatively autonomous "allocation systems:" subsistence (agri. land, staple foods, stone axes, etc.), luxury commodity (tobacco, salt, palm oil, etc.) and ceremonial (shells, ornamental axes, dogs' teeth and pigs). Salisbury's study contributes significantly to the literature of how sociocultural factors influence economic and social development.

	(2)	-	1	-		1	-	-	-
	Gei	cit	lis	rep		ant	eco	pol	soc

Seers, Dudley, "A theory of inflation and growth in underdeveloped economies based on the experience of Latin America," Oxford Econ Pap 14:173-95, 1962.   242

The immediate purpose here is to respond to an earlier paper by G. Maynard on inflation in Argentina and Chile, 1946-55, but a larger purpose is to propose a general theoretical model of the inflationary process in a country which exports primary products, show how well the model fits actual Latin American experience, and suggest what lessons of theoretical and practical importance can be drawn from this experience. The basic approach of the author is a "structuralist" one, and the conclusion is that inflationary experiences in the Latin American countries are to be explained in terms of such factors as needed land reform, level of educational and fiscal adequacy, distribution of wealth, regressive tax systems, etc. , rather than in terms of weaknesses in monetary policy. An appendix contains a brief description and history of the "structuralist school," perhaps the first indigenous school of economic thought to come from an underdeveloped area.

	-	1	3	-		-	2	-	1
	Gei	cit	lis	rep		ant	eco	pol	soc

Sen, Amartya K. , Choice of techniques: an aspect
of the theory of planned economic development, Oxford: Basil
Blackwell, 1960, 122 p.   243
There are three varieties of investment allocation
problems to be confronted in centrally planned economic development: the determination of the total volume of investment, the distribution among the different industries of this
total, and the choice among specific techniques of production
within each industry. This book concerns the last-named
problem, and the central argument is that the best criterion
for choice among different techniques is maximum "reinvestable surplus" yielded by investments, rather than rate of
capital turnover, marginal social product, or considerations
relating to the balance of exports and imports. An interesting feature of this criterion is, that with proper (restrictive)
assumptions, the planning agency is led to a solution which
is exactly the same as that obtained under pure competition,
that is, labor is combined with capital available for investment
until the marginal product of labor is equal to the wage rate.
This in turn suggests the possibility of decentralization once
the availability of capital is no longer problematic.

	7	-	3	-		-	3	-	-
	Gei	cit	lis	rep		ant	eco	pol	soc

Shils, Edward, "The military in the political development of the new states," p. 7-67 in J. Johnson (ed.), The role
of the military in underdeveloped countries, Princeton:
Princeton University Press, 1962.   244
In countries where government policy did not create a
"modern literacy-political or modern technical-administrative
intelligensia," military officers become disproportionately important as advocates of modernity. Their puritanical training makes them react negatively to the "effete and decadent
culture" in cities. Moreover, when the military offers social
mobility to rural-bred sons of small-holders and tradesmen,
military officers are able to identify with rural problems.
These officers, however, are not traditionalists by training.
Modern methods of problem solving are emphasized at the
expense of traditional lore. The nationalism of the military,
in symbolism and sentiment, is less extreme than that of a
political movement. Thus, the military can integrate diverse
ethnic groups into a national community, teach skills useful
for economic development, widen horizons beyond village and
locality, and create a viable sense of nation. A military
oligarchy, however, is not a complete regime. Often, it
defines its role as that of caretaker. Yet it seldom plans for
orderly succession. Moreover, it lacks an ideologically-
coherent program and a perspective on future development.

In these important respects, the military is similar to other modernizing oligarchies. Both military and civilian elites must legitimate themselves through modernizing achievements, showing respect for traditional beliefs, and recruiting intellectuals who can reinterpret traditional beliefs and adapt them to modern needs.

2	1	1	20		-	-	1	-
Gei	cit	lis	rep		ant	eco	pol	soc

Srinivas, Mysore N. , Caste in modern India, and other essays, NY: Asia Publishing House, 1962, 171 p.   245
Of the 11 essays in this collection six are on Indian society in general, its structure and patterns of change; three are on the methods and potential of social anthropology in and for India; and two deal with the important topic of caste. From the point of view of general social organization perhaps the most interesting chapter is "The Indian Road to Equality," in which the author shows how in this highly stratified society the government and people have accepted the goal of social equality and taken steps to achieve it. This has been one of the reasons why the people have tended to become more, rather than less, caste-conscious, and why the castes have become more organized and active as political groupings. Another important essay, on "The Problem of Indian Unity," stresses the view that various particular loyalties--to caste, village, region, religion, etc. --do not necessarily preclude, alongside them, loyalty to the Indian Republic. Srinivas also develops here his interpretation, in "A Note on Sanskritization and Westernization," of how social change, and mobility, occur in a hierarchical society, namely, through emulation by lower caste persons of the practices of those in higher castes.

-	3	1	-		-	-	1	-
Gei	cit	lis	rep		ant	eco	pol	soc

Weiner, Myron, The politics of scarcity: public pressure and political response in India, Chicago: University of Chicago Press, 1962, 251 p.   246
This is a study of the interaction between interest groups and India's government and political institutions. Indian government leaders tend to oppose the entry of pressure groups --communal, labor, business, peasant, student--into the political life of the country. They feel these groupings as intrusions, which place divisive, extravagant, and regionalizing demands on the country, hindering India's struggle for unity and economic development through rational planning. Weiner's view is that this attitude is dysfunctional, because such groups cannot be ignored and will exert covert influence upon political

leaders if their demands cannot be presented openly. He argues that Indian politics must come closer to the American model of compromise because of India's great social diversity. Weiner also advocates that the Indian government shed some of its activities, allowing private groups to perform them. For instance, the free market system needs a greater role. This analysis is highly suggestive.

2	3	2	-		-	-	2	-
Gei	cit	lis	rep		ant	eco	pol	soc

Almond, Gabriel and Sidney Verba, The civic culture: political attitudes and democracy in five nations, Princeton: Princeton University Press, 1963, 562 p.   247

Already recognized as a classic of comparative analysis, this book investigates a topic of long history and great concern --the attitudes of people toward their political systems. This complex of attitudes is termed "political culture" and the citizens of five countries--United Kingdom, USA and Federal Republic of Germany on the more developed side, and Mexico and Italy on the less developed side--were queried with modern survey research techniques to learn which among them were active, articulate and responsive, and which were passive, inarticulate and unconcerned. Respondents' knowledge, sense of trust, feelings of competence, and actual patterns of behavior vis-a-vis their government were investigated. Levels of participation and awareness are highest in the stable polities of the USA and the UK, and there are more "subjects" and "parochials" as one moves down the ladder of national development. Typical defects or "lacks" in the civic cultures of the various countries are also identified. In Germany the cognitive skills of the citizens are well-developed, but the people refrain from strong commitment or participant contribution to the system. Mexico has an "aspirational" culture, in contrast, in which emotional commitment to the polity is strong and favorable, but where cognitive skills are weak, so that there is little actual participation in the political process.

7	2	8	-		-	-	7	1
Gei	cit	lis	rep		ant	eco	pol	soc

Apter, David E. , "Political religion in the new nations," p. 57-104 in C. Geertz (ed.), Old societies and new states: the quest for modernity in Asia and Africa, NY: Free Press, 1963.   248

The thesis of this discussion is that the heavy commitment of the new nations to economic development and their disinclination to approach it in terms of democracy, pluralism and individualism, brings to them autocratic, monolithic political structures with a large assortment of strong community imperatives. This in turn creates a new problem, namely, because productivity and the integration of economic roles become the primary concerns of the government, the government requires exceptional authority which becomes monopolistic. To function properly such authority requires new beliefs about the government, its leaders, their laws and doctrines; in a word, strong new allegiances from the people must replace the old ones. The result is in effect a political religion. Such a religion is found typically in nations which are anxious to modernize and have autocratic polities which are here termed "mobilization systems." The patterns and problems of mobilization systems with their political religions are analyzed and illustrated with examples from China, Ghana, Guinea, Indonesia, Mali, and other nations.

1	1	3	-		-	-	3	-
Gei	cit	lis	rep		ant	eco	pol	soc

Bailey, Frederick G., Politics and social change: Orissa in 1959, Berkeley and Los Angeles: University of California Press, 1963, 241 p.   249
    This is a study of contemporary society in the Indian State of Orissa in which the author attempts to discover the relationship between parliamentary democracy and older forms of social and political organization. His focal points are elections at the village, constituency and state levels. Bailey concludes that the majority of persons in Orissa did not grasp the meaning of "responsible" government or citizen action. Turning to the functions of caste in politics, he contends that the traditional caste was not effective in getting votes or in exerting political pressure, but he predicts that when a caste becomes a caste association it may be able to effectively pursue these functions. Bailey says political action is the most effective means of transforming a society.

2	1	3	-		-	-	3	-
Gei	cit	lis	rep		ant	eco	pol	soc

Bowman, Mary Jean and C. Arnold Anderson, "Concerning the role of education in development," Ch. 7, p. 245-279 in C. Geertz (ed.), Old societies and new states, NY: Free Press of Glencoe, 1963.   250
    Comparisons of income and educational levels in a large number of societies suggest that economic gains associated with growth of a literate minority may level off quickly, the economy remaining on a low plateau, until education has built up to a point at which widespread transformation is possible. Furthermore, while an educated elite is a necessary condition for sustained growth of the economy, it is not a suf-

ficient one and may even impede development. Finally, the polarization of society and the absence of a communications continuum among the subpopulations may inhibit effective economic utilization of any given level of schooling. The last hypothesis focusses both on the factor of communication and on the emergence of an active middle class.

2	2	1	-		-	-	1	-
Gei	cit	lis	rep		ant	eco	pol	soc

Crozier, Michel, The bureaucratic phenomenon: an examination of bureaucracy in modern organizations and its cultural setting in France (Paris, 1963), Chicago: University of Chicago Press, 1964, 314 p.   250a

Bureaucracy is defined and analyzed here as a large organization with inadequate feed-back from its operations, and as therefore unable to correct its own errors. The central interest in the analysis is in power, and in the way in which leaders as well as the various other groupings are confined, if not captured, by the system in such a way that their interests lie essentially in power struggles which take the form of institutionalized conflict or of profiting by the occurrence of crises. The first part is a report of two large organizations, both government controlled, one a clerical organization and the other a manufacturing establishment. In the second part the findings are discussed, and in the last part, Crozier treats French bureaucracy as a part of the larger French culture, showing a substantial parallel between the former and the latter, as in the characteristic "legalism," "formalism," and self-protective defensiveness in disputes. A generic difficulty in France is reliance on too-distant leaders who can change the system of rigidly defined rights and duties only through crises, bringing about a situation in which excessive conservatism alternates with radical reform.

-	-	4	-		2	-	2	-
Gei	cit	lis	rep		ant	eco	pol	soc

Curle, Adam, Educational strategy for developing societies: a study of educational and social factors in relation to economic growth, London: Tavistock Publishers, 1963, 180 p.   251

Although the bulk of attention in this short and very readable book is on education, it is also a good introduction to the field of national development. Curle has a lot to say, with many interesting examples and allusions, about such things as poor administration, justice, ignorance, fear, love, equality, and so on, as well as presenting a strong argument for two general themes or coordinative approaches. Both are social or human being-oriented rather than purely economic: how to

162

create the proper conditions so people can work (jobs, land, training, inspection, etc.) and how to break down resistance to change "by involving people participantly in change" through building trade unions, stressing welfare activities, training teachers, etc.

-	2	3	-		3	-	-	-
Gei	cit	lis	rep		ant	eco	pol	soc

Cutright, Phillips, "National political development: measurement and analysis," Am Sociol R 28:253-64, 1963.

252

This article builds upon the work of Lipset, Shannon and others by constructing a systematic index of political development, based on the extent to which a nation has complex and specialized political institutions, and relating a nation's score on this index to other of its features. The index is constructed for 77 independent nations and correlated with level of communications, education, urbanization and economic development. Most closely associated with political development was the communications development index (newspaper readers, newsprint consumption, volume of domestic mail, and telephones--all per capita), which accounted for 65% of the variation around the regression line. Further, the comparison of predicted with observed values of a nation's political development permits the inference that nations with observed values distant from the predicted values are "under some pressure to move toward the predicted score." For example, the large positive "errors" of the Philippines, Burma, Indonesia and India all suggest a strong tendency toward political "backsliding."

-	2	3	-		1	-	2	-
Gei	cit	lis	rep		ant	eco	pol	soc

Deutsch, Karl W. , The nerves of government: models of political communication and control, NY: Free Press, 1963, 316 p.

253

Part I of this important contribution to political theory consists of an extended discussion of the role played by metaphors in thought and models in science, and prepares the reader to accept the model chosen as most appropriate for the political system. This is the cybernetic model, based on the ideas first elaborated by Norbert Wiener, and Deutsch defends it as the best model because it links two features of the political process which are widely recognized as central--communication and control--and also provides, in the concepts of "feedback" and "information" a way to calculate the adaptiveness or non-adaptiveness of a system to its changing environment. In Part II, the concepts of Part I are used to construct rigorous definitions of familiar terms such as power, consciousness, will, integrity and dignity. Part III treats the health and pathology of a system in terms of the proposed concepts.

7	2	4	-		1	-	3	-
Gei	cit	lis	rep		ant	eco	pol	soc

Eisenstadt, Shmuel N. , The political systems of empires: the rise and fall of the historical bureaucratic societies, NY: Free Press of Glencoe, 1963, 524 p.   254

This work is an ambitious attempt to show that the analysis of a society's political system is the most profitable point of entry for study of the structure and functioning of that society itself. Twenty-seven historical bureaucratic polities are compared with traditional or pre-bureaucratic (5th century Athens, Genghis Khan's Mongol Empire, etc.) and modern systems using a broad variety of secondary sources and typological classifications. The major hypothesis, deemed verified by the author, is that the development of a political system is dependent upon certain major, necessary conditions: the development of an autonomous political sphere, an indicator of which is the emergence of non-ascribed goals on the part of the society's ruler; the extent of differentiation in the social structure, an indicator being the political orientations of different groups in the society; and the availability of "free-floating" external resources (wealth, manpower, "support," etc.). These conditions set the stage for the emergence of political centralization, bureaucratic administration and organs for political struggle.

7	3	5	-		-	-	5	-
Gei	cit	lis	rep		ant	eco	pol	soc

Fallers, Lloyd A. , "Equality, modernity, and democracy in the new states," Ch. 5, p. 158-219 in C. Geertz (ed.), Old societies and new states, NY: Free Press, 1963.   255

In this article Fallers attempts to outline some of the more general consequences for social stratification of economic and political modernization. His general theme is that the system of stratification which emerges from the process of political and economic modernization is a product of interaction between generic forces of modernity and the traditional society and culture upon which modernity acts. He believes that the particular relationship between equality and political democracy that has been found in the systems of stratification in the West appears to be a result of interaction between tradition and modernity in a manner which is not universal. Political democracy is thus a result of special circumstances. It is only in the West that these circumstances are brought

together, although some type of egalitarian politics seems to
be a universal result of the process of modernization.   The
author discusses various traditional societies and the forces
of modernization that have acted upon them, a treatment which
develops further the general theme of the anthology.

Gei	cit	3 lis	rep	ant	eco	2 pol	1 soc
-	-	3	-	-	-	2	1

Feith, Herbert, "Indonesia's political symbols and their
wielders," World Politics 16: 79-97, 1963.   256
    In his study of the widespread use of political symbolism
in Indonesia during the 1958-1963 period, Feith accepts the view
that such practices were based on historical and psycho-cul-
tural factors as well as upon the anomie resulting from the
breakdown of the old order.   However, dramatic symbolism is
seen largely as a result of the peculiar conditions of Indonesian
politics: the unwillingness to impose political privations; the
desire to attract opponents into the ruling political stratum
without the use of repressive measures; the need for Sukarno
to balance the army, the Communist party, and numerous less-
er political factions; the need to balance political elements and
supporters against the technocrats; and the unique importance
of Sukarno's desire to promote a form of political activity at
which he excels.   These considerations may not be dissimilar
to conditions prevailing in other developing nations, and understanding them provides some insight into the policies of other
political leaders of the developing world, especially since such
policies often appear irrational with respect to the goal of economic development.

1 Gei	1 cit	3 lis	3 rep	ant	eco	3 pol	soc
1	1	3	3	-	-	3	-

Geertz, Clifford, Agricultural involution: the process
of ecological change in Indonesia, Berkeley and Los Angeles:
University of California Press, 1963, 176 p.   257
    The thesis of this notable effort to apply the methods
and concepts of both anthropology and ecology to the interpretation of Indonesian economic history and current problems
is summarized in the term "agricultural involution." It refers
to the tendency toward an over-elaboration of labor-intensive
methods in agriculture, and it could act as a powerful barrier
to Indonesia's aspirations for rapid economic development.

Gei	cit	4 lis	rep	3 ant	eco	pol	1 soc
-	-	4	-	3	-	-	1

Geertz, Clifford (ed.), Old societies and new states:
the quest for modernity in Asia and Africa, NY: Free Press
of Glencoe, 1963, 310 p.   258

This book is an outcome of the efforts of the University of Chicago's Interdisciplinary Committee for the Comparative Study of New Nations to shed some light on the process of nation-building. After Edward Shils' critique of the macro-sociological approach and the comparative method in the opening chapter, other contributors analyze such problems as national culture, political legitimacy, the nation-building process, the modernization of social stratification, the adoption and development of legal systems, and the role of education in economic development. Although not quite related to each other, the essays presented in this collection suggest many hypotheses about the process of nation-building.

8	-	9	-	3	-	3	3
Gei	cit	lis	rep	ant	eco	pol	soc

Geertz, Clifford, Peddlers and princes: social change and economic modernization in two Indonesian towns, Chicago: University of Chicago Press, 1963, 162 p.   259

This double case-study analysis of the social and cultural contexts under which entrepreneurial activity emerges as one anthropologist's response to the general question of how much social and cultural change is required for economic development. In both Modjokuto on Java and Tabanan on Bali the business enterprise or economic firm is seen as the basic institutional form needed, and the analysis concentrates on its birth pangs and growing pains, different in each town. The entrepreneurs have come predominantly from a single status group, pietistic, orthodox Moslem traders (the "Peddlars") in Modjokuto, and local Balinese aristocrats displaced from positions of political power by the Revolution in Tabanan (the "Princes"). Obstacles to full success in Modjokuto include the limited capacity of its entrepreneurs to organize large-size firms. In Tabanan, where the employees of firms are former subjects of the employers, size is no problem but the tendency is for the firms' economic goals to be subverted to political or welfare considerations arising out of traditional bonds of mutual obligation.

2	2	5	-	3	-	1	1
Gei	cit	lis	rep	ant	eco	pol	soc

Goodenough, Ward H. , Cooperation in change: an anthropological approach to community development, NY: Wiley, 1963, 543 p.   260

In addition to being a thorough, text-like introduction to the culture and personality approach to the study of social change and a sophisticated practical guide for community development workers, this book is important for its theory of the psychological experiencing of change. The key concept is "dissatisfaction with one's identity," a state of mind produced by new experiences. Such dissatisfaction in turn causes the individual to search for and adopt a course of action which will restore a new self-image. Something analogous must take place in the community's self-image if development is to occur, but this can take place only if the change agent approaches his task properly. He must eschew the goal of trying to get the community to accept his view of the world and values and instead seek to provide significant new experiences for the people in the community. That is, he must avoid the "missionary approach" and follow the "experience" approach. Filled with good information, sound theory and practical guidance, this work stresses the creative role of understanding and cooperation on the local level.

2	-	7	-		7	-	-	-
Gei	cit	lis	rep		ant	eco	pol	soc

Hagen, Everett E., "The nature of a good plan and the machinery for good planning," Ch. 11, p. 325-47 in E. E. Hagen (ed.), Planning economic development, Homewood, Ill: Richard D. Irwin, 1963.   261
The volume as a whole consists of case studies of the planning experience of nine carefully chosen countries--Burma, Pakistan, India, Japan, Mexico, Yugoslavia, Iran, Nigeria, and England--written by persons closely acquainted with each of them. The present essay is one of two summary chapters which offer suggestions about the general features of a good plan, describe the institutional machinery and procedures which are required, identify typical difficulties in implementation and execution, and discuss possible solutions. Although the degree of formal planning and the patterns of conception and execution vary widely from country to country, Hagen concludes that well-designed planning procedures are a definite asset to economic development whatever the mix of public and private sector in the economy. Topics discussed in general but lucid fashion are "planning organization," "five-year plans," "annual planning," and "implementation of the plan."

-	-	3	-		-	3	-	-
Gei	cit	lis	rep		ant	eco	pol	soc

Halpern, Manfred, The politics of social change in the Middle East and North Africa, Princeton: Princeton University Press, 1963, 431 p.   262
The historical background is skillfully described and analyzed in terms congenial to behavioral scientists and with the view of clarifying the political and policy aspects of these countries. The Islamic tradition is seen not so much as a source of directly relevant motivation for or against social

change but rather as a world view or definition of the situation likely to rest easily, for example, with political instability. The crucial factor on the scene is the "new" middle class, not the older bourgeoisie of merchant or trader, but young professionals and skilled technicians. They have the education, discipline, vision and potential for power needed to harness the forces of change. Halpern believes that the maintenance of stability is a central problem to be solved, and that benevolent authoritarianism, with military support, is what is needed to guard against "extremists" who play upon the frustration of the masses. He would advise support of "radicals" who desire change in their countries and can lead the way to modernization through outside help and firm domestic control. Perhaps the most notable feature of this book is its thorough contrast with Fanon's The wretched of the earth.

2	1	5	-	-	-	4	1
Gei	cit	lis	rep	ant	eco	pol	soc

Hauser, Philip M., "The social, economic, and technological problems of rapid urbanization," Ch. 10, p. 199-215 in B. F. Hoselitz and W. E. Moore (eds.), Industrialization and society, UNESCO-Mouton, 1963. 263

Although the underdeveloped areas are characterized by more profound problems, the problems of urbanization in the developed countries are also considered here. In the economic sphere, the developed countries experience a "pull" toward urbanization. Agricultural development and urban technology are sufficiently advanced to enable these countries to afford rural to urban migration whereas the major problem of the underdeveloped areas is that, since this infrastructure is insufficient, they tend to be over-urbanized. Antecedents and consequences of this situation are discussed.

1	-	3	-1	-	-	1	2
Gei	cit	lis	rep	ant	eco	pol	soc

Hirschman, Albert O., Journeys toward progress: studies of economic-policy-making in Latin America, NY: Twentieth Century Fund, 1963, 308 p. 264

A growing number of studies of economic development see it from the point of view of policy formation. Described in Part I are three difficult problem areas--Brazil's attempt to deal with its depressed northeast, land use and land reform in Colombia, and Chile's chronic inflation. Part II is an analysis of policy formation--political techniques, aspects of choice, preferences under uncertainties--and generalizations based on the case studies. Offered are a number of interesting insights into Latin American development: "chosen" and "pressing" problems, "functional" crisis, inflation as a means of avoiding revolution, the compatibility of violence and reform, the relative roles of good and bad actors. Hirschman seeks to make a case for traditional Latin American politics as a good way to achieve development. Such a belief--that development is more the result of haphazard forces than of wise policy planning--is in line with his advocacy of unbalanced growth.

2	3	13	-	4	4	2	3
Gei	cit	lis	rep	ant	eco	pol	soc

Hoselitz, Bert F. and Wilbert E. Moore (eds.), Industrialization and society, The Hague: UNESCO-Mouton, 1963, 437 p.   265

The papers in this anthology were prepared for the North American Conference on the Social Implications of Industrialization and Technological Change sponsored jointly by UNESCO, the Canadian and the United States National Commissions for UNESCO, and the University of Chicago in September 1960. The articles follow a meaningful sequence rarely found in this kind of joint effort. In addition to the introductory section, nineteen papers are arranged under the headings of "Entrepreneurship and Innovation," "Consumption, Savings and Investment," "Government and Public Administration," "Urbanization, Population and Family," and "Education and Communication." There is also a lengthy summary of the findings of the conference. Four appendices at the end deal with some aspects of the development and utilization of social research in developing areas.

8	1	5	-	-	-	1	4
Gei	cit	lis	rep	ant	eco	pol	soc

Kaldor, Nicholas, "Will underdeveloped countries learn to tax?" For Affairs 41:410-19, 1963.   266

In order to meet the hope of accelerated economic progress, underdeveloped countries must learn to tax. The percentage of GNP derived from taxation in these nations is less than half that of developed nations. Ineffective taxation measures in LDC's are usually attributed to low average income. Average income, however, does not tell us much about the taxation potential of a country. A factor much more important than average income is the degree of inequality of income distribution and proportion of income devoted to personal consumption rather than savings. In underdeveloped nations, which are generally characterized by greater inequality of income distribution, a large proportion of income is spent on personal consumption by the upper income groups. Most LDC's do not have a progressive taxation program which is imperative due to the level of inequality. They can and must learn to

tax. The question of whether or not they will remains unanswered.

-	-	3	-		-	3	-	-
Gei	cit	lis	rep		ant	eco	pol	soc

Kuznets, Simon S., "Economic growth and the contribution of agriculture: notes on measurements," Int J Agrar Aff
3: 59-75, 1961.   267
There are three interrelated dimensions along which
one can describe the phenomenon of economic growth: the ag-
gregative, a sustained increase in product; the structural, the
relative importance of various industries, regions and classes
of economic units; and the international, the extent to which a
society's economy benefits from and contributes to the rest of
the world. The contribution of agriculture can be considered
in terms of these aspects in reference to three types. The
first is growth of product within the agricultural sector. The
second is a contribution which makes it possible for other sectors of the domestic economy to emerge or for the economy
as a whole to participate in international trade; this type is
termed a "market contribution." Thirdly, agriculture contributes a transfer or loan of resources to other sectors of
the economy, these being of three subtypes, compulsory
capital transfers (as via central government taxation or forced
requisitions), capital loans, and the provision of labor. This
last type is termed a "factor contribution." Measurement
problems and implications for the assessment of these three
forms of contributions by agriculture to the development are
then discussed.

-	-	1	20		-	1	-	-
Gei	cit	lis	rep		ant	eco	pol	soc

Lagos Matus, Gustavo, International stratification and
underdeveloped countries, Chapel Hill: University of North
Carolina Press, 1963, 302 p.   268
Lagos here attempts to use the concepts of sociology,
especially of social stratification, to characterize international
relations, with special reference to the problem of modernization. Each nation can be placed on a differentiated continuum in terms of its "real status" (wealth, power, prestige),
and each nation by virtue of its political sovereignty and membership in the world community also enjoys a "formal status" of
equality or near equality with other nations. Among the underdeveloped countries there is a large, and widening, gap between "real" and "formal" status, a degradation or "atimia,"
which in turn causes an acute sense of dissatisfaction and
aspiration for better which leads to reactive nationalism and
efforts to modernize. These efforts are further analyzed in

terms of their rationality and probability of success. Throughout, enlightening examples are given of the degree to which
particular countries have or have not acted in a rational way
to raise their real statuses, and a typology of international ac-
tions is offered. Another important side of the book is normative. Lagos presents a "model of action" deemed most appropriate for an LDC, complete with suggested policies and institutions. For example, LDC's are urged to join together in
regional, supra-national communities to achieve strength and
stability which they could not attain individually because of
their small size and limited economic potential. An important and provocative contribution, Lagos' work builds on the
best concepts of the sociological tradition, but at the same
time evokes some doubt in the reader as to whether the world
can indeed be termed a genuine community.

3	1	1	-		-	-	-	1
Gei	cit	lis	rep		ant	eco	pol	soc

LaPalombara, Joseph (ed.), Bureaucracy and political
development, Princeton: Princeton University Press, 1963,
487 p.   269
       This is the second book in a seven volume series en-
titled "Studies in Political Development" sponsored by the Committee on Comparative Politics of the Social Science Research
Council. The contents of this collection can be grouped as
follows: general theoretical considerations, bureaucracy and
economic development, case studies of national bureaucracies,
and a report on the role of international civil services. The
eleven articles and the two opening chapters by the editor add
considerable knowledge to the understanding of the role of
bureaucracies in social change. The contributions by La
Palombara, Eisenstadt and Riggs deserve special mention.

8	2	5	-		2	-	3	-
Gei	cit	lis	rep		ant	eco	pol	soc

Lerner, Daniel, "Toward a communication theory of
modernization," Ch. 18, p. 327-350 in L. W. Pye (ed.), Communications and political development, Princeton: Princeton
University Press, 1963.   270
       Mobility is not enough to bring about modernization.
Societal equilibrium as a ratio between individual mobility
and institutional stability is required. Social institutions affecting this equilibrium are: the economy, the police, the
family, the community, the school, and the media. The media
need to spread in a direct and monotonic relationship with industrial growth if they are to further modernization. This requires capacity to produce media systems and to consume
media products. To avoid having expectations turn into frus-

trations the media have to mobilize energies of persons by
rational articulation of new interests. Lerner develops an
idealized model of media functions based on the notion of
sustained economic development and the present stand of communications research. This is a short, clear evaluation of
the conditions in which communications promote or impede the
process of socialization and modernization.

2	2	-	-		-	-	-	-
Gei	cit	lis	rep		ant	eco	pol	soc

Lipset, Seymour M. , The first new nation: the United
States in historical and comparative perspective, NY: Basic
Books, 1963, 366 p.   271
    Lipset's book is an interpretation of American history
and society in terms calculated to clarify its pattern of societal development. The frame of reference, though both comparative and historical, is mainly to the experience of the
Western industrial, democratic states, especially Britain,
Canada and Australia. The main argument is that the American Revolution and its immediate consequences played a central role in the formation of the American value system
(achievement and equalitarianism are predominant, in contrast
to Britain where ascription and elitism are more important),
and that this latter has been a major factor in ensuring a
stable democratic polity and continuing economic development.
The value of this book for the sociology of development lies in
the proposed similarities and contrasts between American development history and the experiences now confronting the
nations of Asia, Africa and Latin America.

2	2	1	-		-	-	1	-
Gei	cit	lis	rep		ant	eco	pol	soc

McClelland, David C. , "The achievement motive in
economic growth," Ch. 4, p. 74-95 in B. F. Hoselitz and W.
E. Moore (eds.), Industrialization and society, The Hague:
Mouton, 1963.   272
    This is a summary of the author's book, The achieving
society, in which he identifies a motivational force--the need
for achievement--as a necessary condition in accounting for
economic development. The independent variable is measured
primarily in terms of the frequency of occurence of achievement themes in children's readers. The dependent variable
has as its chief indicator kilowatt hours of electricity produced within a country. The data offer substantial support for
the hypothesis.

1	-	2	20		1	-	1	-
Gei	cit	lis	rep		ant	eco	pol	soc

Mair, Lucy, New nations, Chicago: University of
Chicago Press, 1963, 235 p.   273
It is argued in this account of the modernization process
that the key features are new economic opportunities which
initiate and support social and cultural changes. These serve
to change traditional patterns in ways dependent upon local cultures, colonial administration practices, missionary influences,
etc. , but the chief thing is the extension or enlargement of
social ties from small, kin-based (small-scale) communities
to larger, urban, national or micronational (large scale) communities. The claim is made that this treatment by a social
anthropologist goes further than is usual in this discipline,
carrying the analysis further than that of traits, but the book
is disappointing in its failure to follow up its hypotheses, its
confusing presentation of materials and a general "absence of
virtues. "

1	-	6	-		2	-	4	-
Gei	cit	lis	rep		ant	eco	pol	soc

Meier, Gerald M. , International trade and development,
NY: Harper and Row, 1963, 202 p.   274
Using the traditional classical comparative statics approach, Meier relaxes some assumptions and adds relevant
variables to "update" the fundamental principles of development problems. Among the areas covered are: the changing
structure of comparative costs in the course of development;
the significance for poor countries of secular movements in
the terms of trade (and a clear discussion of the various
definitions of terms of trade such as barter, income, and
commodity terms of trade); the relation between capital formation and the maintenance of an equilibrium in the balance of
payments; the developmental role of international capital movements; and the potential for transmitting development through
foreign trade.   Framed in an analytical examination of the
monetary and pure theory of international trade, the importance of the book stems from its attempt to analyze changing
situations in countries with different levels of development and
the changing relationships among these countries.

2	-	4	-		-	4	-	-
Gei	cit	lis	rep		ant	eco	pol	soc

Moore, Wilbert E. , "Industrialization and social change,"
Ch. 15, p. 299-370 in B. F. Hoselitz and W. E. Moore (eds.),
Industrialization and society, The Hague: Mouton, 1963.   275
This lengthy and useful chapter is a summary of the
major results obtained in a large number of studies of industrialization which were supported, either directly or indirectly, by UNESCO. The survey is restricted primarily to the

developing countries, and the focus is on the social implications of changes in the technology of production, this to include agriculture, manufacture and services.

1	1	4	-	1	-	1	2
Gei	cit	lis	rep	ant	eco	pol	soc

Moore, Wilbert E. , Social change, Englewood Cliffs, NJ: Prentice-Hall, 1963, 120 p.   276

Though oriented mainly to the topic of the title, this book is also a good assessment of some of the basic themes and trends of modern sociological theory. It contains, for example, a helpful and succinct discussion of why social change has until quite recently suffered neglect. One reason has been the predominance of an equilibrium model of society, which emphasizes mainly the tendency for restoration of the system to a steady state. To handle the phenomena of change more adequately Moore proposes a "tension-management" model of society. "Tensions" (inconsistencies, strains) invite attention to social change as well as to social order. Topics discussed include "the normality of change," "small-scale change," "changes in societies," "modernization," and "social evolution." An excellent survey, this work offers an extra bonus in the form of some intellectual history and treatment of current issues in the sociological enterprise.

7	3	8	-	4	-	2	2
Gei	cit	lis	rep	ant	eco	pol	soc

Mukerji, Dhurjati P. , "Mahatama Ghandi's views on machines and technology," p. 63-7 in J. Meynaud (ed.), Social change and economic development, Paris: UNESCO, 1963.   277

This paper was written in support of the conviction that "any study of the social changes brought about by technology should be based primarily on an understanding of the conditions of both the society which introduces technology and the society to which it is introduced." While Western sociologists have recognized the common presumption that technological advance is a self-evident good, there has been no formulation of the Eastern value system characterizing Asian countries which are recipients of new technology. To help fill this need, Ghandi's view of the Indian value system is presented. Ghandi himself held to the "ideal" pattern of Hindu values (renunciation of self and body) but his interpretation of that ideal to the masses in the form which won him so many advocates was less ephemeral. He crystallized the values of the Indian masses in his emphasis on non-possession. The motivating factor is "the concept of love, or altruism, the good of all, as opposed to the hedonistic calculus of the greatest good to the greatest

174

number." The value of Mukerji's paper lies in its presentation in concrete terms of a problem often considered, a value system antithetical to the changes which most development programs seek to institute.

Gei	cit	lis	rep	ant	eco	pol	soc
1	-	-	60	-	-	-	-

Pye, Lucian W. (ed.), Communications and political development, Princeton: Princeton University Press, 1963, 381 p.   278

This is the first book in a seven volume series entitled "Studies in Political Development" sponsored by the Committee on Comparative Politics of the Social Science Research Council. The articles are revisions of invited papers originally presented at a seminar held in September, 1961. The book deals with seven different aspects of development: (1) the economic and social conditions necessary for developing a mass communications industry, (2) the relations between the media and the political development, (3) the functions of mass communications in nation building, (4) patterns of the usage of the media by governments and their consequences, (5) the kinds of communications developments and their use for political development, (6) the effective use of the media in politics, and (7) the mass media in relation to traditional communication. Pye's introductory chapter, "Models of Traditional, Transitional, and Modern Communication Systems," and his introductions to the other articles make this collection well-harmonized and helpful.

Gei	cit	lis	rep	ant	eco	pol	soc
8	2	5	-	-	-	4	1

Riggs, Fred W., "Bureaucrats and political development: a paradoxical view," p. 120-67 in J. La Palombara (ed.), Bureaucracy and political development, Princeton: Princeton University Press, 1963.   279

In this major and controversial article it is argued that political development may be impeded by bureaucratic interests. The general thesis is that "premature or too rapid expansion of the bureaucracy when the political system lags behind tends to inhibit the development of effective politics." It is also postulated that "separate political institutions have a better chance to grow if bureaucratic institutions are relatively weak." Riggs analyzes the relation of bureaucracy to the party system, the electorate, interest groups, and the legislature in clarifying these hypotheses. One of the most controversial postulates is that the bureaucratic merit system can have a negative effect on the growth of a new political party system, and therefore on political development, by undercutting one of its major bases, namely the spoils system. An efficient career bureaucracy, while needed for economic and social development, paradoxically may hinder political development by resisting the politicians' attempt to establish effective controls.

1	-	3	3	-	-	3	-
Gei	cit	lis	rep	ant	eco	pol	soc

Schultz, Theodore W., The economic value of education, NY: Columbia University Press, 1963, 92 p.   280
     The Ford Foundation commissioned this survey of the rapidly growing field of the economics of education. Education as an economic quantity can be seen in three relations: as an output of the educational system; as an input in individual, firm and aggregate production functions; and as an input for individual utility and social welfare functions. In this book primarily the latter two are treated, and in terms of investment analysis, by which costs are related to returns. This work is useful as an assessment of the current state of knowledge, for a discussion of major analytical problems, and for an excellent bibliography in an important corollary field.

-	3	-	-	-	-	-	-
Gei	cit	lis	rep	ant	eco	pol	soc

Silvert, Kalman H., (ed.), Expectant peoples: nationalism and development, NY: Random House, 1963, 489 p.   281
     The major theme of this volume of studies by the American Universities Field Staff is the role and quality of nationalism in twelve developing countries in the Middle East, Latin America, Asia, and Africa. Twelve countries are treated as "total societies," and are described with particular attention to "nationalism," and "national integration," as factors influencing their development. The historical analyses of these countries make it easier to trace the varying manifestations and nuances of nationalism among them. An appendix presents some 74 propositions about nationalism.

8	-	3	-	-	-	2	1
Gei	cit	lis	rep	ant	eco	pol	soc

Vernon, Raymond, The dilemma of Mexico's development, Cambridge, Mass: Harvard University Press, 1963, 226 p.   282
     Vernon's study of the roles played by the government and the private sector in Mexico's economic development concludes that the stimulus heretofore provided by the export and import substitution policies is now diminishing, causing some stagnation in the Mexican economy. Local businessmen, he

believes, lack the confidence in the future necessary for an expansion of productive capacity at the same rate as in the past.
Moreover, the government, which has assumed such a critical
role in the past in investments, land, water, the mobilization
of foreign credits, loan distributions to agriculture, and the
control of prices, now finds its role circumscribed by its inability to levy sufficient taxes and operate public enterprises
at a profit and by its reluctance to use deficit financing. The
stagnating economy demands modification of government policies but Vernon sees the president as so dominated by the
Party (PRI) as to make any action unlikely. It is possible that
Vernon has exaggerated the problem, mistaking a cyclical decline in Mexico's growth rate for secular stagnation. Furthermore, his characterization of the institutional forces of the
country may underestimate their ability to cope with the problem, since the Mexican system is responsive to public opinion,
affords considerable scope for personal freedom, permits
peaceful change of administrations, and fosters a good amount
of political stability.

| 2 | 1 | 3 | - | | - | - | 2 | 1 |
| Gei | cit | lis | rep | | ant | eco | pol | soc |

Ward, Robert E. , "Political modernization and political
culture in Japan," World Pol 15: 569-96, 1963.   283
It is suggested here that the way in which political
modernization has been achieved in Japan may be a prototype
for the forms and organizations likely to appear in any modernizing society. Japan's history leads to the following propositions: authoritarian political organization can be extraordinari-
ly effective in the early stages of the modernization process;
authoritarian political forms need not prevent the gradual
emergence of more democratic forms of political organization;
some process of gradual transition from authoritarian to
democratic political forms may be not only desirable but essential to the emergence of political systems which are durable. Furthermore, the experience of Japan suggests that all
durable democracies are the products of lengthy and complex
evolutionary processes, and that the only reasonable candidates
for democratization are societies which are modernized, that
is, societies to which is presented the potential for a thorough
ability to control and change both the physical and social environment, and which have a value system positively oriented
toward the desirability of such an ability.

| - | 3 | 2 | - | | - | - | 2 | - |
| Gei | cit | lis | rep | | ant | eco | pol | soc |

Adams, Richard N. , "Rural labor," Ch. 2, p. 49-78
in J. J. Johnson (ed.), Continuity and change in Latin

America, Stanford: Stanford University Press, 1964.   284

Although of obviously great importance on the Latin American scene, rural labor has attracted little attention from social scientists. There are, to be sure, many forms: reciprocal labor, peasant labor, plantation proletariat, hacienda colono or corvee labor, mining proletariat, forest labor and rural industrial labor. The author discusses a variety of problems and makes many interesting generalizations in terms of labor market and migration, the influence of power domains (for example, many haciendas in the Andes and some in Meso-America still exercise the right of corporal punishment of recalcitrant laborers), and social structure and attitudes. An important topic in the last category is attitudes toward work. Generally, work is considered undesirable; leisure--to be savored and appreciated--is more esteemed. On the other hand, in some of the Peruvian highland and Guatemalan Indian communities "work is greeted with considerable enthusiasm."

Gei	cit	lis	rep	ant	eco	pol	soc
1	-	4	-	1	-	1	2

Arensberg, Conrad M., and Arthur H. Niehoff, Introducing social change: a manual for Americans overseas Chicago: Aldine, 1964, 214 p.   285

Rather elementary, but very readable, this textbook is on "directed change" and what it involves in the less developed areas of the world. It deals with the concepts of culture and cultural borrowing, the general features of underdeveloped peoples, and the ways in which American values are apt to differ from the values of such peoples. Good reading on applied anthropology for those with no previous training in the social sciences.

Gei	cit	lis	rep	ant	eco	pol	soc
-	1	3	-	3	-	-	-

Bendix, Reinhard, Nation-building and citizenship: studies of our changing social order, NY: Wiley, 1964, 314 p.   286

Authority relationships are the focus in this analytical reconstruction of the development of Western Europe, Russia, Japan, Germany and India. The author rejects both single-factor determinisms and the idea that modernity arises at the expense of tradition. Nor does he use an explicit model of society. Rather, Bendix presents history in sociological, often Weberian, concepts stressing the problems and patterns of authority unique to each case. Especially interesting is the concept of "private authority," a kind of coalescence of interests arising out of the tendency for groups to form in new situations. In the transition of Western societies from feudalism there were two critical points: the transformation of the estate system and the consequent subjection of the individual to control by a central authority, and the social protest movements which led to the establishment of the rights of citizenship. In Russia the success of industrialization is linked with constant pressure placed by the party upon administrators at high levels (public authority) alongside collusion between party officials and administrators at lower levels (private authority). Japan and Prussia began late, but both had effective, nationwide public authority which facilitated rapid industrialization. India's government is relatively stable, but its authority cannot be considered national because of the difficulty of reaching the village level.

| 2 | 2 | 5 | - | | - | - | 4 | 1 |
| Gei | cit | lis | rep | | ant | eco | pol | soc |

Berg, Elliot J. , "Socialism and economic development in tropical Africa," Q J Econ 78:549-73, 1964.   287

In Africa most statesmen and intellectuals regard capitalism as old-fashioned, inadequate, morally unacceptable, tainted by association with the colonial period, and they strongly prefer socialism. This latter includes preference for the State as a driving force in development, distrust of the market principle, desire for State control of the distribution sector, large-scale, cooperative, mechanized agriculture, etc. In fact, argues this writer, current conditions in Africa make the kinds of policies espoused by African socialists quite unlikely to be successful. The state lacks the trained people to bear the burden socialists would impose upon it, socialist agricultural patterns are not suited to ecological and economic conditions, and so on. To date socialist policy has had only a limited effect on economic policy, except in a few countries, notably Guinea, where the results have been disastrous.

| - | 1 | 4 | - | | - | 3 | 1 | - |
| Gei | cit | lis | rep | | ant | eco | pol | soc |

Bonilla, Frank, "The urban worker," Ch. 7, p. 186-206 in J. J. Johnson (ed.), Continuity and Change in Latin America, Stanford: Stanford University Press, 1964.   288

What is the impact of the city upon the urban worker? What is the impact of the urban worker upon the Latin American city? In answering the first question Bonilla shows first that the city is literally a schoolhouse providing educational opportunities, and not all in the formal sense, unknown in the rural areas. Secondly, the worker is exposed to new levels of consumption which greatly affect expectations. On this point

Bonilla argues that "high" urban wages are largely illusory, and cause the worker to turn to the government for welfare services. Thirdly, the city politicizes the worker giving him a potential voice in national politics. As to the effect of the worker on the city, the problem is posed mainly in terms of the labor union's role in Latin American politics. Latin American governments have tended to closely regulate union activities. Bonilla notes "the persistence in law and government of the operational principle that business must be persuaded or enticed to compliance but labor can be forced..." Also discussed are the long-term antipathy of Latin American labor unions toward the USA and the consequences of this for American financed development programs.

1	-	3	-		-	-	1	2
Gei	cit	lis	rep		ant	eco	pol	soc

No entry 289

Etzioni, Amitai and Eva Etzioni (eds.), Social change: sources, patterns, and consequences, NY: Basic Books, 1964, 503 p.   290
        This reader or source book contains selections on four aspects of social change: (1) brief theoretical discussions; (2) illustrations of specific social changes; (3) concern for variety of social systems in change and; (4) specific process by which social change develops. There are selections among them from Spencer, Comte, Toynbee, Spengler, Marx, Weber, Toennies, Kroeber, Park, MacIver, Linton, Ogburn, Parsons, Mannheim, and Riesman, with a grand total of fifty-five pieces. The book may be valuable to graduate students in locating the ideas presented and identifying potentially fruitful interconnections among them for subsequent theory and investigation.

8	-	3	-	2	-	-	1
Gei	cit	lis	rep	ant	eco	pol	soc

        Flanders, M. June "Prebisch on protectionism: an evaluation," Econ J 74:305-26, 1964.   291
        Here is a detailed analysis of the "Prebisch Thesis," which has been an extremely influential though highly controversial set of ideas about the role of the setting of international trade in the chances for economic growth for the countries of the "periphery." His main recommendation is that such countries should vigorously protect and subsidize domestic industry. Flanders shows that there are several components to the Prebisch Thesis, two of which are the idea that wage and price rigidity in the "center" prevents the fruits of technical progress from being passed on to the periphery; and the assertion that the periphery has a high income elasticity of demand for imports, while that of the center is low, which causes the terms of trade for the periphery to decline and to retard its

growth. The conclusion is that the Prebisch position requires some questionable and/or rather strictly limiting assumptions before his policy recommendations can be accepted.

| | - | - | 3 | - | | - | 3 | - | - |
| Gei | cit | lis | rep | | ant | eco | pol | soc |

Harbison, Frederick and Charles A. Myers, Education, manpower and economic growth: strategies of human resource development, NY: McGraw-Hill, 1964, 299 p.   292
        Two economists attack the problems of development from the point of view of human resource development, the latter being achieved through three principal means: formal education, on-the-job training, and self-development. (Improvements in nutrition and health are relevant, too, but not analyzed here.) Four levels of development (labelled "underdeveloped," "partially developed," etc.) of 75 countries are identified with an index of proportionate enrollment of relevant age groups in educational institutions. The index is highly correlated with per capita GNP and percent of population in agriculture.Within this framework the shortcomings of each of the four groupings are discussed and specific strategies to overcome them are recommended. For example, the final chapter shows how planning for human resource development can be integrated with general economic and social planning.

| | 2 | 4 | 4 | - | | - | 4 | - | - |
| Gei | cit | lis | rep | | ant | eco | pol | soc |

Harris, Marvin, Patterns of race in the Americas, NY: Walker, 1964, 154 p.   293
        Here is a bold and competent effort to trace the current patterns of race relations in the Western hemisphere back through history to their origins in the geographic, climatic and economic conditions in which the European settlers found themselves. The key factor which determined the fate of race relations was the attempt made by the Europeans to find and control mass labor power to exploit the land and precious metal resources of the New World. In places where it proved difficult or impossible to exploit the labor of the Indians, African slaves were imported. Subsequently, relations between the races depended in good part upon whether plantation or small-scale farming got established first. If the former, as in Brazil, small-scale farming could not develop so strongly and a competitive relation between the free labor of European immigrants and the slave laborers did not occur. If the latter, as in the USA South, the competition between free (white) labor and slave (black) labor produced, after the abolition of slavery, a rigid system of castes by which Negroes and mulattoes were segregated by whites in order to protect their

dominant economic and political positions.

-	1	3	-	2	-	1	-
Gei	cit	lis	rep	ant	eco	pol	soc

Helleiner, Gerald K. , "The fiscal role of the marketing boards in Nigerian economic development, 1947-61," Econ J 74: 582-610, 1964.   294

Originally regarded mainly as fortuitous, Marketing Board trading surpluses (from export taxes, etc.) in Nigeria were in the early years earmarked as a reserve to be used primarily for future stabilization efforts. Later, the view took hold that these reserves could legitimately be used as sources of revenue for the financing of new development programs, and MB funds were allocated to Regional Production Development Boards, general development programs, agricultural research and development, universities, and private enterprises engaged in manufacturing, finance and real estate. Although weaknesses in this practice can be detected, the author concludes that on the whole this pattern of collection and expenditure of revenues was beneficial to Nigerian economic development.

-	1	3	-	-	3	-	-
Gei	cit	lis	rep	ant	eco	pol	soc

Janowitz, Morris, The military in the political development of the new nations, Chicago: University of Chicago Press, 1964, 134 p.   295

Military-civilian relations, types of military leadership and career patterns, and contributions and potential help in the tasks of modernization are discussed with special reference to the nations of Africa and Asia. Among the conclusions, perhaps the most important is that the military in these new nations is recruited from the middle and lower-middle class; there is no connection between military and traditional aristocracy. For this and related reasons the military tends toward nationalism, acceptance of collectivist public enterprise, opposition to corruption in public or private life and a strong "anti-politics" orientation. Military political rule tends to lack certain capacities, such as that for carrying out an overall development plan, and to be authoritarian, but without exception develops only after the failure of politicians to exercise effective leadership.

2	1	4	-	-	-	4	-
Gei	cit	lis	rep	ant	eco	pol	soc

Johnson, John J. , "Introduction," p. 3-20 in J. J. Johnson (ed.), Continuity and change in Latin America, Stanford: Stanford University Press, 1964.   296

Initially the author presents changes in the social, political and economic scene of Latin America occurring since World War I. There is much tension between the established urban parties and the short-range demands of new political groups. The locus of power in the cities lends continuity to politics as well as biasing national policy. Much disequilibrium has resulted from the trend toward the replacement in the economy of agriculture by industrial activity. Resultant urban and industrial problems relating to rapid growth, lack of foreign exchange, shifts from commercial to subsistence agriculture, and the need for high state and public sector investment receive added discussion. Johnson further sketches the format for the rest of the book, which is a study of eight groups--peasant, rural laborer, writer, artist, the military, industrialist, urban worker, and university student. Their problems, aspirations, capabilities, group position and changing character are analyzed. A general theme is the constant interplay between groups with new ideas and groups with old ways, a situation which lends itself to political manipulation.

-	-	3	-		-	-	1	2
Gei	cit	lis	rep		ant	eco	pol	soc

Johnson, John J. , The military and society in Latin America, Stanford: Stanford University Press, 1964, 308 p.
297
In contrast to the stereotyped image of the military as a monolithic, politically conservative force the author argues that the attitudes found among officers in Latin America have changed. Due to the rise of levels of military expertise, more mobility from lower classes and greater professionalization of the armed forces, the military leader has become "more sensitive to the advantages of modernization and technical advancement" and "painfully aware of the extent to which his own country is economically and technologically retarded." Though his evidence is thin, Johnson asserts that the military favor education, are nationalistic, favor state intervention in economic life, etc. but are ambivalent toward communism and land reform.

2	1	4	-		2	-	2	-
Gei	cit	lis	rep		ant	eco	pol	soc

Meier, Gerald M. (ed.), Leading issues in development economics: selected materials and commentary, NY: Oxford University Press, 1964, 572 p.   298
According to its editor, this book departs from the usual approaches of a textbook of readings. Meier distilled from the enormous literature on development a relatively few issues that have emerged to the forefront of the subject but

which are still unsettled and in need of closer analysis. On
each of these leading issues, the editor presents a variety of
materials that should be looked at together. On the other
hand, to ensure cohesion, Meier provides commentary through
a series of connected notes. The result is a valuable reference
book on the leading issues of economic development. The following problems are discussed: (1) the validity of Rostow's
analysis of the stages of growth, (2) the meaning and significance of dualism, (3) problems of capital accumulation, (4)
effects of inflation on development, (5) criteria for allocating
investment resources, (6) the relative emphasis to be given
industrialization and agriculture in the development process,
(7) the influence of international trade on development, (8) the
scope for development planning, and (9) techniques of development planning. This volume makes available a substantial collection of theoretical, applied and policy materials reflecting
the present state of development economics.

	8	-	4	-		-	3	1	-
Gei	cit	lis	rep		ant	eco	pol	soc

Myint, Hla, The economics of the developing countries,
NY: Praeger, 1964, 192 p.   299
Why are some countries underdeveloped? What is appropriate in the way of theoretical models of the process of
development for these countries? An Indian economist and
Senior Lecturer at Oxford provides a succinct and occasionally technical response to these two questions. Population size,
growth and density, and the extent to which primary sectors
(agriculture, extraction) are integrated with a money economy
play an important role in explaining the first problem. The
second is dealt with by a summary and critique of the main current theories of development, which Myint finds inadequate because they involve presuppositions appropriate to economies
already developed but not those of underdeveloped countries,
and for other reasons. Valuable for its attention to demographic and socio-cultural factors, this work also poses policy
alternatives faced by the developing nations: higher present
consumption vs. higher future growth rate, economic equality
vs. economic growth, etc. Myint's discussion is best suited
for those who have already been exposed to some of the concepts and controversies in development economics.

	2	-	8	-		1	5	1	1
Gei	cit	lis	rep		ant	eco	pol	soc

Powelson, John P., Latin America: today's economic
and social revolution, NY: McGraw-Hill, 1964, 303 p.   300
Here is an adroit exposition of the interweaving of economic, political and cultural influences in Latin America. The

main contribution is in the analysis of "dominant intellectual opinions" or contrasting perspectives of Latin America and the USA. Latins have never understood well the mixed economy welfare state in the USA nor have the Americans "del Norte" the unproductive "capitalized feudalism," after Milton Eisenhower, or "adventure-dominated capitalism," to use Powelson's term, understood the pattern in Latin America. It is also asserted that the USA prefers to see individual, person or organization, deal with individual, while Latin Americans are more apt to favor government-guided, collective solutions to economic problems.

(2)	-	-	-		-	-	-	-
Gei	cit	lis	rep		ant	eco	pol	soc

Russett, Bruce M., Hayward R. Alker, Jr., Karl W. Deutsch, Harold D. Lasswell et al, World handbook of political and social indicators, New Haven: Yale University Press, 1964, 373 p.   301
This book compares nations on a great variety of politically and socially relevant indicators, with the view of presenting data necessary for the development of comparative and international politics. The indicators were chosen to operationalize a variable central to several important theories of political or social change. The basic data consists of 75 series taken from as many as 133 different political entities (independent nations and colonies), and each series is carefully described in terms of its sources, advantages and limitations. Part B, "The Analysis of Trends and Patterns," pages 261-364 contains a wealth of important propositions, tabular data to test them and revealing interpretations. For example, Figures B.3-B.5 have the following titles: "Voting turnout tends to be highest in developed countries but not in the richest ones;" "Economic development is associated with political violence, at least in the early stages;" and "The central government's role in the economy increases with development, but may diminish at very high levels.

7	1	3	-		-	1	1	1
Gei	cit	lis	rep		ant	eco	pol	soc

Schultz, Theodore W., Transforming traditional agriculture, New Haven: Yale University Press, 1964, 212 p.
                                                                      302
Schultz disposes of doctrines of the low efficiency or zero marginal productivity of traditional agriculture by showing how in Panajáchel, Guatemala, and Senapur, Northern India, given the existing factors of production, agricultural labor was remarkably efficient. Thus, to transform agricul-

tural production, an initial and necessary step to economic growth and industrialization, reliance should be placed not upon the use of power to effect agricultural reorganization (the command approach), but preferably upon the provision of economic incentives to farmers in a market situation by supplying them with chances for profitable use of new factors. This task, argues the author, will have to be accomplished in the main by government agencies, for profit-oriented firms have little interest in poor agricultural communities, and a major input is the diffusion of knowledge, a form of investment in farm people.

2	3	6	-		-	4	-	2
Gei	cit	lis	rep		ant	eco	pol	soc

Scott, Robert E. , Mexican government in transition. Champaign: University of Illinois Press, 1964, 345 p.   303

Because Mexico has been so long on the road and traveled so far transiting from non-Western to Western-type politics, Scott suggests that a study of its experience and system of government has value in an international context. He credits the central political party, the PRI, with reasonably effectively aggregating important interests of major groups, and he detects a gradual professionalization of the party and government toward providing needed social and economic programs. Scott says that progress toward modernization can be seen in the transition of Mexico's polity from 90 per cent parochial in 1910 to 65 per cent subjects and 10 per cent participants by 1964. The expansion of participation developed as a result of expanded communication and transportation networks and subsequent mental adjustments to personal political involvement. The value of the study would have increased had the author broadened his consideration of political factors to include more emphasis on the role of U.S. and other foreign interests, the intellectuals and military, among other groups.

2	1	6	-		-	-	5	1
Gei	cit	lis	rep		ant	eco	pol	soc

Sinai, I. Robert, The challenge of modernization: the West's impact on the non-Western world, NY: Norton, 1964, 256 p.   304

The thesis of this book is that the LDC's must travel much the same path to modernity as that taken by the West. Three central experiences have produced the dynamic spirit and values of Western nations, the Renaissance, the Reformation and the Enlightenment. A similar, though greatly telescoped cultural re-orientation or "social rebirth," it is argued, must occur in countries like India, Indonesia, Burma and the new

African nations, but cannot take place if these countries attempt to do the job through parliamentary democracy and "floating values." Needed instead are a strong leader, such as Turkey's Kemal Ataturk, a new ideology with the power to foment a thorough cultural revolution, dedicated reformist--innovational elites, and a state organized "to impose collective savings far beyond the limits of what individuals would be likely to save if left to their own devices." Sinai's approach strikes one as hard-headed, sometimes to a fault, but a welcome change from the message of those who optimistically anticipate progress through trade, aid and education. But his argument that cultural revitalization is essential suffers by his cursory attention to underdeveloped Latin America, much of it long exposed already to Western cultural influences, and by his failure to assess the place of the USSR in his scheme.

2	-	6	-		2	-	2	2
Gei	cit	lis	rep		ant	eco	pol	soc

Strassmann, W. Paul, "The industrialists," Ch. 6, p. 161-86 in J. J. Johnson (ed.), Continuity and change in Latin America, Stanford: Stanford University Press, 1964.   305

Two facets of the emergence and continuation of productive industrial entrepreneurship in Latin America are the "objective" social and economic factors of Latin American society, and the "subjective" variation among individual entrepreneurs arising out of social and psychological differences in their environments. These two facets are discussed in a variety of contexts, touching upon the availability of industrialists in relation to industrial supply and demand, possible explanations of the origins of entrepreneurs in Latin America, the differences between the goals set by the society for the industrialist as compared to the goals the industrialist sets for himself, the policies likely to arise from such goal discrepancies, and the political repercussions involved. It is concluded that the industrialists generally act as a conservative force until change is brought about in spite of them, in which case they give sanctimonious approval. The information is most impressive in areas concerning the industrialists' role in the economy and weakest in considering the role of the industrialist politically and ideologically--undoubtedly a reflection of the abundance of economic facts and figures and the dearth of facts regarding these men as individual personalities.

2	-	3	-		-	-	1	2
Gei	cit	lis	rep		ant	eco	pol	soc

United Nations, The economic development of Latin America in the post-war period, NY: UN, 1964, 147 p. (Doc. E/CN. 12/659/Rev. 1)   306

One cannot find a better and more comprehensive survey of the economic and social development and problems of this area. Overall trends, both economic and social, analysis of the patterns country by country with good tabular data, charts and interpretations, and much emphasis on the roles of population, foreign trade and export-import experiences make this an invaluable compilation. The most important general conclusion is also the reason why the survey was published--the tendency for Latin American development to slow down or to show considerable fluctuations in the post-war period. One of the main factors explaining this is found in the fact that the value of Latin American exports rose very little between 1948 and 1960. Significantly, however, those countries with the highest rates of growth were also those which showed the greatest expansion of exports.

| - | 1 | 4 | - | | - | - | 1 | 3 |
| Gei | cit | lis | rep | | ant | eco | pol | soc |

von der Mehden, Fred R. , <u>Politics of the developing nations</u>, Englewood Cliffs, NJ: Prentice-Hall, 1964, 143 p.

307

Here is a concise survey of the major patterns exhibited in the political life of the underdeveloped nations of Africa, Asia, and Latin America. Eighty-four countries are treated and interest is centered on their two basic problems, how to maintain a stable government and how to establish a unified state. In six parts, the following topics are treated: the colonial heritage, the search for national identity, political parties, political elites, political action by the military, and ideology. There is no index, but a selected bibliography is at the end of each chapter.

| 7 | 1 | 3 | - | | - | - | 3 | - |
| Gei | cit | lis | rep | | ant | eco | pol | soc |

Ward, Robert E. and Dankwart A. Rustow (eds.), <u>Political modernization in Japan and Turkey</u>, Princeton: Princeton University Press, 1964, 502 p.   308

This is the only book among a seven volume series entitled "Studies in Political Development" that applies the case method rather than a strictly functional approach. The series was sponsored by the Committee on Comparative Politics of the Social Science Research Council. Seventeen experts on Japan and Turkey examine eight aspects in each nation's development. The areas examined include traditional society, environmental and foreign contributions, economic growth, education, mass media, civil bureaucracy, the role of the military, and party leadership. Most of the articles in the collection concentrate on the take-off period of economic and

political modernization before 1945, but it seems generally
agreed that political development tends to take a longer time.
At the end the editors provide a brilliant synthesis of the comparisons of the two countries by especially emphasizing the
uniqueness of national experience.

8	-	4	-		-	-	4	-
Gei	cit	lis	rep		ant	eco	pol	soc

Whiteford, Andrew H. , Two cities of Latin America:
a comparative description of social classes, Garden City, NY:
Doubleday, 1964, 266 p.   309
This study points to the existence of a substantial middle class in two Latin American cities, Popayan, Colombia,
and Queretaro, Mexico. Whiteford looks in detail at the characteristics identifying members of three broad social sectors--
upper, middle and lower--and further subdivides these usual
class groupings into more sharply defined social strata. He
details the criteria for membership in any given part of the
social hierarchy, compares interclass relationships, and
describes the significantly different limits and means of upward social mobility. Whiteford concludes that the middle
class enjoys greater emancipation in the more developed Mexican city and that the extremes of the social strata are oblivious
to the life-styles of their social opposites. Data for the study
were gathered from 1949 to 1958.

7	-	3	-		2	-	1	-
Gei	cit	lis	rep		ant	eco	pol	soc

Worsley, Peter, The Third world, Chicago: University
of Chicago Press, 1964, 317 p.   310
This is as much an interpretation of recent world history as a version of the situation faced by the third or underdeveloped world. The main arguments are (1) that colonial
economic exploitation served as the midwife for the emergence
of the third world; (2) that both the white capitalist world and
the white communist world, thanks largely to Stalin, are set
over in opposition, as "millionaire" nations, with little in the
way of perceived significant differences between them; and
(3) that key variables in the process of sociopolitical development are nationalism and populism. The latter is a single,
nation-wide, ethnically and ideologically united front of the people, all supporting a big push toward development and leading
to a single party political system. The dominant characteristics of the third world countries are a sense of being different
and needy, both expressed in populist nationalism, the clearest
version of which is found in the one-party "solidarist" societies
like Guinea or Sudan. Moreover, based on a sense of unity because of recent shared experiences and needs these countries

are building an increasingly strong power bloc to confront both the West and the Soviet bloc. This work is useful as a "big picture" but the unity, both domestic and international, is exaggerated.

2	-	3	-		-	-	2	1
Gei	cit	lis	rep		ant	eco	pol	soc

Zollschan, George K. and Walter Hirsch (eds.), Explorations in social change, Boston: Houghton Mifflin, 1964, 832 p.
311

The papers in this volume were prepared for a written symposium. The construction of a written symposium provides a measure of continuity and orderly sequence of thought lacking in the ordinary reader. The editors present a prevailing theme in arguing that "social theory, particularly in America ... became practically synonymous with an emphasis upon the regular and repetitive--the normative and functional." The discussions by the contributors on this main theme are grouped under the following headings: "General Perspectives on Change," "Working Papers in the Theory of Institutionalization," "Social System Models of Change," "Psycho-Social Models of Change," and "Broad Historical Perspectives on Change."

8	-	3	-		2	-	-	1
Gei	cit	lis	rep		ant	eco	pol	soc

Apter, David, The politics of modernization, Chicago: University of Chicago Press, 1965, 369 p.   312

This ambitious effort theorizes, with new classification schemes and functional analysis, about political systems in relation to modernization. Types of polities are conceived in terms of value emphasis (instrumental vs. consummatory) and type of authority (pyramidal or pluralistic vs. hierarchical), and specific types are proposed as best adapted for societies in different stages of development. Thus, "mobilization" polities are best for the transition from the traditional to the modernizing stage and again from the latter to the (third and last) industrialism stage, but "neomercantilist" systems are best for the long modernization period, and "reconciliation" political systems (instrumental values, pyramidal authority) fit best in nations already industrialized, though these, too, entrain dysfunctional consequences, such as individual alienation. Other important contributions by Apter include the formulation of six types of traditional societies, each with differential receptivity and potential in respect to modernization; discussion of the roles of value, ideology, stratification, political parties, information, coercion, occupational careers, and personal motivation in different political systems; and, perhaps most important, a vivid emphasis upon the variety of conditions and choices faced by developing societies.

3	-	12	-	1	-	6	5
Gei	cit	lis	rep	ant	eco	pol	soc

Aron, Raymond and Bert F. Hoselitz (eds.), Social development, Paris: Mouton, 1965, 349 p.   313

A series of papers read at a UNESCO symposium on social development in Paris in May, 1961, were edited and collected in this volume. There are contributions from economists, philosophers, political scientists, and sociologists representing different countries of the world with varying levels of socio-economic development. The topics discussed include not only the process of industrialization in the modern world but also an examination of "the total historical development of human society...from the standpoint of...the rationalization, moralization and universalization of human thought and behavior." The papers in general tend to reflect the idea that the urgent research task in the areas of social development is to investigate the causal and sequential regularities observable in the transition of societies from lower to higher levels of complexity, and to develop a theory which permits one to make conditional predictions about such processes.

8	-	4	-	-	-	-	4
Gei	cit	lis	rep	ant	eco	pol	soc

Boserup, Ester, The conditions of agricultural growth: the economics of agrarian change under population pressure, Chicago: Aldine, 1965, 124 p.   314

This writer rejects the Malthusian view that autonomous changes in agricultural technology determine the rate of population growth, and argues the contrary case. She asserts that the growth of population is the chief source of innovations in agriculture, land-use patterns, land-tenure systems, and other features of society. Population growth leads to a food crisis, which forces technological innovations and more intensive utilization of the land. In addition, to raise total food output men must reduce leisure time and increase hours worked. Data from India, Japan and Java are presented in support of the thesis.

2	-	3	-	-	2	-	1
Gei	cit	lis	rep	ant	eco	pol	soc

Bruton, Henry J., Principles of development economics, Englewood Cliffs, NJ: Prentice-Hall, 1965, 376 p.   315

This is a textbook without footnotes, tabular data or anecdotes but of admirable (if dry) rigor. The author's view is that the basic problem faced by the LDC's is one of raising

per capita income , and that neoclassical economic concepts
and theory (with small modifications) are adequate to describe
the sources and process of development. In presenting his
analysis, relying heavily on the production function concept,
Bruton critizes "popular catchphrases" and "issues" such as
the "take-off," "industrialization vs. agriculture," the "big push,"
etc. , as highly simplified views more apt to hinder than clarify
understanding of the growth process. One of the best texts,
this work is strong in its pure theoretical bones, and weak for
its lack of responsiveness to the great variety of structures and
conditions among the LDC economic systems.

-	-	4	-		-	3	1	-
Gei	cit	lis	rep		ant	eco	pol	soc

Coleman, James S. (ed.), Education and political development, Princeton: Princeton University Press, 1965, 620 p.
316

In this fourth book of a seven volume series, "Studies
in Political Development," sponsored by the Committee on
Comparative Politics of the Social Science Research Council,
three aspects of the political process and their educational
implications are selected for analysis: (1) political socializa-
tion--the part the school plays in identifying the individual with
the existing political system; (2) political recruitment--train-
ing for leadership and expertise; and (3) political integration--
the problem of national unification, particularly, reducing the
gap between the elites and the masses and overcoming religious,
ethnic, and locality divisiveness. The book is divided into four
parts of which the first three deal with aspects of education in
relation to the above-mentioned dimensions of political development. The fourth part provides a summary and suggestions
with reference to educational planning for integrated social and
political progress. The editor's contributions of introductory
chapter and full-length introductions for each of the four chapters make this volume extremely valuable. There is a bibliographic guide to education and political socialization at the end.

8	-	5	-		2	-	2	1
Gei	cit	lis	rep		ant	eco	pol	soc

Harbison, Frederick and Charles A. Myers (eds.), Manpower and education: country studies in economic development,
NY: McGraw-Hill, 1965, 343 p.   317

This volume presents a collection of papers on the high-
level manpower problems encountered by a number of developing countries, and the programs developed to remedy deficiencies. The countries studied are Argentina, Peru, Chile, Puerto
Rico, Iran, Indonesia, Communist China, Senegal, Guinea, the
Ivory Coast, Nyasaland, and Uganda. Most of the contributions

are from economists. The only two exceptions are sociologist
William Foote Whyte's paper on "High-level manpower for
Peru," and historian C. Y. Hsu's paper on "The impact of industrialization on higher education in Communist China." In their
introduction, Harbison and Myers characterize education as
"...both the seed and the flower of economic development."
Nevertheless, they both caution that much of a country's expenditure for education can be wasted in terms of economic
progress if the wrong kinds of education are emphasized.

8	1	4	-		-	4	-	-
Gei	cit	lis	rep		ant	eco	pol	soc

Heath, Dwight B. and Richard N. Adams (eds.), Contemporary cultures and societies of Latin America: a reader
in the social anthropology of Middle and South America and the
Caribbean, NY: Random House, 1965, 586 p.   318
      The 28 articles comprising this anthology are grouped
into four sections "Delineation of Cultural Entities," "Land,
Agriculture and Economics," "Social Organization" and "Views
of the World." All but one of the selections were published
previously, although four appear for the first time in English.
The articles deal with Latin America as a whole, with regions,
and with individual countries, and they constitute a fair sample
of the best work currently available and also of the "extremely
loose and unsatisfactory" level (in Adams' words) of our understanding of the social aspects of Latin America. One reviewer
comments, in addition, that the papers "give us a deceptively
quiet, static and calm view...at a time when violence and
revolution are current affairs in at least half of the countries
studied..."

-	-	4	-		1	-	-	3
Gei	cit	lis	rep		ant	eco	pol	soc

Hicks, Ursula, Development finance: planning and control, NY: Oxford University Press, 1965, 187 p.   319
      A brief review of some of the problems of, and strategy
for, development, this work stresses the maintenance and
improvement of existing public investments in basic services
of communications, education, and health, and the introduction
of new ways of producing goods and services--improved use
of land, exploitation of mineral resources, etc. The author
advises that while the central government need not bear all the
costs or responsibility for balanced growth, it must finance
infrastructure costs and guide in the optimum use of the economy's resources. The basic principles of expenditure choice,
monetary and fiscal controls and guides, and budgetary control
are set forth in practical terms, in order that the book be of
"direct assistance to planners and administrators."

2	-	3	-		-	3	-	-
Gei	cit	lis	rep		ant	eco	pol	soc

Little, Ian M. D. , and Juliet M. Clifford, International aid, London: George Allen and Unwin, 1965, 360 p.   320

Little and Clifford are concerned here with the effects of international economic aid and with the ways in which such aid may be rendered more effective. The authors distinguish between commercial loans and real economic aid. Failure to make such distinction has led to too much concern among donor nations with their short-run interests and to a blurring of the long-run goals of their aid. It is legitimate for donor nations to have economic and political interests. Rich Western nations, specifically, may and should want to create stable nations as their safeguard against communism. But aid-giving will backfire if donor countries persist in extracting short-run economic advantages from LDC's through their aid programs. The book's main point is that the best way of attaining their true ends is for donor countries to orient their aid toward a rapid and balanced development of the recipients. In maximizing the effectiveness of aid, some considerations are crucial. One is the absorptive capacity of recipient countries; capital will be wasted in nations that do not have the technical-administrative resources to handle it effectively and in countries whose governing elites are corrupt or apathetic. Another is the primacy of developmental goals; aid will be partially wasted if invested in projects according to their cheapness or their prestige value as "showcases." Then there is the economic criterion of aid-giving; with capacity for absorbing capital constant, aid should be given not only as a complement to internal savings, but also as supplement of foreign exchange shortages.

2	-	3	-		-	2	1	-
Gei	cit	lis	rep		ant	eco	pol	soc

McCord, William, The springtime of freedom: evolution of developing societies, NY: Oxford University Press, 1965, 330 p.   321

This book treats a crucial problem--whether democratic or authoritarian government is the best road to the achievement of development. The problem can be treated at two levels, that of values and that of tactics. The author espouses democracy as his own value position and also as the best means to social, economic and political development. Social development is "to construct a society receptive to modernization without utterly destroying traditional civilizations." The challenge of economic development is to find "how to make the bitter choices involved in economic growth without recourse

to political tyranny," and the political goal is to achieve these
changes while preserving the rule of law, preserving personal
liberties and promoting popular political participation. Such a
way of phrasing the goals of development almost necessitates
democratic means or tactics. The author's analysis wavers
between values and tactics as grounds for the justification of
democracy. He does not come to grips with the problem of the
relative costs of the two alternatives. Such an evaluation is
difficult, but is precisely the problem many LDC's face. On
the other hand, the most consistent argument in the book is
based on the author's historical evidence that once authoritarian measures have been adopted, they have not been relaxed,
except in the case of post-emergency situations in established
democracies. In general, the author leaves too much to the
rhetoric of his values and does not analyze data systematically. The comparison of Russia and Japan as alternate developmental models does not establish the basis for comparison,
nor which of these two countries at the beginning of its developmental process was more similar to the majority of the
LDC's today.

2	-	4	-		-	-	2	2
Gei	cit	lis	rep		ant	eco	pol	soc

Martz, John D. (ed.), The dynamics of change in
Latin American politics, Englewood Cliffs, NJ: Prentice-
Hall, 1965, 283 p.   322
Political scientists and historians make up most of the
contributors of this collection of 27 papers on Latin American
politics and government. Part 1 treats politics and social
change, Part 2 the nature and elements of change, and Part 3
the agents of change. The contributors tackle a wide variety
of problems, ranging from "Conditions Favoring the Rise of
Communism in Latin America," to "The Role of the Military
in Latin American Politics." There is no index.

8	-	4	-		-	-	2	2
Gei	cit	lis	rep		ant	eco	pol	soc

Nash, Manning, The golden road to modernity: village
life in contemporary Burma, NY: Wiley, 1965, 333 p.   323
First-hand personal observation or "microanalysis"
plus broad sensitivity to the problem of identifying conditions,
forces, and factors leading to modernity constitute the method
and problem of this book. Two villages in Upper Burma are
carefully described on the basis of expertise acquired by the
author's residence there and intimate association with the people
in each village for at least 5 months. The resulting product is
important for several reasons: its detailed analysis of poverty
and the traditional orientation to it of a static agricultural

area, the exploratory analysis of the relevance of Buddhist values and institutions to the presumed modernized future, and the emphasis upon the extent to which the villagers are not involved in the national society. As to poverty, the valuation of leisure and the performance of religious rites seem to offer acceptable alternatives to the pursuit and enjoyment of wealth. The role of Buddhism is left uncertain. For example, it is judged as giving a lot of importance to the individual, a pattern which is felt to be inimical to organization for economic cooperation, but which at the same time opens the way for innovators, deviants and new modes of behavior. The lack of experience with and orientation toward the modern world leads to the concept of "multiple society" and the notion of plural cultures inside Burma. In summary, the virtue and vice of the method are left in prominent relief. The materials are detailed, interesting and suggestive, but do not lend themselves well to generalization. From the latter perspective the title is ironic, for the golden road to modernity is not to be found in this book.

2	-	4	-		4	-	-	-
Gei	cit	lis	rep		ant	eco	pol	soc

Peterson, Harold, "The wizard who oversimplified: a fable," Q J Econ 79:209-12, 1965.   324

In this kingdom it was considered very important and interesting to play chess in the school for princes. A wizard was hired to teach it. He never had played chess himself, but he nevertheless taught, with the aid of a 700 page treatise containing "a few simplifying assumptions" leading to a model, a set of principles, and decision rules. However, the king learned of this and became greatly distressed to find that the wizard did not take the trouble to observe actual chess players in order to learn the practical usefulness of his treatise, nor did he teach the princes to play chess in the real world.

-	-	3	-		-	3	-	-
Gei	cit	lis	rep		ant	eco	pol	soc

Pye, Lucian W., "The concept of political development," Annals Am Acad Pol Soc Sci 358:1-13, 1965.   325

Ten different definitions of the concept of political development are analyzed and distilled, and as a result the author dispels some of the confusion over its meaning. The essential dimensions are three in number: concern with equality unrelated to the nature of the political culture; the capacity of the political system, related to the development of authoritative governmental structures; and differentiation or specialization of governmental organizations, related to the various non-authoritative structures and groups of society. In consequence, the pattern and processes of political development revolve around the relations among the participants in political culture, the structure of authority, and the general conduct of affairs through politics.

-	1	3	1		-	-	3	-
Gei	cit	lis	rep		ant	eco	pol	soc

Shils, Edward A. , Political development in the new states, The Hague: Mouton, 1965, 91 p.   326
This study examines the utility for modernization of various political systems available to underdeveloped countries. Shils contends that modernity hinges on the character of the elite and that a state once embarked on the road to moderniza- tion has irreversibly turned its back on a traditional oligarchic system. Shils' position is that the present low level of de- velopment of individuality in the new states is more congenial to oligarchical than democratic regimes, but that democratic regimes have more likelihood of arousing individuality and that the LDC's have more to gain from it than any of the oli- garchical alternatives. Shils is particularly strong in his ex- plication of modernity and development and in his discussion of the role of the elites.

2	1	4	-		-	-	4	-
Gei	cit	lis	rep		ant	eco	pol	soc

Waterston, Albert, Development planning: lessons of experience, Baltimore: Johns Hopkins Press, (for the Eco- nomic Development Institute, International Bank for Recon- struction and Development), 1965, 706 p.   327
A comparative analysis of development planning in over 100 countries in Asia, Africa, and the Americas, this is a comprehensive source, with many interesting examples, for the study of national planning,attempting to identify when, how and why planning has been successful or unsuccessful, and drawing relevant lessons of experience from the comparisons. Part I concerns the planning process, with emphasis on the problem of plan formulation and implementation. Part II treats the setting up of organizations and administrative pro- cedures for preparing and implementing development projects, sectoral programs, and regional and national development plans. The appendices provide a chronological listing of national plans by country or dependent territory as well as a comprehensive bibliography. Besides the careful documentation of problems and policies in many of the nations studied, Waterston places planning in its historical perspective, with concise definitions of degrees and purposes of planning as applied to the particu- lar nation. Although the conclusions are generally left to the reader, two patterns are prominent. One is the tendency for

a "plan" to be formulated and presented to aid donors for monetary purposes without a hint of "consistency" in goals for the economy; in fact, many plans have been submitted without any intention of following through with the goals espoused. The second is the common experience of discouragement and frustration when long term plans fail to produce the expected results.

| (2) | | - | 1 | - | | - | 1 | - | - |
| Gei | cit | lis | rep | | | ant | eco | pol | soc |

Watson, Andrew M. and Joel B. Dirlam, "The impact of underdevelopment on economic planning," Quart J Econ 79: 167-94, 1965.   328

This article comes to grips with the unpleasant but true fact that "the societies that most want comprehensive economic planning are those least prepared to benefit from it." Inappropriate attitudes, lack of indispensable information, shortages of crucial skills, and absent or underdeveloped institutions are among the handicaps which appear universally in the LDC's to thwart the economic planner in his efforts to use sophisticated techniques or to evolve a grand design for development. This article brings a wealth of detail to bear on this important problem, argues for a strong dosage of realism to be injected into the presumed close relation between planning and development, and suggests some shifts of emphasis. One such shift recommended is that major attention be given to removing the obstacles to successful planning. In this connection the authors propose projects such as the following:

> the development of essential statistical series and the making of reasonable projections; the survey of essential resources such as minerals, ground water and soils; the study, evaluation and, where suitable, detailed programming of the widest possible range of projects (including those for legal, fiscal, and administrative reform); and above all, the development of a more enlightened and capable labor force at all levels...

A second shift recommended by the authors is that the political leaders of the LDC should recognize that much more can be achieved if maximum activity, with necessary conditions, be encouraged in the private sector, even if this means a considerable measure of foreign domination over economic life.

| - | - | 3 | - | | - | 3 | - | - |
| Gei | cit | lis | rep | | ant | eco | pol | soc |

Young, Crawford, Politics in the Congo: decolonization
and independence, Princeton: Princeton University Press, 1965,
659 p.   329
         This book is a detailed narrative and analytic political
history of the groping, sometimes violent, of a new-born society toward some kind of viable political system. The background is found in Belgian colonial rule, which created a strong
colonial society, but which refused to face the need for adapting to the rise of African nationalism. Consequently, decolonization was an immensely difficult and disorderly experience, which is here recorded in terms of the nature and role of
the new Congolese elites, the political aspects of ethnicity, the
form taken by the new nationalist movement, and the role of
the UN. A final section concentrates on the patterns associated with recovery and rebuilding, made necessary by the
breakdown crisis of 1960.

| - | - | 3 | - | - | - | 2 | 1 |
| Gei | cit | lis | rep | ant | eco | pol | soc |

Black, Cyril E. , The dynamics of modernization: a
study in comparative history, NY: Harper & Row, 1966, 206 p.
                                                            330
         Modernization is "the dynamic form that the age-old
process of innovation has assumed as a result of the explosive
proliferation of knowledge in recent centuries." Thus, Black
sees knowledge as the force motrice, and views modernization
as a process continuum dating from earliest times rather than
as a "transition" from traditionalism, which is a more popular
view. The process has five aspects, intellectual, economic,
social, political and psychological, each with its distinctive
province of variation and rates of change which are not always
coordinated. Most attention in this book is given to the political side of things, particularly in terms of the responses
given by national leaders to the critical problems faced by their
societies. These problems present themselves in a chronological series as "phases" and constitute crises which often produce domestic or international violence. Four in number, they
are "the challenge of modernity" (new knowledge of the possibility of change, etc.), "the consolidation of modernizing leadership" (a break with the agrarian way of life, creation of a
politically organized society, etc.), "economic and social transformation" (nationalism, industrialization, urbanization), and
"the integration of society" (reduction of local ties, efficient use
of resources, etc.). In addition, a typology of 7 patterns of
development is proposed, and 170 societies are classified in
one or another pattern according to 5 criteria. In sum, Black's
book offers a rich and broad scheme for the clarification of
historical patterns of development, with many wise generali-

zations and has an excellent bibliographic essay at the end.

3	-	9	-	1	-	4	4
Gei	cit	lis	rep	ant	eco	pol	soc

Clinard, Marshall B. , <u>Slums and community development: experiments in self-help</u>, NY: Free Press, 1966, 395 p.
331

What sets this book off from the many other case-studies and textbooks on community development is that it is in effect a text in applied sociology. While other books are based on tacit but unverified value-assumptions, this one is based on a thorough comparative analysis of what is almost a universal social phenomenon, and on the cumulative findings in social psychology over the last few decades. Clinard espouses the somewhat starry-eyed "C D" approach, so the most important contribution of this book is in its first two parts, which prepare the ground sociologically and historically. The apparently successful Delhi Project in Urban Community Development, described in Part III, serves merely as a case study to elucidate the problems and processes involved. Part IV is an analysis of the project, with a view to generalization and application to other parts of the world. The key-concepts, as in the whole "C D" approach, are self-help and indigenous leadership.

(2)	-	-	-	-	-	-	-
Gei	cit	lis	rep	ant	eco	pol	soc

Currie, Lauchlin B. , <u>Accelerating development: the necessity and the means</u>, McGraw-Hill, 1966, 255 p.   332

Currie favors rigorous governmental controls for accelerating development. His ultimate goal is to provide the "poorer half" with a minimum standard of living. External aid is unreliable or too little. Agrarian reform would only worsen the lot of the mass of subsistence farmers because of prevailing economic conditions. Instead, he proposes a "breakthrough plan." The plan entails the rapid transfer of large groups of people into the cities and their employment there. It would require economic policies similar to those of wartime. His plan would be fulfilled only when the agricultural portion constitutes ten percent of the total labor force, when the population growth rate is less than one percent, and when there is general equality of income and opportunity. This probably could be obtained only if wartime-like controls were functioning at peak efficiency for a generation. Much of this book is devoted to a detailed description of how his plan would operate in Colombia. While the book suffers from a disorganized style, inadequate measurements, and a number of strong biases, and while its boldness has stimulated great

controversy, it may well be that Currie has stated plainly what
has come to be the majority point of view among informed ob-
servers.

| 3 | - | - | - | | - | - | - | - |
| Gei | cit | lis | rep | | ant | eco | pol | soc |

Eisenstadt, Shmuel N. , "Breakdowns of modernization,"
p. 573-91 in J. L. Finkle and R. W. Gable (eds.), Political
development and social change, NY: Wiley, 1966.   333

This paper is concerned with the case of several LDC's
in which an initially modern political structure "broke down" and
was replaced by a more primitive and less democratic one.
Eisenstadt's basic interpretation of these happenings is that
such breakdowns do not occur because of lack of structural
modernization, but precisely because the fast pace of changes
taking place becomes too much for the weak modern political
framework. Modernization brings a lot of formerly isolated
groups, "primitive" and "civilized" alike, into increasing interaction with one another. This increasing interaction and its
concomitant conflicts occur within a political organization lacking the institutionalized norms and the power for regulating
these processes. According to Eisenstadt, the reason why
modern political elites fail to regulate the processes of modernization lies in the orientations of the power groups emerging
from traditional society. These groups are generally closed
and self-regarding; they rigidly demand rewards from the existing order without regard for the long-run goals of the nation.
The state becomes a provider of uneconomic rewards and privi-
leges. It ceases to be the promoter and guider of development
and the strong regulator of the turbulences of modernization.
Only in countries such as Turkey, Mexico, and Russia where
political elites have been able to impose their will against the
self-seeking demands of different groups and to establish a
clear hierarchy of developmental goals has the process of
modernization continued without stagnating breakdowns.

| 2 | 1 | 4 | 2 | | - | - | 3 | 1 |
| Gei | cit | lis | rep | | ant | eco | pol | soc |

Eisenstadt, Shmuel N. , Modernization: protest and
change, Englewood Cliffs, NJ: Prentice-Hall, 1966, 166 p.
                                                      334

Although there is little new data offered in this book,
the author commendably attempts to bring order to already
available facts and theories about societal development. He
sets out what he considers to be the basic characteristics of
modernization and then examines the problems of sustaining
growth. Eisenstadt's intention is to discover what conditions
enable a society to develop an institutional framework capable

of absorbing the changes inherent in modernization. After looking at the change experiences of Western Europe, the United States, the Soviet Union, Japan, Latin America, other communist regimes and formerly colonial societies, the author concludes that protest orientations are inherent in the process of modernization. Whether the society coheres or disintegrates depends on ideological commitments of the elites, the nature of the relationship between the elites and other strata, and the structural flexibility of the society. The book contains a good description of some conditions for protest and the forms protest usually takes, but it does not relate social discontent and disorganization to types of protest movements.

2	-	5	-		1	-	2	2
Gei	cit	lis	rep		ant	eco	pol	soc

Horowitz, Irving L. , Three worlds of development: the theory and practice of international stratification, NY: Oxford University Press, 1966, 528 p.   335

Here is a sociologist's exploration of the interaction in today's world of economic, political, military and social forces--more specifically, of these forces as they can be grouped into one or another of "three worlds" of the USA and its Western allies, the USSR and its Eastern allies, and the non-aligned, developing nations of Africa, Asia and Latin America. The book is unique for its scope--topical, geographical and disciplinary. The main argument probably is that the LDC's form a relatively homogeneous group or "world" and stand to profit from the other two worlds by choosing the best of what these latter have to offer, technological virtuosity from the first and economic planning from the second. The book is useful as a wide-ranging summary of current facts and issues and contributes some conceptual innovations of its own, e. g. , the "fusion effect" whereby the third world leans toward "mixtures" rather than "pure systems" (capitalism, socialism, etc.). Mixed in is the author's own fusion effect, in the shape of a conspicuous amount of social criticism and idiosyncratic opinions, a style which will appeal to some readers and alienate others. Among other traits of the book are 22 pages of general propositions about societal development in the last chapter, and a misnamed subtitle; "stratification" in the usual sense plays only a minor role, for the author's main commitment of interest is to the distribution, exercise and implications of power in social life.

2	-	6	-		-	-	4	2
Gei	cit	lis	rep		ant	eco	pol	soc

Huntington, Samuel P. , "Political modernization: America vs. Europe," World Pol 18: 378-414, 1966.   336

The major trend in European politics in the 17th century involved the rationalization of authority and the differentiation of structure. Authority was centralized in the absolute monarchs on the continent and in Britain in Parliament, and specialized political structures performing legal, administrative and military functions emerged. This did not happen in America. Instead, the traditional political institutions, later drastically changed in Europe, were exported to America in the 17th century and perpetuated at colonial, state and national levels. The colonization experience, the relative security of American society from external threats, and the absence of an aristocratic class and feudal tradition are all responsible for this perpetuation of Tudor institutions. They made possible the development of a modern society in America without the centralization of power required to demolish the traditional order in other countries. Their unique experience, urges the author, makes it difficult for Americans to understand contemporary patterns of political modernization, and to accept the fact that the American way is largely irrelevant to the possibilities confronting the LDC's today.

		3				2	1
Gei	cit	lis	rep		ant	eco	pol	soc

Huntington, Samuel P. , "The political modernization of traditional monarchies," Daedalus, Summer, 1966, p. 763-788.
337

The modern political system differs from a traditional one mainly in respect to the amount of power in the system. The primary problem facing a monarch who wishes to expand the amount of power in the political system is how to do it. The three categories of contemporary monarchies are parliamentary, oligarchical and ruling, and they encounter various difficulties in the march toward modernity. For example, reform and liberty seem to be incompatible and so do success and survival. In general, the outlook for the remaining traditional monarchies is not a happy one. How violent will be their end, and who will perpetrate the violence are two key questions.

		4				2	2
Gei	cit	lis	rep		ant	eco	pol	soc

Inkeles, Alex, "The modernization of man," Ch. 10, p. 138-150 in M. Weiner (ed.), Modernization: the dynamics of growth, NY: Basic Books, 1966.   338
While the societal conditions of modern man may be summarized in terms of urbanization, education, mass communication, industrialization and politicization, he also has attitudes, values and feelings. According to Inkeles, modern

man manifests: readiness for new experience, an openness to innovation and change, a disposition to form opinions about many problems and issues both in and outside of his immediate environment, a democratic bias, an orientation to the present or the future rather than the past, a favorable attitude toward planning, a belief that man can learn to dominate his environment in order to advance his own purposes and goals, a confidence that the world is calculable, an awareness of the dignity of self and others, faith in science and technology, a great belief in distributive justice. These themes are identified as qualities of modernity because they are intimately related to an individual's successful adjustment as a citizen of a modern industrial society.

(2)	-	-	-		-	-	-	-
Gei	cit	lis	rep		ant	eco	pol	soc

Inkeles, Alex and David H. Smith, "The OM scale: a comparative sociopsychological measure of individual modernity," Sociometry 29:353-377, 1966.   339
Psychic modernity may be defined as a set of attitudes, beliefs, behavior, etc. which characterize persons in highly urbanized, highly industrialized and highly educated social settings. Over 150 interview items attempting to measure psychic modernity were administered as part of a four hour interview to 5,500 men from six different developing countries--Argentina, Chile, India, Pakistan, Israel and Nigeria. Using a subset of 119 strictly attitudinal items (excluding informational and behavioral measures), the present paper attempts to derive a brief, reliable, valid, and cross-culturally useful measure of the relative standing of individuals on a scale of modernity. The resulting measure was called "OM," standing for "Overall Modernity." Two major types of OM measures were derived, one using item analysis methods and one using criterion group methods. The final short OM scale suggested consists of items meeting both selection procedures simultaneously. The authors describe the derivation of the OM scale from theoretical and empirical research, and how the scale has been successively modified.

(2)	-	-	-		-	-	-	-
Gei	cit	lis	rep		ant	eco	pol	soc

Johnson, Chalmers A. , Revolutionary change, Boston: Little, Brown, 1966, 191 p.   340
A generalized and succinct statement of the nature and sources of revolution is provided in this effort to build upon both traditional political theory and current thinking about society as a social system. Society is seen as in a state of mov-

ing equilibrium in which a value system is relatively synchronized with the society's environment (the division of labor, technological development, etc.). Revolution, a violent action based on a sense of societal failure, occurs in disequilibrated systems arising out of endogenous or exogenous changes in values or environment. Crucial roles are played by elites, the system's capacity for non-violent change and a relatively unpredictable factor termed an "accelerator." In addition to providing an abstract model, the author contributes suggestions for the measurement of equilibrium (suicide rates, amount of ideological activity, etc.), and the proposition that as the world becomes a community international wars will decrease but revolutions will increase. This is an invaluable book, and the best available on revolution in relation to development, though difficult problems of measurement remain unsolved.

3	-	2	-		-	-	2	-
Gei	cit	lis	rep		ant	eco	pol	soc

Kuznets, Simon S. , Modern economic growth: rate, structure and speed, New Haven: Yale University Press, 1966, 509 p.   341

This is a comparative historical analysis of the economic growth experience within the last 200 years of the world's 16 developed countries. Ten are European, five European "offshoots" and from Asia comes Japan. Conceptual definitions, analytic techniques and processed data are all presented with critical but affectionate care, and several new conceptual tools are contributed by the author himself. Among these are the "economic epoch," a relatively long period (100+ years) with a distinctive pattern of association between technological and institutional factors. Past economic epochs are identified as "medieval city-economy," "feudalism," and "merchant capitalism." The present epoch is designated the "scientific epoch." Each epoch has a linked "epochal innovation," which begins in one or two, typically small, "pioneer" countries and then spreads osmotically to other "follower" countries. This notion is expressed in the concept of "sequential international growth," which is the name for the author's theory of how economic growth comes to the nations of the world. Among other features it differs from the theory of Rostow in that growth takes place within one all-inclusive epoch rather than stages, and in that the interdependence and time sequence of entry of one country relative to others plays a more prominant role. Among other important conclusions are (1) income tends to become more equally distributed among the population as development proceeds, and (2) a general theory of growth applicable to all countries cannot be constructed.

3	4	-	-		-	-	-	-
Gei	cit	lis	rep		ant	eco	pol	soc

Levy, Marion J. , Jr. , Modernization and the structure
of societies: a setting for international affairs, Princeton:
Princeton University Press, 1966, 855 p. , 2 vols.   342
This is the most detailed, consistent and comprehensive
theoretical statement in the sociological literature dealing explicitly with both societal development and, what many see as
a logically prior topic, the nature of human society itself. Part
I is a comparative analysis of relatively modernized and relatively non-modernized societies, in which the distinguishing
variable is defined by the ratio of inanimate to animate sources
of power use in a society. Part II discusses aspects of social
structure in relatively familiar terms--rational vs. traditional
cognitive patterns, universalistic vs. particularistic membership criteria, role differentiation, economic allocation, etc.
Part III deals with organizational contexts of social life and
in Part IV with problem foci in modernization and stability.
Among the strategic problems of transition to modernity are
the problem of control and coordination of effort and the much
debated issue of the prerequisites to modernization. Prerequisites (conditions necessary for achieving a given system)
are distinguished from requisites (conditions necessary for
maintaining a given system). Among Levy's general propositions are these: (1) prerequisites to modernization for late-
comers are not necessarily the same as they were for early-
comers, (2) prerequisites for one set of late-comers are not
necessarily the same as for others, and (3) requisites are not
necessarily the same as prerequisites.

2	-	6	-		3	-	2	1
Gei	cit	lis	rep		ant	eco	pol	soc

Lewis, W. Arthur, Development planning: the essentials of economic policy, NY: Harper & Row, 1966, 278 p.
343
The main topical headings in this introduction to the
subject are "plan strategy," the "arithmetic of planning" and
the "planning process." Under the first are treated project
evaluation; optimum foreign trade policy at different stages of
development; optimum patterns of income distribution;
principles of public expenditure, taxation and so on. The
arithmetic chapter discusses the determinants and estimation
of rates of growth: how to achieve balanced supply among
industry by input-output analysis;   how to estimate optimum
allocation through linear programming, etc. Throughout,

theoretical analysis is combined with practical advice in a
clear, richly packed, occasionally opinionated style of presentation.

-	-	5	-		-	4	1	-
Gei	cit	lis	rep		ant	eco	pol	soc

Moore, Barrington, Jr. , Social origins of dictatorship
and democracy: lord and peasant in the making of the modern
world, Boston: Beacon, 1966, 559 p.   344
    This is an ambitious effort to understand the role of
the landed upper classes, the peasants and commercialized
agriculture in the great revolutionary transformations of major
world powers from agrarian societies to modern industrial
ones.   Three typical paths or "routes" are identified: (1)
democratic-capitalist as in England, France and the USA; (2)
capitalist but culminating in 20th century fascism as in
Germany and Japan; and (3) communism as exemplified in
Russia and China. In the first pattern the landed upper class
either collaborated in a bourgeois impulse toward modernism
or was swept aside in revolution or civil war. The same is
true of the peasantry, except in the USA which never had a
true peasantry. The second pattern involves a relatively
weak commercial and industrial class which had to rely on
dissident elements of the older, still dominant, landed ruling
classes in order to press for modernization. These societies,
however, never go through violent revolutions; instead the
ruling elites institute reactionary political reforms. In the
third pattern huge agrarian bureaucracies and peasant populations both inhibited modernization. But the peasantry, subject
to great stress from the encroachment of the modern world,
provided the main destructive force overthrowing the old
order and propelling the country toward modernity. Under
communist leadership, however, they also became the primary victims in the process. Six chapters deal with England,
France, USA, China, Japan and India (which fits well into
none of the three routes), and there are three chapters seeking theoretical implications and projections.

3	-	4	-		-	-	2	2
Gei	cit	lis	rep		ant	eco	pol	soc

Packenham, Robert A. , "Political-development doctrines in the American foreign aid program," World Pol 18:
194-235, 1966.   345
    The information upon which this article is based comes
from public statements made by Executive Branch Officials
between 1947 and 1963, and 54 formal interviews with Washington officials of the Agency for International Development
in 1962-63. The question to be answered is: To what extent

is political development--formation of effective, stable, democratic polities--an important factor in the decision-making of the officials who administer USA foreign aid programs? The answer is that although this is the stated goal of foreign aid, the administrators of the programs devote little explicit attention to the consequences of aid for political development. It is widely assumed that economic development leads to political development, but there are many doubts about the link between aid and political development, small knowledge about political development, and ignorance of the fact that such knowledge exists.

Gei	cit	lis	rep	ant	eco	pol	soc
-	-	3	-	-	-	3	-

Parsons, Talcott, Societies: evolutionary and comparative perspectives, Englewood Cliffs, NJ: Prentice-Hall, 1966, 120 p.   346

Parsons divides societies into "primitive," "intermediate" and "modern," (with appropriate sub-type distinctions) in which the appearance of written languages divides the second from the first, and a formal legal system emphasizing "procedure" the third from the second. The criterion of evolutionary direction is taken to be a tendency toward increase in "generalized adaptive capacity." In the present volume Parsons concentrates on the "intermediate" stage, pointing out that social anthropologists have devoted a large amount of attention to primitive society. He reserves the second companion volume in this Prentice-Hall series for his analysis of modern society. Included are ancient Egypt, the Mesopotamian Empires, China, India, the Islamic Empires, Roman Empire and the "seed-bed" societies of Israel and Greece.

Gei	cit	lis	rep	ant	eco	pol	soc
7	-	5	-	1	-	1	3

Pye, Lucian W., Aspects of political development, Boston: Little, Brown, 1966, 205 p.   347

The major value of this overview of political development in the underdeveloped areas is its condensed analysis of significant issues--democracy, personality and changing values, law, insurgency, communications, and the role of armies. Discussion is at the level of principles of governmental and political behavior, with illustrative references to specific cases. For example, governments faced with rebellion are in the rigid position of having only one objective, the maintenance of their claim to legitimacy, whereas rebels can change claims, issues and goals according to their military successes. In assessing the political progress of the developing countries, the author concludes that the failure of many countries to achieve any immediate succeses in development plans has caused widespread disillusionment and an almost universal crisis of authority. But some countries have progressed, and differential rates of development are themselves causing tensions among developing countries which did not exist in the 1950's when the nations of Asia and Africa formed a roughly unified bloc. Such tensions are likely to increase. The relative decline of the cold war and the increasing Sino-Soviet split suggest that future policies of the USA and Russia toward the developing countries will be less ideologically oriented and more pragmatic.

1	-	5	-	-	1	2	2
Gei	cit	lis	rep	ant	eco	pol	soc

No entry 348

Weiner, Myron (ed.), Modernization: the dynamics of growth, NY: Basic Books, 1966, 373 p.   349
This volume contains twenty-five lectures originally prepared for broadcast by the Voice of America in a series entitled "Forum Lectures," later revised and edited for publication. The book is divided into five parts: perspectives and conditions, the modernization of society and culture, the modernization of politics and government, the modernization of the economy, and conclusion. In his introduction, Weiner attempts to define modernization and also prepares the groundwork for the articles dealing with various aspects of the modernization process. In his concluding remarks, Pye tries to relate modernization to international understanding and betterment of the world. The tone of the lectures was kept at a level which the overseas audiences of the Voice of America could understand. They are informative reading for the interested layman.

8	-	7	-	2	-	1	4
Gei	cit	lis	rep	ant	eco	pol	soc

Zolberg, Aristide R., Creating political order: the party-states of West Africa, Chicago: Rand McNally, 1966, 168 p.   350
Here is a review of the accumulated experience and analysis of a decade of the new political institution developed in the emerging African nations--the party-state. How did they come into being, and what purpose do they serve? And is it useful to continue the debate over whether they are, can be, or will be democratic, or totalitarian? Included for analysis and comparison are Ghana, Guinea, Ivory Coast, Mali and Senegal, and the author's discussion includes their structural form (a partnership of party and state), their

ideology (unity, rationality and order are dominant themes),
and the manner in which a new order is created via the merging of party and government under a leader whose rule is likely to be patrimonial in nature.

-	-	4	-		-	-	4	-
Gei	cit	lis	rep		ant	eco	pol	soc

Index

211

221, 271, 335. See also: Names of individual countries.
"Aspects of technical change, Some," 52
Ataturk, Kemal, 304
Australia, 85, 110, 271
Authoritarianism, 248, 295. See also: Democracy, Totalitarianism
Authoritarianism vs. democracy as best means for development, 321
Authority, 167, 286, 312, 325, 336, 347. See also: Power.
Autonomous development, 94
Autonomous political sphere, 254
Awakening valley, The, 39

Backwash effect, 128
Bailey, Frederick G. , 115, 249
Balance of payments, 274
"Balanced and unbalanced growth in under-developed countries," 234
Balanced growth doctrine, 58, 91, 122, 234
"Balanced growth in economic development," 58
Balandier, George, 43
Baldwin, Robert E. , 126
Bali (Indonesia), 259
Banfield, Edward E. , 135
Banfield, Laura F. , 135
Bantu (East Central Africa), 28
Baran, Paul A. , 49, 116
Barnett, Homer G. , 64
Barriers and stimulants to change, 226
Banks, 108
Bauer, Peter T. , 44, 117, 152
Beals, Ralph, 65, 66
Bechuanaland Protectorate, 28
Becoming more civilized, 172
Belgian Congo, 108, 329. See also: Africa.
Belgium, 329
Bellah, Robert N. , 118, 136
Bemba (Northeastern Rhodesia), 28
Benda, Harry J. , 168
Bendix, Reinhard, 107, 286
Benne, Kenneth B. , 193
Bennis, Warren G. , 193
Berg, Elliot J. , 287
Big push theory of economic development, 130, 141, 315
Binder, Leonard, 222
Bisipara (India), 115
Black, Cyril E. , 330
Black man's ordeal, 51

213

Blackmer, Donald L. M., 209
Blanksten, George I., 67, 169
Bloomfield, Arthur I., 108
Blossoms in the dust, 210
Boeke, Julius H., 24
Bolivar, Simon, 4
Bolivia, 27, 50, 134. See also: Latin America.
Bolivian national revolution, The, 134
Bonilla, Frank, 288
Boserup, Ester, 314
Bourguiba, Habib, 168, 235
Bowman, Mary Jean, 250
Braibanti, Ralph J. D., 194
Brazil: described as total society, 33; community study of village culture of, 78; changes in village and plantation life in, 124; political development in, 142; Vargas of, 169; characteristics of urbanization in Rio de Janeiro, 214; policy-making for economic development in, 264; mentioned, 180, 293. See also: Latin America.
Brazil: people and institutions, 33
"Breakdowns of modernization," 333
Breakthrough plan, 332
Britain: economic history of, 17, 21; international investments of in 18th and 19th centuries, 85, 126; social change in during Industrial Revolution, 162; tribalism in Africa under rule of, 179; and effort to force culture change on Hausa, 186; taxation in commonwealth LDC's, 237; political culture of, 247; planning experience of, 261; route to modernization of, 344; mentioned, 16, 65, 97, 107, 159, 172, 207, 271. See also: Europe.
British Foreign Office, 191
Bronfenbrenner, Martin, 88
Bruno, Michael, 223
Bruton, Henry J., 315
Buddhism, 323
Buganda, Kingdom of (Uganda), 191
Buitron, Anibal, 39
Bureaucracy, 83, 107, 250a, 254, 279
Bureaucracy and political development, 269
Bureaucratic phenomenon, The, 250a
"Bureaucrats and political development," 279
Burma, 73, 170, 238, 252, 261, 323
Business cycles, 9
Businessman, 207

Cairncross, Alec K., 89
Callard, Keith B., 119
Camelot Project, 217

Canada, 85, 94, 194, 271
Cancian, Francesca, 170
Cantel (Guatemala), 147
Capital: a critique of political economy, 8, 228
Capital formation, 74, 89, 98, 171, 215, 267
"Capital formation and economic development," 58
Capital movements, 21, 74, 84, 85, 274
Capital requirements of LDC's, 117, 215
Capital symbolized, 51
Capitalism, 3, 8, 11, 12, 15, 24, 53, 76, 81, 116, 158,
    172, 185, 287, 300, 335, 341
Cargo cults, 133
Carroll, Thomas F., 204
"Case study of response to price," 152
Caste, 13, 16
Caste and the economic frontier, 115
Caste in modern India, 245
Castes and tribes of Southern India, 13
Central banks in LDC's, 108
Chan Kom: a Maya village, 25
Chan Kom (Mexico), 25, 29, 41
Change: functional analysis of, 170; guided, 181; planning
    of, 193; role of man in sociocultural, 198; role of man
    in rapid social, 221. See also: Social change.
"Changing community attitudes and values in Peru," 181
Challenge of modernization, The, 304
Charisma, 192. See also: Leadership.
Chenery, Hollis B., 68, 120, 153, 171, 195, 223
Children of Sanchez, The, 206
Chile, 142, 264, 317, 339. See also: Latin America.
Chin, Robert, 193
China: sociology of familism in South, 20; modernization of,
    100, 344; communist elite in, 168; split with Russia of,
    347; mentioned, 185, 233, 248, 317, 346. See also: Asia.
Choice of techniques, 243
Christianity, 16, 38, 45
Cities of Latin America, Two, 309
Citizenship, 192, 286
Civic culture, The, 247
Civil liberties, 211, 321
Civil service, 269
Clairmonte, Frederick, 172
Clark, Colin, 44
Clark, Paul G., 153
Class struggle, 8
Classical economics, 1, 3, 14
Clifford, Juliet M., 320
Clinard, Marshall B., 331

Cleven, Nels A., 27
"Closed corporate peasant communities in Mesoamerica," 131
Coale, Ainsley J., 137
Coercion, 192, 312. See also: Conflict, Violence.
Coleman, James B., 79
Coleman, James S., 148, 165, 166, 173, 316
Collectivism, 295
Collectivization of agriculture, 32, 199
Collier, John Jr., 39
"Colonial situation, The," 43
Colonial social accounting, 69
Colonialism: and race relations, 40, 43, 51, 240; and living
    standards, 69; and development of nationalism, 79, 80,
    240; and Latin American development, 109, 236; Marxist
    critique of, 116; and education, 121; and types of polities,
    173, 183; as force opposing traditional societies, 179,
    208; and intellectuals, 190; opposition to, 191, 200; and
    uneven change, 197; administrative practices of, 273; as-
    sociated with capitalism, 287; heritage of, 307; and eco-
    nomic exploitation, 310; in political history of the Congo,
    329; in USA 336
Colombia, 264, 309, 332. See also: Latin America.
Comas, Juan, 50
Command economies, 98
Commerce, see International trade, Trade.
"Commercial policy in the underdeveloped countries," 160
Common markets, 180
Communal society, 155
Communications, 250, 270, 347. See also: Mass Media
Communications, and political development, 278
Communications development Index, 252
Communism: as mass movement, 45, 155; vs. capitalism as
    means for economic growth, 86a, 185; patterns of indus-
    trialization of, 107; U.S.A. fear of, 184; and nationalism
    as affected by industrialization, 231; ambivalence of Latin
    American military to, 297
Community development, 331
Community in the Andes, A, 151
Community projects, 50
Community studies, 25, 29, 39, 41, 47, 56, 76, 78, 115,
    124, 140, 146, 147, 151, 181, 225, 259, 323, 331
Commuters, 225
"Comparative advantage and development policy," 195
Comparative analysis, 36, 37, 96, 148, 165, 166, 258
Comparative analysis of planning, 327
Comparative costs, 274
"Comparative politics in non-Western countries," 96
Competition, 7, 53, 63

217

projects in India, 146; labor and industrialization problems of, 187; in relation to comparative advantage, 195; debate over route to in Russia, 199; role of revolution in, 200, 340; general structural theory of, 201; in relation to USA foreign policy, 209; attitudes toward in Indian villages, 210; factors affecting success and failure of, 226; educational strategy for, 251; value system antithetical to, 277; authority relationships in, 286; human resource, 292; financing of, 294, 319; populist nationalism in, 310; best means to--democratic or authoritarian, 321; processes and structures of planning for, 327; role of state in acceleration of, 332; role of self-help and indigenous leadership in, 331. See also: Economic development, Political development, Social development.

"Economic growth and income equality," 97
"Economic growth and the contribution of agriculture," 267
Economic imperialism, British, 21
Economic planning, see Planning
Economic progress, 111
"Economic progress and occupational distribution, " 44
Economic theory: contributions to "pure," 9; limits of for
    understanding LDC's, 128
Economic stagnation, 282
Economic surplus, 116
Economics of development anthologies, 204, 298, 317
Economics of development textbooks, 72, 101, 126, 128,
    143, 154, 201, 227, 299, 315
Economic value of education, The, 280
Economics of the developing countries, The, 299
Economics of under-developed countries, The, 117
Economics of welfare, The, 18
Ecuador, 39, 50. See also: Latin America
Education: adult, 146; in Peru, 151, 181; and inflation, 242;
    and urban residence, 288; as human resource, 292;
    favored by military, 297; and political development, 316;
    role of in economic development, 250, 258, 317; as an
    economic quantity, 224, 280
Education and political development, 316
Education, manpower and economic growth, 292
Educational strategy for developing societies, 251
Egypt, 346
Eisenhower, Milton, 300
Eisenstadt, Shmuel N., 121, 197, 254, 269, 333, 334
Ejidos, 38
Elections, 249
Elites: In New Zealand, 95; in China and Japan, 100; in
    mass society, 155; non-Western leaders as, 168; and
    traditional masses, 173; five types of, 183; predisposi-
    tions of, 194; functions of in social mobilization, 196; as
    innovators, 198; and cohesiveness, 235; military as, 244;
    as necessary condition, 250; as measure of absorptive
    capacity, 320; in the Congo, 329; and protest orientation,
    334; and revolution, 340
Emerging nations, The, 209
Emerson, Rupert, 80, 175, 176
Empathy, 144
Empires, 354
Entrepreneurs, 14, 95, 107, 121, 182, 225, 259
Equality, 131. See also: Social stratification, income dis-
    tribution
"Equality, modernity, and democracy in the new states," 255
Equilibrium: analysis in economics, 10, 19; theory of

poverty, 31, 340; theory of vs. industrialization theory, 86; as state of LDC's economy, 125 as model of society, 276

Epstein, Arnold L., 140

Epstein, T. Scarlett, 225

Erasmus, Charles J., 198

Erlich, Alexander, 199

Essay on the principle of population, An, 2

Essays on sociological aspects of political and economic development, 197

Etawar, Uttar Pradesh (India), 146

Ethics, See Morality

Etzioni, Amitai, 490

Etzioni, Eva, 290

Europe: and Protestant ethic in development of, 12; industrialization of Eastern, 30; and urban population growth, 32; and urbanization in Middle Ages, 71; influence of on Africa and West Indies, 174; industrialization of, 228, 334; authority relations in development of, 286; political modernization of, 336; and modern economic growth, 341; mentioned, 6, 66, 93. See also: Names of individual countries

Europeans, 31, 43, 241

Evans-Pritchard, E. E., 28

Evolution, 10, 14, 19

Evolutionary theory, 104

"Expansion and employment," 34

Expansionist growth, 94

Expectant peoples, 281

Experts, 226

Exploitation, 116, 200

Explorations in social change, 311

Exports, 212, 306

External economies, 10, 86, 91

"External economies and the doctrine of balanced growth," 91

Extremadura (Spain) 177

Extremism, 190

Fair trade agreements, 111

Family, 20, 35, 56, 101, 124, 135, 147, 157, 206, 236

Familism, 20, 135

Fanaticism, 45

Fanon, Frantz, 51, 200, 262

Farmers, 48, 53, 56, 147. See also: Agriculture, peasants

Farquhar, John N., 16

Fascism, 45, 155

Feith, Herbert, 256

223

ment in, 286; village agricultural production in, 302; and Delhi Project, 331; route to modernization of, 344; mentioned, 185, 227, 299, 314, 339, 346. See also: Asia

"Indian-European relations in colonial Latin America," 103

Indians (American), 64, 105, 147, 177. See also: Community studies

Indicators, political and social, 301

Indigenismo, 35

Individual experience of development, 144

Individualism, 46, 76, 117, 139, 236, 248, 323, 326

Induced development, 94

Industrial structure, 98

Industry and trade, 17

Inflation, 34, 58, 122, 204, 242, 264, 298

Inflationary process in Latin America, 242

Indigenous Institute of Peru, 181

Individualism and the role of the state in economic growth," 139

Indonesia, 229, 248, 252, 256, 257, 259, 317. See also: Asia

"Indonesia's political symbols and their wielders," 256

Industrial entrepreneurs in the Latin American economy, 305

Industrial Revolution and social change in Britain, 162

Industrialism and industrial man, 183

"Industrialists, The," 305

Industrialization: in Russia, 32; 199; role of in development, 49, 183; effect of on traditional societies, 77, 147; in China and Japan, 100, communist and non-communist patterns of, 107; patterns of in LDC's, 171, 187; rate of and modernization, 213; of Europe in the 19th century, 228; political effects of in LDC's, 231; readings on, 265; in Russia, Japan, and Prussia, 286

Industrialization and labor, 47

"Industrialization and social change," 275

Industrialization and society, 265

Information, 312. See also: Knowledge

Inkeles, Alex, 338, 339

Innovation, 3, 5, 64, 89, 129, 213, 239, 314, 323, 330, 341

Innovation: the basis of cultural change, 64

Inquiry into the nature and causes of the wealth of nations, An, 1

Input-output analysis, 153, 165, 166, 343

Institutional transfer, 87

Insurgency, 347

Integration, see National integration

Intellectual between tradition and modernity, The, 216

Intellectuals, 83, 145, 168, 200, 216, 231, 244

227

228

314, taxation of, 54; scarcity of, 76, 208; reform, 134, 172, 204, 242, 297, 332

conflict with West, 145; and agricultural price changes, 152; intelligentsia as political elites within, 168; political systems of, 173, 307; labor problems of, 187, 317; resource allocation in, 195; role of revolution in, 200; role of agriculture in, 205; nature of social status in, 207; foreign aid required by, 215; political religion in, 248; social research in, 265; and international stratification, 268; policy alternatives of, 299

Leach, Edmund R., 170

Leadership: in the village, 25; traditional, 41; and "religiofication," 45; self-oriented, 80; of Nkrumah, 87; on Manus Island, 110; and charisma, 114; failure in Pakistan, 119; in Northern Rhodesia, 140; in Peru, 181; of intellectuals, 190; in Mexico, 211; in Tunisia, 235; in India, 246, 331; too-distant in France, 250a; and political symbolism, 256; military, 295, 297

Leading issues in development economics, 298

Leibenstein, Harvey, 91, 120, 125

Legalism, 250a

Lenin (Ulianov), Vladimir I., 11

Leisure, 284, 323

Leninism, 190

Lerner, Daniel, 144, 270

Levy, Marion J., Jr., 100, 165, 342

Lewis, John P., 233

Lewis, Oscar, 46, 56, 57, 157, 206

Lewis, W. Arthur, 72, 84, 101, 343

Liberalism, 172, 190

Lieuwen, Edwin, 184

Life in a Mexican village, 46

Linear programming, 153, 343

Linkages, 141

Linton, Ralph, 29, 290

Lipset, Seymour M., 158, 173, 252, 271

Lipton, Michael, 234

List, Friedrich, 172

Literacy, 83, 144, 196, 219

Little, Ian M. D., 320

Localistic modernism, 167

Location theory, 71

"Long run terms of trade between agriculture and manufacturing, The," 159

Lorimer, Frank, 32

Luxemburg, Rosa, 15

McCarthyism, 155, 188

McClelland, David C., 207, 272

McCord, William, 321

Machine age Maya, 147
MacIver, Robert, 290
Madagascar, 40
Madero, Francisco I. , 168
"Mahatma Gandhi's views on machines and technology," 277
Mair, Lucy, 273
Malagasy (Madagascar), 40
Malenbaum, Wilfred, 185
Mali, 248, 350. See also: Africa
Malinowski, Bronislaw, 36
"Malinowski's contribution to social anthropology," 36
Malthus, Thomas R. , 2, 5, 24, 137, 314
Mambwe (Northern Rhodesia), 150
Managerial policies and ideologies, 107
Man in rapid social change, 221
Man takes control, 198
Mannheim, Karl, 290
Mannoni, D. Otare, 40
Manpower and education, 317
Manufacturing, 1, 141, 159
Manus Island (New Guinea), 110
Maori (New Zealand), 95
Marginal analysis, 9
Marginal groups and development, 95, 182
Marginal growth contribution, 120
Markets: local vs. national, 11; and imperialism, 15; size
    of, and division of labor, 22; role of in balanced growth
    theory, 58, 122; role on international scene, 82, 128,
    160; capital, 108; free vs. planning, 143, 246, 287;
    labor, 150, 284; and price incentive in an LDC, 152;
    role of in Soviet collectivization, 199; and contribution
    of agriculture, 267, 302
Marshall, Alfred H. , 10, 17, 18, 19
Martinique, 200
Martz, John D. , 322
Marx, Karl, 8, 11, 14, 15, 189, 200, 201, 228, 290
Marxism, 11, 14, 15, 51, 95, 116, 145, 227
Marxist concept of surplus, 201
Mass media, 144, 196, 270, 278
Mass movements, 45, 155
Mass society, 155
Matossian, Mary, 145
Maya, 29, 41, 147
Mayer, Albert, 146
Maynard, Geoffrey, 242
Mead, Margaret, 73, 110
"Meaning and measurement of economic growth, The," 156

231

Measurement of development, 63, 69, 156, 224, 267
"Mechanics of economic development, The," 61
Medicine, 181
Medieval city economy, 341
Meier, Gerald M. , 126, 274, 298
Meiji Restoration in Japan, 118
Melanesia, 133
Mellor, John W. , 205
Menger, Karl, 9
Mental health, 73
Merchant capitalism, 341
Merchants, 100
Merida (Mexico), 29
Merit system, 279
Merton, Robert I. , 47, 127
Mesoamerica, 131
Mesopotamian Empires, 346
Mexican agrarian revolution, The, 23
Mexican government in transition, 303
Mexico: agricultural revolution in, 23; culture of, 35, 46;
    economic study of two villages of, 47; rural-urban migra-
    tion in, 56; role of middle class in political development
    of, 129; agricultural estates of, 132; political development
    in, 142, 211, 303; anthropological study of families in,
    157, 206; PRI (Party of Revolutionary Institutions) of,
    169, 211; militarism in, 184; political culture of, 247;
    planning experience of, 261; role of state in development
    of, 282; urban social strata of, 309; mentioned, 50, 57,
    180, 198, 333. See also: Latin America.
Middle East: modernization of, 144; intelligentsia as political
    elites in, 168; politics of social change in, 262; national-
    ism in, 281. See also: Names of individual countries
Migration: rural-urban, 56, 150, 214, 263; of unskilled
    labor, 84; from Europe to New World, 85, 177; into
    Israel, 197; in Latin America, 203, 214, 284
Migration of British capital to 1875, The, 21
Military, 81, 116, 168, 184, 202, 244, 295, 297, 307
Military and society in Latin America, The, 297
Military assistance, 184
Military in the political development of the new nations,
    The, 295
Mill, John Stuart, 7
Miller, Walter B. , 102
Millikan, Max F. , 208, 209
Mills, C. Wright, 188
Miner, Horace, 57, 186
Mintz, Sidney, W. , 132
Missionaries, 16, 146, 273

Mobilization political system, 248, 312
"Modern Latin American culture," 35
Modern religious movements in India, 16
Modernism, 144
Modernismo, 35
Modernization: of China, 100; of Japan, 100, 136, 283, 308;
    role of revolution in Bolivian, 134; religious aspects of
    in Turkey and Japan, 136; in Middle East, 144; tra-
    ditionalism in political, 167; psychological, 174; role of
    military in, 202; rate of industrialization as aid to, 213;
    role of personal psychology in, 238; and egalitarian
    politics, 255; of Asia and Africa, 258; international
    stratification as function of, 268; communication theory
    of, 270; role of economic opportunities in, 273; need
    for social rebirth to promote, 304; of Turkey, 308; role
    of political systems in, 312; Burmese villages fail to
    achieve, 323; role of political development in, 326, 333,
    336, 337; dynamics of, 330; role of protest in, 334;
    strategy of, 342; role of social classes in, 344; the
    dynamics of growth, 349
Modernization and the structure of societies, 342
"Modernization of man, The," 338
Modernization: protest and change, 334
Modernization gap, 213, 228, 341. See also: Social
    stratification of nations.
Modern economic growth, 341
Modern society, 188
Modernity as psychic trait, 339
Modjokuto (Indonesia), 259
Monarchies, 337
Monetarists vs. structuralists, 204
"Monetary policy in underdeveloped countries," 108
Money, credit, and commerce, 19
Monopoly, 1, 17, 115
Moral basis of a backward society, The, 135
Morality and development, 75, 221, 226
MDC's (more developed countries), 99, 228, 341
Morgan, Theodore, 159
Morocco, 192
Moore, Barrington, Jr., 344
Moore, Clement H., 235
Moore, Wilbert E., 47, 187, 265, 275, 276
Morse, Richard M., 236
Mukerji, Dhurjati P., 277
Multiple society, 129, 232. See also: Dualism.
"Multiple society in economic development, The," 129
Multiplier, 59
Muslims, 259

Muquiyauyo (Peru), 151
Mutual aid associations, 179
Myers, Charles A., 292, 317
Myint, Hla, 299
Myrdal, Gunnar, 111, 128

Nair, Kusum, 210
Nash, Manning, 129, 147, 323
Nasser, Abdel Gamal, 168
Nation-building and citizenship, 286
National community, 200
National identity, 81, 307
National Institute of Economic and Social Research, 69
National income, 26, 60
National integration, 27, 81, 119, 166, 173, 196, 281, 330
"National political development," 252
National planning, 327. See also: Planning.
Nationalism: as mass movement, 45, 310; sources of, 70,
    175, 208, 310; sources and types in Africa, 79, 140,
    175, 191, 235, 240, 329; paradoxes of, 80; and inter-
    nationalism, 175; role in development, 176, 310, 330;
    and elite types, 183; of intellectuals, 190; integrative
    function of, 217, 235, 240; and communism, 231; of
    military elite, 244, 295, 297; propositions about, 281
Nationalization, 134
Native problem, 50
"Nature of a good plan and the machinery for good planning,
    The," 261
"Nationalism and political development," 176
Nationalism and social communication, 70
"Nationalism in tropical Africa," 79
Near East, 166
Need achievement, 207
Needler, Martin C., 211
Negritude, 51
Negroes, 66
Nehru, Jawaharial, 168
Neo-classical economics, 10, 315
"Neo-Destour party of Tunisia, The," 235
Neo-isolationism, 88
Neo-mercantilist polity, 312
Nerves of government, The, 253
Ne Win, 168
New Guinea, 110, 241
New lives for old, 110
New Zealand Maori, 95
New nations, 273
Ngwato (Bechuanaland Protectorate), 28

Niehoff, Arthur H. , 285
Nigeria, 73, 152, 186, 261, 294, 339. See also: Africa
Nkrumah, Kwame, 87, 168
"Non-Western intelligentsia as political elites," 168
"Non-Western political process, The," 148
North Africa, 262
North American Conference on the Social Implications of
    Industrialization and Technological Change, 265
Northern Rhodesia, 69, 140, 150, 179. See also: Africa
"Notes on the theory of the 'big push'," 130
Nuer (East Africa), 28
Nurkse, Ragnar, 85, 91, 212, 58, 74
Nutrition, 181
Nyasaland, 69, 179, 317. See also: Africa

Occupational careers, 312
Occupational distribution, 44
Old societies and new states, 258
Oligarchies, 173, 244, 326
Oligopoly, 53
"OM scale, The," 339
Opportunities and development, 273
Oppositionalism, 190
"Ordeal of the black man, The," 51
Organization as a development factor, 17, 27, 28, 89, 135,
    224
Orissa (India), 249
Otavalo (Ecuador), 39
Overpopulation, 74, 84, 88
Overurbanization, 123, 203, 262

Pacific Northwest, 64
Packenham, Robert A. , 345
Pakistan, 119, 194, 261, 339. See also: Asia.
Pakistan: a political study, 119
Palau (Southwest Pacific), 73
Palauans, 64
Paliau (leader on Manus Island), 110
Panajachel (Guatemala), 76, 302
"Paradoxes of Asian nationalism" 80
Park, Robert E. , 290
Parsons, Talcott, 77, 118, 162, 165, 170, 182, 188, 290,
    346
Participation in society: in Mexico, 41, 303; in Italy, 135;
    in the Middle East, 144; in India, 146, 249; and democra-
    cy, 158; as indicator of social mobilization, 196; in
    stages of development, 202; in five countries, 247; in
    France, 251; of workers in politics, 288; in Burma, 323

institutional transfer in, 87; analysis and theory of, 96, 328, 347; difficulties of in LDC's, 121; in Latin America, 142; nationalism in, 176; and intellectuals of new states, 190; in Morocco, 192; and social mobilization, 196; sociological aspects of, 197; of Mexico, 211, 303; in Tunisia, 235; military in, 244, 295; role of state in Indian, 246; and communications, 252, 278; index of, 252; necessary conditions for systems, 254; consequences of for social stratification, 255; and bureaucracy, 269, 279; of USA, 271; role of education in, 316; and democracy, 321; and alternative political systems, 326; and USA foreign aid programs, 345; of party-states in Africa, 350

Principles of political economy considered with a view to their practical application, 5
Principles of political economy and 'taxation,' On the, 3
Private authority, 286
Private enterprise, 88, 233
Private vs. public sector, 86, 149, 246, 282, 328
Problems of capital formation in underdeveloped areas, 74
"Problems of industrialization of Eastern and South-Eastern Europe," 30
Productivity, 58, 84, 92, 120, 224, 248
Profits, 14, 18
Progress of underdeveloped areas, The, 55
Property ownership, 5, 8, 48, 124, 227, 198. See also: Private vs. public sector
Prospero and Caliban, 40
Protectionism, 1, 84, 160, 172, 180, 212, 291
Protest movements, 133, 240, 334
Protestant ethic and the spirit of capitalism, The, 12
Prussia, 286
Psychological traits, 6, 47, 64, 77, 106, 146, 180, 200, 239, 240, 247, 284, 288, 338, 339
Public finance in underdeveloped countries, 237
Public opinion, 282
Public services, 72
Public utilities, 85
Punta del Este Conference, 1967, 205
Puerto Rico, 132, 317
Pye, Lucian W., 96, 148, 238, 278, 325, 347, 349

Quer'etaro (Mexico), 309
Quiet crisis in India, 233
Quintana Roo (Mexico), 29

Race and race relations, 40, 43, 51, 56, 133, 200, 293
Racialism, 40
Radicalism, 31
Rangachari, K., 13
Rao, Vijendra K. R. V., 59
Rates of industrial growth, 213, 306
"Rates of industrial growth in the last century, 1860-1958," 213
Reconciliation polity, 312
"Reconstruction of foreign tax systems," 54
Recreation, 147
"Recruitment of white-collar workers in underdeveloped countries," 83
Redfield, Robert, 25, 29, 41, 46, 57, 75
Reinvestable surplus, 243

239

Relative backwardness, 139, 228
Religion: and urbanization, 56; and stratification, 106;
    Catholicism, 110; as cargo cults, 133; political, 248;
    Buddhism, 323; mentioned, 101, 124
"Religious aspects of modernization in Turkey and Japan,"
    136
Religious movements, 16, 45, 240
Report on industrialization and the Gold Coast, 72
Republican native culture, 35
Requisites and prerequisites of society, 342
Research and development, 181
Resources, 94, 95, 98, 171, 195
Revolution: Marxist theory of, 8, 49; Mexican, 23, 28;
    as mass movement, 45; Bolivian, 134; and non-Western
    intellectuals, 168; and nationalism, 176; and elite types,
    183; as precondition for development, 200, 202; inflation
    and, 264; and Latin America, 318; as social change, 340
Revolutionary change, 340
Ricardo, David, 63, 126, 172, 201
Rich lands and poor, 128
Riesman, David, 144, 290
Riggs, Fred W., 269, 279
"Rise of African nationalism, The," 240
Rogers, Everett, 239
"Role of agriculture in economic development, The," 205
"Role of cities in the economic growth of underdeveloped
    countries, The," 71
"Role of national income estimates in an underdeveloped
    area," 60
"Role of traditionalism in the political modernization of
    Ghana and Uganda, The," 167
Roman Catholicism, 110
Roman Empire, 16, 346
Rosenstein-Rodan, Paul N., 30, 91, 130, 215
Rostow, Walter W., 112, 161, 189, 298, 341
Rotberg, Robert I., 240
Rural cultural missions, 38
"Rural labor," 284
Rural Mexico, 38
Rural-urban contrast, 33
Rural-urban differences in Latin America, 219
Russett, Bruce M., 301
Russia: Lenin's analysis of, 11; population growth patterns
    of, 32; industrialization of, 32; and Siberia as possible
    recipient of International Investment, 85; subordination of
    economic enterprises in, 107; Communist elite in, 168;
    debate over development of, 199; problems of economic
    and social change in, 228; reasons for success of

industrialization in, 286; modernization example of, 304, 321, 333, 334, 344; as one of three worlds of development, 335; and future policies toward developing countries, 347. See also: Europe

Rustow, Dankwart A. , 308

Salisbury, Richard F. , 241
Sanitation, 181
Satellitic growth pattern, 94
Saving, 3, 34, 58, 69, 74, 88, 101, 215, 302, 320
Say's law, 130
Scale, economies of, 224
Schultz, Theodore W. , 280, 302
Schumpeter, Joseph, 95, 201
Scientific revolutions, structure of, 232
Scientific theory of culture and other essays, A. , 36
Scitovsky, Tibor, 86
Scott, Robert E. , 303
Sectoral growth, 171, 267
Sectoral integration, 299
Sectoral relations, 61, 101
Seers, Dudley, 60, 242
Self-help, 331
Sen, Amartya K. , 243
Senapur (India), 302
Senegal, 317, 350. See also: Africa
Separatism, 80, 167, 191
Sequential international economic growth, 341
Serfdom, 23
Service, Elman R. , 103
Sex ratios, 219
Shannon, Lyle W. , 173, 252
Shils, Edward A. , 190, 216, 244, 258, 326
Shintoism, 145
Siane, 241
Siberia, 85
Silvert, Kalman H. , 202, 217, 281
Sinai, I. Robert, 304
Singer-Prebisch thesis, 42, 159, 160, 180, 291
Singer, Hans W. , 42, 58, 61
Single party systems, 211, 235, 310
Skills, 171, 224
Slavery, 293
Slums, 157, 206, 214
Slums and community development, 331
Smith, Adam, 1, 126, 201
Smith, David H. , 339
Smith, T. Lynn, 33

Smelser, Neil J. , 162, 165, 170
SMP (social marginal product) criterion, 68
Social change: theory of, 31, 162, 229; as disruptive, 73;
    required for economic development, 259; the individual
    as agent of, 260; politics of, 262; textbooks on, 276,
    285, 290; American theories of, 311
Social change, 276
Social change in the industrial revolution, 162
Social change: sources, patterns, and consequences, 290
Social change in Latin America, 164
Social change, On the theory of, 229
Social development, 313
Social development: in Mexico, 41; in the colonial situation,
    43; as implemented by technical aid programs, 55; as
    affected by industrialization, 77; role of state in, 139;
    ideologies in, 145; transition to, 209; as affected by
    economic development, 225; in New Guinea, 24; as
    provoked by political action, 249; of USA, 271; readings
    on, 313; and fate of traditional civilization, 321; as an
    evolutionary process, 346. See also: LDC's.
Social deviance development theory, 95, 182
"Social, economic, and technological problems of rapid
    urbanization, The," 263
Social marginal productivity, 68, 120
Social mobilization, 196, 235
"Social mobilization and political development," 196
Social movements, 45, 133
Social origins of dictatorship and democracy, 344
Social protest, 286
Social rebirth, and modernization, 304
"Social requisites of democracy, Some," 158
Social research in underdeveloped countries, 265
Social Science Research Council, Committee on Comparative
    Politics of, 269, 278, 308, 316
Social sciences in implementing technical aid programs, 55
Social security, 179
Social stratification: role of middle class; 5, 129, 178, 183,
    198, 295; equality, 6, 97, 255, 325, 341; marxist
    theory of, 8, 49; role of peasantry, 11, 106; in the
    village, 41,76, 124; of the nations, 42, 99, 111, 128,
    213, 268, 335, 341; in Latin America, 66, 105, 230,
    309; as condition for development, 95; in Japan and
    China, 100; caste, 115, 225, 249; in Asia, 123; open
    class system, 158; and power, 172; elites and masses,
    173, 194, 250, 334; sources of, 179, 198, 225, 255; and
    intellectuals, 190; and role of slum, 214; and national-
    ism, 217; and social mobility, 244, 295, 297; moderniza-
    tion of, 258. See also: Caste, Elites

"Social stratification in Latin America," 66
Social theory and social structure, 127
Social welfare, 92, 122
Socialism, 8, 81, 190, 287, 335
"Socialism and economic development in tropical Africa,"
    287
Socialization, 196
Societal equilibrium, 270
Sociocultural values: of race differences, 31, 51; sources of,
    71, 77; on capital, 88; convergence in, 95; as precondi-
    tion, 12, 114, 194; Gandhian, 146, 277; in Guatemalan
    village, 147; on equality, 158; consummatory and in-
    strumental, 167, 312; in Peru, 181; of venturesomeness,
    239; as political symbolism, 256; in Japan, 283; on
    democracy, 321; Buddhist, 323; on self-help, 331; in
    conception of society, 340; as source of tension, 347
"Sociological approach to economic development, A," 95
Sociological aspects of economic growth, 182
"Sociological aspects of political development in under-
    developed countries," 121
Societies: evolutionary and comparative perspectives, 346
Sociology anthologies, 55, 164, 193, 194, 265, 290, 311,
    313
Sociology textbooks, 127, 221, 276
Soga (Uganda), 90
"Some characteristics of urbanization in...Rio de Janeiro,"
    214
"Some signposts for policy," 178
Spanish Americans of New Mexico, 73
Spread effect, 128
Stages, 59, 104, 202, 298, 312, 341
Stagnation, 98, 130
State's role in development: under capitalism, 49; stimulate,
    provide social overhead capital, 58, 82, 120, 319; as
    mobilization device, 114, 332; arguments against, 117,
    172, 180; and individualism, 139; in Mexico, 282; com-
    parative analysis of, 286; and preference for socialism,
    287; with unions and business, 288; in Latin America,
    300; mentioned, 7, 101, 234, 297
Structuralist School, 242
Subtheories of economic development, 98
Successful development, 32, 39, 41, 81, 151, 181, 331
Suffrage, 134
Suicide rates, 340
Sukarno, 256
"Summary and conclusions. , 1. rapporteurs report, Part
    One:" 203
Sunspots, 9

Trade, 1, 44, 116, 122. See also: International trade.
Trade union, see Labor union
Tradition, values and socio-economic development, 194
Traditional cultures, 226
Traditionalism, 37, 39, 167, 208, 216, 259, 330
Transforming traditional agriculture, 302
Tribal cohesion in a money economy, 150
Tribalism, 179
Tropics, 78, 84
Trotsky, Leon, 199
True believer, The, 45
Trumpet shall sound, The, 133
Tschopik, Harry Jr., 37
Tsimshian, (Northwest America), 64
Tunisia, 235
Turkey, 45, 126, 304, 308, 333
Tusik (Mexico), 29
"Two concepts of external economies," 86
"Types of Latin American peasantry," 106
Types of production, 26
Typology of Latin American subcultures, A," 105

Uganda, 90, 167, 191, 317. See also: Africa
Ulianov, see Lenin.
Unbalanced growth, 264
Underdeveloped countries, see LDC's.
"Underdeveloped countries and the pre-industrial phase in
    the advanced countries," 99
Underdevelopment seen as a new phenomenon, 201,228
Unemployment, 59
United Nations: Department of Economic Affairs of, 48;
    Economic Commission for Latin America of, 159, 180,
    220; UNESCO, 78, 265, 275, 313; Bureau of Social
    Affairs of Population Branch, 219; mentioned, 306, 329
United States: democratic system of, 6; economic history
    of, 17; and 19th-century British investment, 21, 85;
    and urban population growth, 32; foreign investment of,
    85; and progress of underdeveloped countries, 86a, 209,
    233; need of to liberalize trade position, 111; relations
    of with Latin America, 164, 178, 184, 288, 300; analy-
    sis of economy and growth of, 170, 224, 271, 334; in-
    fluence of on Africa and the West Indies, 174; Senate
    Committee on Foreign Relations of, 209; and ethics of
    foreign social science research, 217; and policy toward
    Iran, 222; political culture of, 247; race relations in,
    293; political modernization of and LDC's, 336, 344;
    political development doctrines in foreign aid programs
    of, 345; future policies of toward LDC's, 347;

mentioned, 65, 94, 107, 110, 111, 155, 159, 188, 198, 205, 207, 303, 335
Universities, 83
University of Chicago, Interdisciplinary Committee for the Comparative Study of New Nations of, 258
Urban employment in Latin America, 220
"Urban worker, The," 288
Urbanization: and industrialization, 71, 92, 182; in Middle East, 144; as source of mass society, 155; as indicator of social mobilization, 196; in Latin America, 203, 219, 220, 236; problems of, 263; effect on workers of, 288; as social transformation, 330
"Urbanization without breakdown," 56
Uruguay, 50, 81, 142. See also: Latin America.
Uruguay: portrait of a democracy, 81
USSR. See Russia

Vargas, Getulio D. , 169
Venezuela, 4. See also: Latin America
Verba, Sidney, 247
Vernon, Raymond, 282
Vicos (Peru), 181
Villa Rojas, Alfonso, 50
Village and plantation life in northeastern Brazil, 124
Village that chose progress, A, 41
Viner, Jacob, 63
Violence, 87, 100, 200, 264, 318, 329, 330
Voice of America, 144, 349
Voluntary associations, 140, 155, 158, 240
von der Mehden, Fred R. , 307
Vorontsov, Vasili P. , 11
Vries, Egbert de, 221

Wagley, Charles, 78, 105
Wairas, Leon, 9
War, 15, 98, 110, 155, 200, 208, 340, 347
Ward, Robert E. , 283, 308
Waterston, Albert, 327
Watson, Andrew M. , 328
Watson, William, 150
Wealth, 158, 225, 254, 323
Wealth, authority and prestige in the Ica Valley, Peru, 230
Weber, Max, 12, 286, 290
Weiner, Myron, 246, 349
Welfare, 259
Welfare economics, 18, 120
Welfare state, 300
West Africa, 44